All the Blessings of Life

of Life

REVISED

THE BEST STORIES OF
F. W. BOREHAM

PUBLISHED BY
JOHN BROADBANKS PUBLISHING

F. W. Boreham

Lover of Life: F. W. Boreham's Tribute to His Mentor (Revised and Expanded)

All the Blessings of Life: The Best Stories of F. W. Boreham (Revised)

Second Thoughts – Includes an Introduction by Ravi Zacharias

The Chalice of Life: Reflections on the Significant Stages in Life

A Packet of Surprises: The Best Essays and Sermons of F. W. Boreham

Angels, Palms and Fragrant Flowers: F. W. Boreham on C. H. Spurgeon

Geoff Pound

Making Life Decisions: Journey in Discernment

All the Blessings of Life

REVISED

THE BEST STORIES OF
F. W. BOREHAM

John Broadbanks Publishing
Eureka, CA

2010

John Broadbanks Publishing
Eureka, CA
2010

10 9 8 7 6 5 4 3

Printed in the United States of America

ISBN-13 978-0-9790334-7-6
ISBN-10 0-9790334-7-0

Proofreader: Jeff Cranston
Cover Design: Laura Zugzda
Interior Layout: Stephanie Martindale

Contents

FOREWORD

ABOUT THIS BOOK

This volume is a compilation of the best stories of F. W. Boreham. Such a rating is subjective and the compiler of this book could do another marathon reading of Boreham books and come up with a different selection. If you do not find your favorite Boreham story in this book it may be because it was included in *A Packet of Surprises: The Best Essays and Sermons of F. W. Boreham.*

While language has changed markedly in the one hundred years since he began writing, only minor punctuation and spelling changes have been made to these stories. Because the author communicated in a former age no changes have been made to modify the text into inclusive language with political correctness. Readers will need to make some subtle adaptations in the retelling of the Boreham stories as he made references and exhibited biases that may no longer be relevant in one's local and contemporary contexts.

ABOUT THE STORYTELLER

While many readers of this new volume will be devoted 'Borehamaniacs' or 'Borehamphiles,' others may be sampling Boreham for the first time. For such readers the biographical essay by Irving Benson has been included as it provides an introduction and the setting for understanding the life and work of this storyteller. More detailed accounts are contained in Boreham's autobiography, *My Pilgrimage* and T. Howard Crago's biography, *The Story of F. W. Boreham.*

Frank Boreham's discovery of the power of stories was instilled within him when he was a child. Sunday night was story time in the Boreham household. Listen to Frank Boreham recall this never-to-be-missed ritual around the fireside in England's Tunbridge Wells:

> "There mother gathered her boys about her; read with us the collects and the lessons that were being used in church; and then held us spellbound with a chapter or two of some delightful book. It is wonderful how many books we got through on those Sunday evenings. Then, before we said good night, we turned out the gas and just sat and talked by the light of the dying embers. Most of us were sprawling on the hearth-rug, sitting on hassocks, or kneeling around the fender. It always ended with a story. And, of all the stories that I have since heard and read, none ever moved me like those stories that in the flickering firelight, Mother told."[1]

F. W. Boreham knew that while the experience of being spellbound by stories is a good first step it did not make him into a scintillating storyteller. He therefore committed himself to developing the art of storytelling. As a seminary student in London he listened to the effective preachers of his day, who included, Dwight L. Moody, Charles Haddon Spurgeon and Joseph Parker. He would drop into the British House of Commons to observe the way politicians like William Gladstone would get their point across. When he became a pastor in Mosgiel, New Zealand, Boreham frequently visited the Dunedin Law Courts to study the way eminent barrister, A. C. Hanlon, argued his cases.

---

[1] F. W. Boreham, *Arrows of Desire*, (London: The Epworth Press, 1951), 125.

Throughout his life Boreham wrote and refined his stories in order to master the difficult art of telling a story well. Such diligence was rewarded as Dr. Boreham became recognized as one of the leading Christian preachers and writers in the first half of the twentieth century. In the second half of the last century, well-known preachers such as Billy Graham, Ravi Zacharias (USA) and Gordon Moyes (Australia) have frequently expressed their indebtedness to the writings of F. W. Boreham. Scores of lesser-known speakers and writers have discovered Boreham and have scoured his books in search of an apt illustration for their sermons and articles.

SUCCESSFUL STORYTELLER SECRETS

What were the spheres from which his stories were gleaned and how did Boreham become such an interesting communicator and an effective storyteller?

Many of the stories in this volume come from *human experience* or from Boreham's own *life story*. Challenging his readers to consider what they were bequeathing, Boreham expressed his verdict in stating, "Experience—the most priceless hoard that living creatures ever amass—is bequeathed as a heritage from generation to generation."[2] When he wrote the story of his life in *My Pilgrimage* he encouraged all his readers to do the same saying:

> "The lives of the Nobodies and the Nonentities offer a virgin field of novelty and freshness.... There is no drama like the drama of reality; no lure like the lure of life; no business half as intriguing as other people's business. The person whose biography is not worth writing has never yet been born."[3]

Furthermore, F. W. Boreham had a rich fund of stories because he was an avid *reader of books*. From that day

---

[2] F. W. Boreham, *Mercury*, January 4, 1936.
[3] F. W. Boreham, *My Pilgrimage*, 7-8.

when, with the help of his mentor, Boreham was converted to serious reading the young preacher commenced the practice of buying and reading at least one substantial book every week. From this discipline he not only found ample ideas and illustrations for his weekly preaching, but he was stimulated and resourced to write for over forty-seven years weekly editorials for leading newspapers, which became the germs from which the essays in his books subsequently developed.[4]

In addition to the Bible, Boreham devoured newspapers, reread novels and loved biographies. Studying the stories of people helped Boreham to perfect the biographical style of preaching. The subjects of the stories in this volume reveal an eclectic range of books that Boreham consulted—works of history, spiritual classics, geology, travel, poetry, politics, archaeology, adventure and inventions.[5] Commending the reading of good books to budding storytellers and preachers F. W. Boreham said:

> "The ideal reader, the man who reads well, the well-read man, preserves the ecstasy and rapture of reading all through the years. There are worlds so wonderful that he cannot deny himself the raptures they offer…. Let a man assiduously cultivate and jealously preserve the high art of reading well and he will soon take his place among earth's really well-read men."[6]

---

[4] F. W. Boreham, *The Man Who Saved Gandhi*, (London: The Epworth Press, 1948), 9-10. This book has been republished as *Lover of Life: F. W. Boreham's Tribute to his Mentor - Revised and Expanded* (Eureka, CA: John Broadbanks Publishing, 2009).

[5] The range of subjects F. W. Boreham wrote about can be observed by visiting the web sites at: http://thisdaywithfwboreham.blogspot.com and http://fwboreham.blogspot.com.

[6] F. W. Boreham, *Ships of Pearl*, 172-173, 175-176.

A large number of F. W. Boreham's stories in this book come from *nature*—either from first-hand experience or his reading of nature books. Through a series of accidents and illnesses he had experienced the therapeutic and recuperative value of visiting the bush or holidaying at the beach. He loved the way stories from nature could evoke surprise and wonder. According to Boreham:

> "A world that could no longer surprise us would be a world that had run out of bombshells. Half the fun of waking up in the morning is the feeling that you have come upon a day that the world has never seen before, a day that is certain to do things that no other day has ever done. Half the pleasure of welcoming a new-born baby is the absolute certainty that here you have a packet of amazing surprises ... here is novelty, originality, an infinity of bewildering possibility."[7]

F. W. Boreham viewed nature as one of the greatest educational influences in life,[8] saying, "We have the trees as teachers and preachers, and many a man has learned the deepest lessons of his life at the feet of these shrewd and silent philosophers."[9] He told many stories from nature because he believed its greatest contribution was that it "hinted"[10] disclosed truths about the Creator, and like the pointers of the Southern Cross—they "possess no value or importance of

---

[7] F. W. Boreham, *Faces in the Fire* (London: The Epworth Press, 1916), 14.

[8] F. W. Boreham, *Mercury*, October 6, 1923. Benjamin Disraeli, the Earl of Beaconsfield said, "Nature is more powerful than education." Benjamin Disraeli, *Contarini Fleming: An Autobiography* (New York: D. Appleton & Co, 1870), 19.

[9] F. W. Boreham, *Mercury*, June 11, 1932.

[10] F. W. Boreham, *The Three Half-Moons*, 125.

their own; but they point to things that no man can afford to miss: that is their only glory."[11]

F. W. Boreham would say that a person who wants to build a bank of good stories will need to *travel*. He loved to cite the story in which Lord Chesterfield was asked about the best way to acquire a good education and he answered, "There are three main ways, travel, travel and travel."[12]

Frank Boreham took this advice to heart and there are many stories he told in which it is clear that his understanding and his communication was stimulated and enriched by travel. Writing about the way his eyes were opened to the treasures of London when after years of absence he returned to the United Kingdom, Boreham said, "I never saw London until I left it."[13] Inherent in this quote is the truth that travel *per se* will not extend our education or make us a good storyteller. One needs to have the eyes to see or as Boreham learned from James Cook, the secret "lies in the traveler's ability to detect the treasures that are best worth gathering."[14]

A further source of good stories is in the *arts*. F. W. Boreham made a point of attending the theater to watch good plays although he never enjoyed viewing movies at the cinema. He visited the local art gallery on a weekly basis and the savoring of paintings was always included in his travel itineraries. Notice how many of his stories and sermons commence with a reference to a painting.

Push Your Keel into New Seas

Human experience, books, nature, travel and the arts were some of the many avenues of life down which F. W. Boreham

---

[11] F. W. Boreham, *The Crystal Pointers,* 8.

[12] F. W. Boreham, *The Passing of John Broadbanks*, 195; F. W. Boreham, *The Prodigal*, 35.

[13] F. W. Boreham, *When the Swans Fly High*, 75-79.

[14] F. W. Boreham, *The Passing of John Broadbanks*, 204.

found his stories. When he was asked to speak about effective communication Frank Boreham would encourage people to be adventurous:

> "I do suggest that a man should be incessantly forcing his mind along new lines, familiarizing himself with unfamiliar themes, pushing his keel into new seas and exploring worlds on which his eyes have never before gazed."[15]

It is often the discovery of some new scene or truth that not only provides the story content but gives us the eagerness and excitement that is essential in the sharing of a good story. During his retirement when F. W. Boreham was a much sought after international conference speaker in the USA, Canada and the United Kingdom, he kept urging pastors to stay fresh and interesting by "always forcing your minds along unfamiliar tracks, to be constantly breaking fresh ground, to be everlastingly exploring new worlds."[16]

LIKE A DOG ON A COUNTRY ROAD

To become a colorful communicator who is able to connect with the wide range of interests represented in every audience F. W. Boreham offered this final gem:

> "If a man is to keep himself alive in a world like this, infinity must be sampled. Like a dog on a country road I must poke into as many holes as can. If I am naturally fond of music, I had better study mining. If I love painting, I shall be wise to go in for gardening. If I glory in the seaside, I must make a point of climbing mountains and

---

[15] F. W. Boreham, *Ships of Pearl*, 170-1.

[16] F. W. Boreham, *The Blue Flame*, (London: The Epworth Press, 1930), 248.

scouring the bush. If I am attached to things just under my nose, I must be careful to read books dealing with distant lands. If I am deeply interested in contemporary affairs, I must at once read the records of the days of long ago and explore the annals of the splendid past. I must be faithful to old friends, but I must get to know new people and to know them well. If I hold to one opinion, I must studiously cultivate the acquaintance of people who hold the opposite view, and investigate the hidden recesses of their minds with scientific and painstaking diligence. Above all I must be constantly sampling infinity in matters of faith. If I find that the Epistles are gaining a commanding influence upon my mind, I must at once set out to explore the prophets.... 'The Lord has yet more truth to break out from his Word!' said John Robinson; 'and I must try to find it.' "[17]

Geoff Pound

---

[17] F. W. Boreham, *Mushrooms on the Moor*, 18-19.

DR. FRANK W. BOREHAM: THE MAN AND THE WRITER

A Biographical Essay by Rev. Dr. C. Irving Benson

Here was a man for whom life never lost the halo of wonder—that is the abiding impression of my long friendship with Frank Boreham. What a relish he had for living and how vastly he enjoyed being alive! He was interesting because he was interested in everybody and everything.

His fifty books won for him a multitude of friends across the seven seas. But the man himself was greater than all that he wrote. His books were only the 'fancies that broke through language and escaped.'

There was more in him than could be uttered in one lifetime. 'If there is anything in the doctrine of reincarnation,' he said, 'I intend to spend at least one of my future spans of existence as a novelist, working up into thrilling romances the plots that I have collected in the course of my life as a minister.'

There was a Dickensian quality in his mind, a quickness to sense the possibilities of a story, a situation or a scene. But the chief charm of his books lies in their rich veins of autobiography. Pick up any one of them and you will not read far before striking some personal experience, confession or adventure. He poured himself into his writing. When the French King Henry III told Montaigne that he liked his books, the essayist replied: 'I am my books.' So it was with Frank Boreham.

His work is distinguished by a quiet insight, a gentle humor, a homely philosophy and a charming literary grace, but supremely he was a man with a message. He wrote because he had something to say.

When he was a baby in arms his mother took him for a walk on a summer afternoon along the Southborough Road out of Tunbridge Wells. She rested awhile on a seat in the shade of a hedge. A gipsy caravan came along and trudging beside it was a wrinkled old crone. Catching sight of the mother with her baby, she hobbled across to the seat. Lifting the white veil she looked into the child's face, and holding the tiny hand she said in a husky voice: 'Put a pen in his hand and he'll never want for a living.'

He was a born teller of stories, with a perennial freshness and an ingenious, inventive, imaginative mind. He was scarcely out of school when he began sending articles to London papers and magazines. Had he kept to his youthful ambition to be a journalist he would have been a first-rate interviewer. It was amazing what he drew out of unlikely people.

When you met him you were impressed by his quietness, modesty and fine courtesy. There was no hint that here was a writer and preacher with a world reputation. His gentle, sensitive face seemed rather shy but became expressive as he talked. His voice was clear and kindly, with a lingering Kentish flavor.

If the word 'genius' may be used of him, it should be applied in the realm of friendship. You find it in his many essays on John Broadbanks, but he bestowed it upon a host of people, indeed he offered it to everybody he met. As a brother minister he was an apostle of encouragement and as a pastor he had a rare skill in the art of comforting.

To know him was to love him. He went through life scattering benedictions. I never heard him say an unkind or a mean thing about anybody. He did not attack people, always maintaining that the best way of proving that a stick is crooked is to lay a straight one beside it. 'People want helping and you don't help them by scolding them.'

I do not remember his name being associated with any controversy. With Fundamentalist, with High Church and Evangelical, with Roman Catholic and Protestant, he had no discernible quarrel. With true catholicity of spirit he moved among them with the easy grace of a man who picked flowers from all their gardens.

Early on, Sir Robertson Nicoll raised the question in the *British Weekly* as to whether it was as easy as it looked to write in Boreham's style. But the truth was that the apparent ease with which he wrote was only seeming, for what appeared to be spontaneous was the result of sustained hard work.

Every morning he was in his study at eight o'clock writing down every idea and fancy and experience that came to him. They might not appear in sermons or articles for years, but he accumulated a vast store of material on which he drew as he needed it. His fingers itched to write, and he loved to have a pen in his hand. He always reveled in writing and he could not stay his hand even when he tried. When he told me that *The Passing of John Broadbanks* would be his last book, I smiled. It was not long before another volume appeared with the title *I Forgot to Say,* and he kept on remembering themes he had forgotten through half a dozen more books.

For all his understanding, he was incapable of understanding why a man should dictate to a secretary or—worse still—use a typewriter. His clear, flowing handwriting never made a compositor swear. Until he was an old man he refused to have a telephone in the house, maintaining that he could not have accomplished all he did if there had been the constant interruptions of phone calls.

Many a man envied his dispatch, his punctual attention to affairs so that he was never overwhelmed. And yet he seemed to be leisurely, and his methodical habits reminded me of Beau Brummel's definition of a well-dressed man—so well-dressed that you do not notice it.

His essays were grown—not manufactured. A story, an idea, a fancy came to him and he quickly captured it with his pen. Then, in living and reading, a host of associated ideas gathered round it until the theme ripened in his mind.

Look, for example, at his essay on 'Strawberries and Cream.' Strawberries are delicious. Cream is also very nice. But it is strawberries *and* cream that make an irresistible appeal. He muses on that unrecorded yet fateful day when some audacious dietetic adventurer took the cream from his dairy and poured it on the strawberries from his garden, and discovered with delight that the whole was greater than the sum of its parts. Then you see the idea growing that things are enhanced by being brought together. Away he goes writing of husband *and* wife; William *and* Dorothy Wordsworth; new potatoes *and* mint. Maybe it took years for all these ideas to grow together in his mind.

Read his paper on 'Dominoes.' He begins by telling how he was unexpectedly invited to have a game of dominoes. Now dominoes, he sees, stand for sympathy—the game is to match your neighbor's piece—and one of the delightful things about life is that the most unlikely people are found to play at dominoes. Working out this thesis he instances one of O. Henry's whimsicalities, in which a burglar, on discovering that his victim, like himself, is liable to rheumatism, drops his nefarious intention, and eagerly discusses symptoms and remedies with the astonished householder—in short, they play at dominoes. A sequence of illustrations, each piercing deeper into the heart of the subject, follows this opening until we come to Paul, the master of dominoes, who knew how to become all things to all people, and to One greater than Paul. Finally, he tells how a woman missionary showed a hundred magic lantern slides to a gathering of Japanese mothers. Not a flicker of response did she find until at last she threw on the sheet the picture of Christ toiling with His Cross. Instantly, the room was alive with interest and quick tears flowed. They felt that here was One who had suffered as they suffered, One whose deep and terrible experience answered to their own. These Japanese mothers felt that the scene fitted their lives as key fits lock, as glove fits hand, as domino fits domino.

The discerning can see how the idea suggested by the dominoes came first, how he then read O. Henry by the fireside, and so on until he lighted on the missionary story. The ideas grew together over a period until he gathered them all in the essay.

The essays would appear at intervals in a succession of newspapers and magazines to which he contributed. Then, after much revision, they were prepared for a book. But even then the book would be ready and under critical observation for two or more years before it went to the publisher.

Near the end, on the day his son drove him to the Royal Melbourne Hospital, Dr. Boreham first took him into the study and entrusted to him a bundle of articles—enough to supply the editors of the various papers for which he wrote for six months! Was there ever such a man?

Although his style was his own, he confessed the lasting influence that Mark Rutherford had upon him. His earlier tendency to glittering alliteration mellowed into a graceful, engaging style. There was an exuberance about his adjectives and he always had more than he could use. A man's adjectives are often more characteristic than his nouns. His nouns are names for common objects which he is more or less forced to use; his adjectives are the distinguishing marks he places upon them, and reveal his individuality. There is much to be learned of the spirit of Frank Boreham from a study of his adjectives.

Always he kept his values adjusted, and the evangelist was never lost in the genial fireside essayist. John Wesley's Journal had a permanent place on his desk, and day by day he traveled through the year with the great itinerant who was ever about his Master's business.

Frank Boreham preached a great Gospel. There was fancy and artistry, but all his paths led to the Cross. The preacher of small subjects is doomed, he said. 'The pulpit is the place for magnificent verities. It is the home of immensities, infinities, eternities. We must preach more upon the great texts of Scripture; we must preach on those tremendous passages whose vastnesses almost terrify us as we approach them.'

One day he tossed over to me a tart letter from a woman commanding him to preach the Gospel. She was apparently misled by one of his intriguing titles. All who heard Frank Boreham knew full well that, however far away on the circumference he began, he always came to the very heart of the Gospel. The letter hurt him and I advised him to consign it to the waste-paper basket and forget it. 'I have already answered it,' he said. 'I wrote and told her that I appreciated her concern for the preaching of Christ's Gospel and asked her to pray for me that I may be a faithful minister of the Word.' As I have already mentioned, he had no secretary to handle the considerable flow of letters that came into his box from many lands. Each letter was answered expeditiously, either briefly on a post card or at length, as it deserved.

When asked whether he found his main satisfaction as a writer or a preacher, without any hesitation he answered, 'As a preacher and a minister. Of course,' he added quickly, 'it is like asking a man which of his two children he loves best! I glory in my pulpit—the greatest moments of my life have been spent there—but I am scarcely less fond of my pen. I do not like to choose between them. I want to be a preacher and a scribbler to the end of the chapter.' He was more interested in souls than subjects.

He browsed among many books, but the atmosphere he breathed was of one Book. You set out with him and he lured you through pleasant valleys, plucking flowers by the way, but he never mistook the by-path meadow for the King's high road, and finally he led you to the uplands of God. In his preaching he worked from the surface of a text to its deep heart.

'I have been on a visit to the uttermost star' is the exciting beginning of an essay, but before he is through he has you listening to the Good Shepherd telling: 'A bruised reed shall He not break; a smoking lamp shall He not quench.'

Emma Herman, the mystic, said after hearing him preach, that there was something about his treatment of a theme that was reminiscent of the great Dutch manner of painting which, by the magic play of light and shade, can make a peasant's kitchen romantic as a fairy palace.

When in 1936 he was invited to address the General Assembly of the Church of Scotland in Edinburgh, the Moderator, Professor David Lamont, introduced him as 'the man whose name is on all our lips, whose books are on all our shelves, and whose illustrations are in all our sermons'—which recalls the vicar who was heard to say that he hoped he would never meet Boreham for he would be ashamed to look him in the face because he had preached so many of his sermons!

No man can be at the top of his form in every line that trickles from his pen. The clock only strikes twelve twice a day. In writing thousands of essays a man must sometimes fall below his standard of attainment. Nobody knew better than he that it was so in his case. The high standards he set for himself kept him critical of his own work. He would try and try again, but sometimes he failed and there must be a pile of essays which he did not regard as worth a place in his books.

He found it good to form a set of friendships outside the circle in which he habitually moved, and his other great interest, after preaching and writing, was revealed in an illuminating sentence: 'I only miss a cricket match when the house is on fire.' No member of the Melbourne Cricket Club was more regularly in his place than he. He loved the game and found it a perfect holiday. When he went to the beach or the bush his mind chased quarries for sermons or articles, but watching cricket he forgot everything but runs and wickets.

On nights when sleep was hard to come by, instead of counting sheep he would replay cricket matches in his mind. Lying awake in the darkness, he saw again the green oval 'fanned by the balmy breath of summer and fragrant with the peculiar but pleasant odor of the turf.' He relived the fluctuations and fortunes of the game and thus, so long as he remained awake, remained awake pleasantly, and in the process generated a state of mind in which it was easy to fall asleep.

His royalties must have been considerable, but he gave much of his income away. I learned, for example, in one of his unguarded moments, that he provided the capital cost to establish a Mission Dispensary with wards at Birisiri in Eastern Bengal and had given a capital sum for its maintenance. But it was unusual for anyone to discuss anything about his gifts. In the spirit of generosity, he followed the admonition: 'Let not thy left hand know what thy right hand doeth.' He knew that the best way to do good is not to tell anyone—not even oneself. He had little stomach for committees, but he served for years on the Baptist Mission Board.

Dr. Boreham usually sported a flower in his buttonhole, but riding into Melbourne one day on a crowded tram he realized that he had forgotten it. In Swanston Street, a large, lame old lady climbed on board with difficulty and all eyes turned to the bunch of golden wattle she carried. It was in the winter month of July and the sight of the bright blossom was like the promise of sunshine on a rainy day. As she alighted a few streets further on she plucked off a handful of lovely blossom and gave it to a newspaper boy. He took them without a word of thanks, and while she watched the tram beginning to move he tossed it on the floor. Dr. Boreham was horrified. Diving down among the feet of the passengers he rescued it and asked the boy, 'Don't you want it?' 'No,' he muttered contemptuously, 'what's the good?' So Dr. Boreham stuck it in his own buttonhole and wore it proudly. All that afternoon people remarked on the wattle. 'The wattle's out!' said one with brightening face. 'Like the breath of spring!' said another. The posy sang to everyone he met of the coming spring. He thought of the woebegone face of the old lady as she stood looking after the vanishing car. She had tried to do a nice thing, and although her gift had been thrown away she had succeeded.

At many a gathering of ministers Dr. Boreham told this incident and warmed the hearts of his hearers. Though love's labor often seemed lost, he said, it had results that would surprise them. Lift up your hearts!

Characteristically, Dr. Boreham used to say that he was born on the day when bells pealed across Europe announcing the dramatic termination of the Franco-Prussian War. That was March 3, 1871.

His education at the local school was plain and practical, and he became a clerk in the office of a nearby brickworks. There he had an accident, which left him with a limp through all his days.

Three months before he was seventeen he went up to London in answer to an advertisement and joined the office staff of the South London Tramways Company. Proficiency in shorthand, which he had mastered during his convalescence in Tunbridge Wells, brought him quick promotion. The office years were, he always said, of incalculable importance. He learned to be methodical, to be systematic in the handling of correspondence, and to be courteous, tactful and discreet in handling people.

The impact of London on his young spirit was the turning point of his life. London appalled him. He stood one day under the shadow of St. Paul's, shivering in the crowd at his own utter loneliness. Amid the hops and clover and the orchards of his native Kent he could shout as he wished and never a soul would hear him. That was a tranquil loneliness in which he reveled, but the loneliness of the surging crowd seemed intolerable.

In those first days in London there fastened on his mind a conviction that he needed Something or Someone to nerve him to live in London to some purpose, and in that mood of wistfulness his situation dramatically changed. There in his solitude, he said, 'Christ laid His mighty hand upon me and made me His own.' He could not recall any sermon or book, any minister or missionary, any church or society that played any part in this vital experience which changed his life.

The young Christian became acquainted with a group of city missionaries whose friendship fortified and energized the new life that had sprung up within him. They took him to their mission halls and their open-air meetings, sometimes inviting him to speak. Then in the late summer of 1890 he went with them to Brenchley in Kent to work and witness among the hop-pickers. He always said that was the most delightful holiday he ever had in England. Through those soft September days he reveled in the charming old village, the rambles through the poppy-splashed fields and through woods showing their first autumn tints. But his most vivid memory was of the great tent in which the missioners held their evening meetings. The appeals for personal decision—'wooingly persuasive but never tediously protracted'—brought to his eager mind a powerful realization of the realities of which they spoke.

His first enthusiasm was to be a foreign missionary with the China Inland Mission. Dr. Hudson Taylor did not encourage him and tenderly pointed out the opportunities of doing missionary work at home. The injury sustained in boyhood which had left him with a limp would, he feared, seriously hamper him in China. Under the guidance of a saintly, scholarly Baptist minister who befriended him, he applied to Charles Haddon Spurgeon for admission to his Pastor's College and was accepted. He was the last student Spurgeon personally chose. His college course lasted for two and a half years. Then Thomas Spurgeon, who had ministered at the Auckland Baptist Tabernacle in New Zealand, returned to succeed his father at the Metropolitan Tabernacle. Before leaving, the Church at Mosgiel had commissioned him to send them a suitable minister. The college tutors recommended Boreham, and so it came about that at twenty-four he sailed in January 1895 for New Zealand.

Mosgiel, a few miles from Dunedin, was a Scottish settlement. Save for a small woolen mill, it belonged to the cow and the plow and the pleasant murmur of bees. The original settlers were still there. The people were largely Scottish and he was very English, but from the first he loved them. He did what love does—he discovered them. There was a wealth of human tenderness behind their faces rugged as granite cliffs. They furnished him with as many characters as James Barrie saw through the 'window in Thrums' or Ian Maclaren found in Drumtochty, and he described them in a style worthy to be mentioned in the same breath with theirs.

There was Gavin, one of the Deacons, who 'fairly squirmed under a quotation from Dante or Browning,' and Tammas, the Church Treasurer, a massive old man of wrinkled countenance who looked searchingly at you over his spectacles. 'The man who got Church money out of Tammas was regarded in the light of a genius.' There was a night when Gavin and Tammas quarreled at a Deacons' meeting and then woke him up in the middle of the night to apologize and asked him to pray with them.

Oh peaceful Mosgiel! There were no cinemas, motor cars, planes or wireless, and in that tiny town free from distractions, he was able to fill the church on a week night with a Bible class. Instead of being run off his feet with a thousand fatiguing but futile engagements, he had time for reflection, for learning how to preach, and for pursuing the art of reading. He resolved to buy a book a week and to read a book a week, and he faithfully kept his pact.

It was at Mosgiel that Boreham learned to be a writer, for it was in that quiet manse among the farms of that faraway parish that he made his first literary ventures. He began a weekly column in the local paper and very quickly became a regular contributor to the Dunedin city newspaper.

Looking back upon his first ministry, he would say that from attending a criminal on the gallows to being asked by a bashful lover to propose to a blushing maid on his behalf, he tasted every pain and pleasure of a minister's life.

After twelve years at Mosgiel he was called in 1906 to the Hobart Tabernacle, the leading Baptist church in Tasmania. From the first time he entered the pulpit he realized that he was preaching with a self-possession, and with an enjoyment that made his ministry, as he said, 'a perfect revelry.' Ten of the happiest and most satisfying years of his life were spent there. Hobart was a popular tourist resort, and at almost every service there were men and women whose names were household words throughout the Commonwealth.

When Boreham decided to publish a book of his essays, he looked round his shelves to choose a book the format of which appealed to him. His choice fell upon Percy Ainsworth's minor classic The Pilgrim Church. Thus he sent off the manuscript to the publisher of it. Dr. A. J. Sharp liked it but knew nothing about the author. Tasmania seemed a far cry and it was rather risky to take on this unknown F. W. Boreham. Still, he wanted to publish it, so he wrote asking if the author would pledge himself to take 300 copies. Boreham felt himself unable to accept such responsibility and wrote to say so. But on the way to post the letter he met a leading Hobart bookseller who asked if he had sent the manuscript.

'Yes,' he replied, 'and here's my answer.' When he had told the whole story, the bookseller asked if the Publishing House would be likely to offer his firm the same terms. The upshot was that the first letter was destroyed and another written. The same offer was made to the bookseller. *The Luggage of Life* appeared, and Boreham was launched upon his career as a writer. Every year thereafter he brought forth a new book, which went through edition after edition and sold by the hundreds of thousands. Dr. Sharp once made the interesting remark to me that Boreham was the Publishing House's 'greatest catch' since John Wesley's day.

In June 1916 he accepted the invitation to the Armadale Church. Armadale is an attractive suburb of Melbourne between the river Yarra and Port Phillip. His great preaching—attractive, interesting and evangelistic—drew crowds of eager hearers. Trams and trains set down a constant stream of people bound for Dr. Boreham's church. Some of them became members, others were inspired to be more devoted members of their own Churches, all were confirmed in the Faith. Dr. Boreham became a spiritual power in the life of Melbourne and, indeed, throughout Australia.

A Bunch of Everlastings carries this dedication: 'At the Feet of Those Three Elect Ladies, the Churches at Mosgiel, Hobart and Armadale, I desire, with the Deepest Affection and Respect, to lay this Bunch of Everlastings.'

Retirement in 1928 did not close but extended his ministry. 'I must preach!' he wrote to me urgently when he left Armadale, and Churches everywhere welcomed him. He liked to think of himself as a kind of shuttle, going to and fro between the Churches, weaving them closer to each other.

Through all the ministering years, he was loved and companioned by the lady—Stella Cottee—whose love he had won during his student pastorate at the village of Theydon Bois in Epping Forest. She was not out of her teens when she voyaged alone across the world to become the first mistress of the Mosgiel Manse. Her quiet grace and lovely serenity, blended with good sense, imaginative thoughtfulness and steadfast courage, inspired and sustained, protected and defended him, and smiled away his fears. He knew more than all of us how much she gave to make him the man we admired and loved. They walked and worked together and she was beside him on 'the long last mile.' This must be said of him—that he was at his brightest and best with his wife and children around him in the blessed peace of his home.

Frank Boreham had his share of sorrows, but they were never wasted sorrows, for 'aye the dews of sorrow were lustered by His love.'

He needed no honors, but his friends rejoiced when McMaster University conferred upon him the degree of Doctor of Divinity in 1928 and Queen Elizabeth made him an Officer of the Order of the British Empire in 1954.

The man whom Billy Graham wanted to meet in Australia above all others was F. W. Boreham. So one fine summer morning I drove him out to Wroxton Lodge in Kew overlooking the valley of the river Yarra. It was a day to remember—the young evangelist greeting the revered old minister in his 88th year.

Dr. Boreham's mind was alert as ever, and as we settled down he said pointedly: 'What interests me in you, Dr. Graham, is the way in which you preach. You break all the laws of oratory and yet you succeed. We were always taught to begin quietly and slowly, winning interest, developing an argument, gathering force and proceeding to a climax. But you begin with a climax and sustain it.'

Dr. Graham smilingly explained that he had listened to speakers in pulpits and on platforms, studied them on the radio and television, and had come to the conclusion that with people who were listening and viewing in their homes it was necessary to win them in the first two minutes.

I coaxed Dr. Boreham to tell Dr. Graham some of his best stories—particularly his memories of Dwight L. Moody with his rugged personality like a volcano in ceaseless eruption, a miracle of tireless energy with his flaming evangelism and zeal for souls.

Before we left I asked the dear old Doctor to bless us, and there Dr. Billy Graham and I knelt, while with face uplifted to Heaven and his hands on our heads, he poured out his great heart in a consecrating prayer which will follow us through the years like the sound of a grand Amen.

His day was then far spent. On a May day in 1959 he came to the end of the earthly road, ready to explore what he knew lay on 'the other side of the Hill.' We gathered in the Armadale church knowing that our company represented a multitude of friends the world over whose lives he had blessed. After we had thanked God for the gift of this good and gracious and gifted man and his fruitful life, we laid all that was mortal of him in a plot of earth in the Boroondara burying ground not far from the resting place of John G. Paton, the apostolic missionary to the New Hebrides.

As I walked slowly away on that Australian autumn day, the golden poplars were like great torches of clear yellow flame and the lawns were strewn with scarlet and russet and bronze leaves blown by the clean wind. Yet I thought not of Autumn, but of Christ's gay springtime that sang in this man's heart. And that night as I sat by the fire with the long deep thoughts that such a day brings, there came to me the words of

Dante: 'If the world might know the heart he had within him, much as it praiseth, it would praise him more.'

C. Irving Benson was a friend of Frank Boreham, a leading church leader in Melbourne and pastor of the Wesley Church.

This biographical essay on F. W. Boreham was first published as the preface to the 'memorial volume': F. W. Boreham, *The Last Milestone* (London: The Epworth Press, 1961), 7-20.

THE
STORIES

ALL THE BLESSINGS OF LIFE

It is great to be alive—at any age. As a small boy, following in the Prayer Book the liturgy of the Church, I was always impressed by one phrase in the General Thanksgiving: *We bless Thee for our creation, preservation and all the blessings of this life.*

In those days I only dimly discerned the meaning of the phrases that followed—inestimable love, redemption, the means of grace, the hope of glory, and so on. All this, to me, was enfolded in a golden haze. But I loved that opening expression of gratitude. I felt that it belonged to me. I was glad to be alive, and this particular clause gave me the opportunity of saying so. It is certainly good to be alive today.

F. W. Boreham, *Cliffs of Opal*, (London: The Epworth Press, 1948), 172.

APPROPRIATING THE INEXHAUSTIBLE

One afternoon, a man chanced to pass a Tourist Agency and saw in the window a colored representation of Niagara Falls. He entered; secured a copy of the telling advertisement; and pasted across the foot of it 'More to Follow!'

Could anything be more to the point? However great the demand that the falls may make upon the river, there is always more and more water to come! However great the demand that my needs have made upon the divine grace, there is always more and more at my disposal!

This vision of grace overwhelming and overflowing, rebukes the paltriness of my appropriation.

I recall the story that Macaulay tells in his essay on Lord Clive. When Clive was on his trial, answering his impeachment before his peers, he was charged, among other things, with having taken a sum of two hundred thousand pounds from the Indian princes.

'Two hundred thousand pounds!' exclaimed Clive. 'Two hundred thousand pounds! Is that possible?' He described the way in which the Indian princes had admitted him to their treasure-chests, displaying to his astonished eyes heaps of glittering gems, wealth incalculable, gold beyond the dreams of avarice. 'I was invited,' Clive exclaimed, 'to help myself, to take as much as I would! And is it possible that I contented myself with a paltry two hundred thousand pounds? Great God, I stand astonished at my own moderation!'

So must every person feel who stands with me beside this reservoir. He ponders the monumental, majestic, mountainous phraseology with which the New Testament sets forth the illimitable riches and indescribable wonders of the divine grace. The most tremendous terms falter and seem ashamed of their own pitiful inadequacy. The infinities of grace make the very universe appear tiny. Yet the amazing thing is that we have actually appropriated so insignificant a fragment of the glittering hoard. We have been mendicants when we might have been millionaires. We must learn a higher wisdom. We must lay daring hands upon the inexhaustible supplies that we have so shamefully neglected and live in the enjoyment of an affluence that we have never before known. Ashamed of the past, we must turn shining and expectant faces to the future, giving glory to God for all the grace we have not tasted yet.

F. W. Boreham, *Boulevards of Paradise* (London: The Epworth Press, 1944), 202-203.

BE YOURSELF

John Constable's name will always be held in honor on several grounds. His landscapes are admittedly incomparable. His cloud-effects and sky-effects have never been surpassed. The delicacy of his color-sense has been the admiration and the despair of all his disciples.

But the finest thing about him was his fidelity to his own ideal. He insisted on seeing every object through his own eyes and in depicting it as he himself saw it. As Sir Charles John Holmes says, 'he hated painters who take their ideas from other painters instead of getting them direct from Nature.' It was the glory of Constable that he shattered, and shattered forever, a particularly stubborn tradition. As the late E. V. Lucas said, 'he brought the English people face to face with England—the delicious, fresh, rainy, blowy England that they could identify. Hitherto there had been landscape painters in abundance; but here was something else: here was *weather!*'

There is a famous story to the effect that Henry Fuseli, the historical painter, who, in Constable's time, was keeper of the Academy, was seen one day engrossed in the contemplation of one of Constable's paintings. It represented an English landscape in a drizzling rain. Lost to all the world, the old man became saturated in the spirit of the picture that he was so ardently admiring, and, to the astonishment of the onlookers, he suddenly put up his umbrella!

So triumphant a thing is truth! Let every person who is charged with the solemn responsibility of expressing his soul for the public good take notice! Let no painter paint in a certain way simply because he fancies that it is in that particular way that painters are expected to paint! Let no preacher preach in a certain way simply because he fancies that it is in that particular way that preachers are expected to preach!

I remember one evening standing at a street-corner listening to a chain of testimonies being given at an open-air meeting. They were all excellent; but—they were all exactly alike! I could see at once that each speaker was saying what he imagined that he was expected to say. Then there stepped into the ring a man whose lips were twitching with emotion: he said one or two things that sent a shudder down the spines of his hearers: but the force of his testimony was overwhelming. He had done, in his sphere, precisely what Constable did in his.

Let each painter, each preacher, each person whose duty it is to write a newspaper article or lead a Christian assembly to the Throne of Grace, realize that his view of God and of Humanity and of the Universe is essentially an individualistic view. He sees as nobody else sees. He must therefore paint or preach or pray or write as nobody else does. He must be himself: must see with his own eyes and utter that vision in the terms of his own personality. He must, as Rudyard Kipling would have said, paint the thing *as he sees it* for the God of *things as they are*. And, expressing his naked and transparent soul by means of his palette, his pulpit or his pen, he will find sooner or later—sooner rather than later—that truth, like wisdom, is justified of all her children.

F. W. Boreham, *I Forgot To Say* (London: The Epworth Press, 1939), 131-133.

BEARING ONE ANOTHER'S BURDENS

After granting me seven years of such happy intimacy, Mr. Doke [Boreham's mentor] left New Zealand and I saw him no more. It was a year or two later that he and Mr. Gandhi met. Mr. Doke had recently settled as minister at Johannesburg; and Mr. Gandhi was in South Africa as the legal representative of the Indian population, who, just then, were involved in a serious clash with the authorities. Mr. Doke's sympathies were with the Indians, and he immediately got into touch with Mr. Gandhi. Each was astonished at the other's diminutive stature. They did not look like a pair of champions. Mr. Doke says that he expected to see 'a tall and stately figure and a bold masterful face.' Instead of this, 'a small, little, spare figure stood before me, and a refined earnest face looked into mine. The skin was dark, the eyes dark, but the smile which illumined the face, and that direct, fearless glance, simply took one's heart by storm. He was only thirty-eight, but the strain of his work showed its traces in the sprinkling of silver in his hair. He spoke English perfectly and was evidently a man of great culture.'

On the wall of Mr. Gandhi's office hung a beautiful picture of Jesus; and, the moment that Mr. Doke's eyes rested upon it, he felt that he and his new friend were bound by a most sacred tie.

'I want you,' he said to Mr. Gandhi, 'to consider me your friend in this struggle. If,' he added, with a glance at the picture on the wall, 'if I have learned any lesson from the life of Jesus it is that we should share the burden of those who are heavy-laden.'

F. W. Boreham, *I Forgot To Say* (London: The Epworth Press, 1939), 140.

BECOMING ALIVE

In his *Priest of the Ideal* Stephen Graham makes one of his characters rebuke another because of his failure to recognize the intrinsic splendor of life. 'Why, man,' he exclaims, 'your opportunities are boundless! Your whole life should be a miracle! Instead of merely making a *living*, you can *live!* Instead of finding a *calling,* you can listen for *the call!* You are; but you have also *to become!* A wonderful world about you is beckoning you, enticing you *to become!*

To become! … I am only in the making as yet.

F. W. Boreham, *Home of the Echoes* (London: The Epworth Press, 1921), 57.

BEFRIENDING ONE'S FEARS

I wish I could do for Cecil what a very eminent physician recently did for a young patient to whom he was called. It is Dr. H. E. Fosdick who tells the story. The boy's nerves were being frayed and lacerated by a terrible dream that came to him, night after night, with pitiless regularity. As soon as he dropped off to sleep he found himself confronted by a frightful tiger. At their wits' ends, his parents called in a specialist in child psychology. After thinking it over, the great man took the child on his knee.

'See here, sonnie,' he said, 'they tell me that every night you meet a tiger. Now, really, he is a nice, kind, friendly tiger, and he wants you to like him, so, the next time you meet him, just put out your hand and say, *"Hello, old chap!"* and you will find that he will chum up to you and become a pet!'

That night, after a period of pleasant repose, the boy manifested all the symptoms of his former terror. He tossed about, ground his teeth, puckered his face, and broke into a violent perspiration. Then, all at once, we are told, his muscles relaxed. 'He thrust a small hand out from under the bed-clothes and murmuring softly: *"Hello, old chap!"* his frightened breathing quieted into the perfect restfulness of natural sleep.'

He had discovered that the tiger, however terrible in aspect, was not necessarily hostile, after all!

F. W. Boreham, *A Witch's Brewing* (London: The Epworth Press, 1932), 229.

BEING RECONCILED WITH ONE'S LOT

Life has a wonderful way of coaxing us into a frame of mind in which we not only become reconciled to our lot: we actually fall in love with it. No memory of my early days on this side of the world is more vivid than the recollection of a horrid terror, a cold paralyzing apprehension, that often made me start in the night. I, a young Englishman, loving every stick and stone in England, had come out to New Zealand. Suppose I were to *die here!* My bones to be buried in New Zealand soil! It was an appalling thought, and I broke into a clammy perspiration whenever it took possession of my mind!

Later on, another nightmare, just as dreadful, came to keep it company, and I was haunted by the two of them. I married: little children gladdened our home: and we were as happy as two people could be. But suppose, I would say to myself, suppose these children grow up to regard themselves as New Zealanders, totally destitute of the emotions that bring a tug at their parents' hearts and a tear to their parents' eyes at every mention of the dear Homeland! How those ugly thoughts tyrannized me, shadowing even the sunniest of our early days under the Southern Cross!

When, later on, we found ourselves once more in England, we made two startling discoveries: we discovered that England was even more lovely and more lovable than, in our most sentimental moments, we had pictured her. But we discovered, simultaneously, that our hearts insisted on turning wistfully back to the lands in which so many of our years had been spent. The visits home were, from first to last, a dream of unalloyed delight; we were overwhelmed and touched to tears by the most astonishing kindnesses and hospitalities, yet, in the midst of it all, we found that we had become citizens of the distant south. The wattle and the gum thrust their roots very deeply into one's heart in the course of the years. It is a

way that life has, and a very wonderful way, of putting us on
the happiest of terms with the place in which we are destined
to live and with the work that we have been appointed to do.

F. W. Boreham, *My Pilgrimage* (London: The Epworth Press, 1940),
137-138.

BELIEVING IN PEOPLE

The novelist Laurence Sterne was a member of an extraordinary family. They were incessantly on the move. They seem to
have gone into a place; stayed there until a child had been born
and a child buried; and then jogged on again. He would be a
bold historian who would declare, with any approach to dog-
matism, how many babies were born and buried in the course
of these nomadic gipsyings. They seem to have lived for a year
or so in all sorts of towns and villages, and, with pitiful monot-
ony, we read of their regret at having to leave such-and-such
a child sleeping in the churchyard. 'My father's children,' as
Sterne himself observes, 'were not made to last long.' Laurence
himself, however, was one of the lucky ones.

At the age of ten, having survived the jaunts and jolts
to which the wanderings of the family exposed him, he was
'fixed' in a school at Halifax, and was profoundly impressed
by the conviction of his Yorkshire schoolmaster that he
was destined to become a distinguished man.... On one
occasion the ceiling of the school room was being white-
washed. The ladder was left against the wall. 'One unlucky
day,' says Sterne, 'I mounted that ladder, seized the brush,
and wrote my name in large capital letters high up on the
wall. For this offence the usher thrashed me severely. But
the master was angry with him for doing so, and declared
that the name on the wall should never be erased. For, he
added, I was a boy of genius, and would one day become
famous, and he should then look with pride on the letters

on the schoolroom wall. These words made me forget the cruel blows that I had just received.'

The words did more. They implanted a glorious hope in the boy's breast: they inspired efforts that he would never otherwise have made: they account, in large measure, for his phenomenal success.

If the schoolmaster who welcomed the awkward little ten-year-old in 1723 lived, by any chance, until 1760, he must have felt that his handful of hopeseed had produced a most bounteous harvest. For, in 1760, *Tristram Shandy* took the country by storm. It was chaotic: it was incoherent: it was an audacious defiance of all the conventions: but it was irresistible. Its originality, its grotesque oddity, its rippling whimsicality set everybody chuckling.

Immediately after its publication, Sterne went up to London. He was the lion of the hour. His lodgings in Pall Mall were besieged from morning to night. 'My rooms,' he writes, 'are filling every hour with great people of the first rank who vie with each other in heaping honors upon me.' Never before had a literary venture elicited such homage. And when, a few months later, he crossed the Channel, a similar banquet of adulation awaited him in France.

F. W. Boreham, *The Three Half-Moons* (London: The Epworth Press, 1929), 89-91.

Believing, Loving and Obeying

When Samuel Rutherford was staying for a while at the house of James Guthrie, the maid was surprised at hearing a voice in his room. She had supposed he was alone. Moved by curiosity, she crept to his door. She then discovered that Rutherford was in prayer. He walked up and down the room, exclaiming, 'O Lord, make me to believe in you!' Then, after a pause, he moved to and fro again, crying, 'O Lord, make me to love you!' And, after a second rest, he rose again, praying, 'O Lord, make me to keep all your commandments!' Rutherford, ... had grasped the spiritual significance of the divine order. 'O Lord, make me to believe in you!'—the commandment that ... includes all the commandments! 'O Lord, make me to love you!'—for love, as Jesus told the rich young ruler, is the fulfillment of the whole law. 'O Lord, make me to keep all your commandments!' The person who learns the Ten Commandments ... will see a shining path that runs from Mount Sinai right up to the Cross and on through the gates of pearl into the City of God.

F. W. Boreham, *A Handful of Stars* (London: The Epworth Press, 1922), 66-67.

BLESSED

The *blessed* of the Beatitudes is suggestive of natural fruitfulness; it stands related to the roses round my lawn, to the corn in yonder valleys and to the autumnal harvest of the orchard. It has to do with joys that arise spontaneously and inevitably from certain fixed conditions.

It is the word *Macaria,* a name that was once given to the Island of Cyprus because that island was said to be so fertile as to be able to produce upon its own shores everything that its inhabitants could either require or desire. Such is the blessedness of the poor in spirit. The Kingdom of Heaven—the only true *Macaria*—is theirs; and, when they at last finish their long fight with self and sin, they shall inherit that happy land where all their chastened appetites shall be fully gratified and all their purified cravings be abundantly appeased.

Well may Sextus Rufus hint that Cyprus, the Isle of Macaria, famous for its fertility and wealth, presented a constant temptation to the Romans; they lusted to seize upon it and make so rich a prize their very own. The wonder is that the Kingdom of Heaven—the brighter, grander, fairer Macaria—does not entice all earth's knightliest spirits to venture along the lowly track that winds its way through the Valley of Humiliation in quest of such abounding and abiding felicity. Blessed are the lowly and the contrite, for the true Macaria shall be theirs!

'Blessed are the poor in spirit, for theirs is the kingdom of heaven.' It was the King of the Kingdom who said it; and, depend upon it, He knows the laws by which His happy subjects win their glorious victories and gain their glittering crowns.

F. W. Boreham, *The Heavenly Octave* (London: The Epworth Press, 1935), 23-24.

BLESSING OF A PURE CONSCIENCE

The moral and spiritual significance of sleep can scarcely be overestimated. I fortify myself at this point by an appeal to Victor Hugo, and Victor Hugo was a philosopher. He is describing Jean Valjean in the act of robbing the good bishop who had pitied him in his distress, and had admitted him to the hospitality of his home and the confidence of his heart. In creeping through the silent and darkened house, the culprit came to the bed on which the bishop slept. 'A moonbeam passing through the tall window suddenly illuminated the bishop's pale face. He was sleeping peacefully, his head thrown back on the pillow in an easy attitude of repose, and his hand, which had done so many good deeds, hung out of the bed. His entire face was lit up by a vague expression of satisfaction, hope, and beatitude—it was more than a smile, and almost a radiance. He had on his forehead the inexpressible reflection of an invisible light, for the soul of a just man contemplates a mysterious heaven during sleep. A reflection of this heaven was cast over the bishop, but it was at the same time a luminous transparency, for the heaven was *within* him, and was *conscience*. Jean Valjean was standing in the shadow, with his crowbar in his hand, motionless and terrified by this luminous old man. He had never seen anything like this before, and such confidence horrified him. *The moral world has no greater spectacle than this, a troubled, restless conscience, which is on the point of committing a bad action, contemplating the sleep of a just man.'* The moral world, says the brilliant Frenchman, has no greater spectacle than this! No statement that I have made is half so sweeping as that!

F. W. Boreham, *The Golden Milestone* (London: Charles H. Kelly, 1915), 17-18.

I have quoted Victor Hugo for the sake of the philosophy of that golden sentence. The illustration in itself is inconclusive, seeing that it is taken from romance. And so, beside that scene taken from French fiction, I place an almost identical scene taken from English history. An hour or two before the execution of the Earl of Argyle, one of the traitor lords came to the castle and asked to see his lordship. 'He was told,' Macaulay says, 'that he was asleep. The visitor thought this was a subterfuge, and insisted on entering. The door of the cell was softly opened, and there lay Argyle on the bed, sleeping, in his irons, the placid sleep of infancy. The conscience of the renegade smote him. He turned away sick at heart, ran out of the castle, and took refuge in the dwelling of a lady of the family living hard by. There he flung himself on a couch, and gave himself up to an agony of remorse and shame.

His kinswoman, alarmed by his looks and groans, thought that he had been taken with some serious illness, and begged him to drink a cup of sack. "No, no," he said, "that will do me no good." She prayed him to tell her what had disturbed him. "I have been," he said, "in Argyle's prison. I have seen him, within an hour of eternity, sleeping as sweetly as ever a man did! But as for me—"

Now is not this an exact counterpart to the scene in *Les Miserables?* And is it not an abundant confirmation of Victor Hugo's affirmation that 'the moral world has no greater spectacle than this, a troubled, restless conscience, which is on the point of committing a bad action, contemplating the sleep of a just person'? That golden saying should be learned by heart.

The Church, of course, is the true Sleepy Hollow. She has excelled in the production of heroic and magnificent sleepers. That is why I insist that every candidate for her membership should be searchingly questioned as to his ability to sleep.

F. W. Boreham, *The Golden Milestone* (London: Charles H. Kelly, 1915), 18-19.

I like to remember, also, that the night before Latimer and Ridley lit at Oxford that candle which has never been put out, Ridley's anxious brother offered to spend that last terrible night with them. 'No, no, brother,' smiled the Bishop, 'I mean to lie down and sleep as gently as ever I did!' And, to the amazement of the warders who kept guard, he was as good as his word, rising in the morning from his quiet slumber to greet the flames that bore his soul to the skies! Great sleepers, these!

F. W. Boreham, *The Golden Milestone* (London: Charles H. Kelly, 1915), 20.

BREAKING DOWN PREJUDICE

After F. W. Boreham had a train accident, in which he lost part of his leg and almost lost his life, he tells about the nurse who looked after him in the hospital:

My nurse, Teresa Taylor, was a tall and charming Irish lady, of ample means and genuine refinement, who regarded her nursing as her mission and insisted on handing her salary back to the hospital. I can forgive any man for falling in love with a nurse, for I fell head over heels in love with her. There were, however, the gravest difficulties! To begin with, she was a devout and whole-souled Catholic while I was a convinced young Protestant. That was serious. And then, to make matters worse, there was the minor circumstance that I was only fourteen while she was over forty.

Thus it came to pass that love's young dream was shattered; but to my dying day I shall cherish the fact that, in hours of anguish and delirium, her face seemed to me like the face of an angel. Night and day, through weary weeks, she watched tirelessly beside me; no vigil too long, no trouble too great. I used to guess at what the doctors had said by closely scrutinizing her face. She would walk off with them when they left me. If she came back crooning to herself some jaunty little Irish melody, I knew that the doctors were satisfied. If she came back looking as though the weight of the world were on her shoulders, I knew that I was fighting an uphill battle; and once, when things were very dark with me, I caught the glint of tears in her eyes.

A few weeks later, when I was making headway rapidly, she would exchange meals with me. My bread and butter was cut and spread by machinery—each slice just like every other slice. Her bread was cut by hand; the slices were irregular; and the butter was in neat little pats on the side of the plate. And each little delicacy that came her way she at once brought to me.

We both cried when, the long, long struggle over, we said goodbye to each other. I have never since been able to look upon a nurse without blessing her; and, whenever I have been tempted to a too vigorous criticism of Roman Catholicism, I have been confronted by the imperishable memory of Teresa Taylor. She would have thought it heaven to lay down her life for her Church—or for her patients.

F. W. Boreham, *My Pilgrimage* (London: The Epworth Press, 1940), 41-43.

BREAKING THE NEWS

As a general rule, things that are broken are broken by the clumsy. When eggs are broken, or when dishes are broken, or when promises are broken, it is because some one has blundered. But to this general rule there is one striking exception. Careless people may break our china; careless people may break our hearts; but, when it comes to breaking the news, careless people would be worse than useless. However dexterous and skillful at ordinary tasks, the man who is called upon to break the news feels himself to be destitute of all the courtesies and delicacies of human life.

One of the most distinguished of our Australian artists, Mr. John Longstaff, has a particularly fine picture bearing the title, *Breaking the News*. It is the painting that won for him his traveling scholarship. It represents the interior of a cottage, the door of which stands open. A stalwart and bearded miner, gray and kindly, is doing his best to convey to the young mother, who holds a baby in her arms, the cruel tidings that a terrible catastrophe has overtaken the mine, and that her husband is numbered among the victims. When the news-breaker entered, the woman was evidently preparing the evening meal. The plates are warming by the fire; the table is laid; a fork on the floor has fallen from her hand in her sudden agitation. Through the open doorway the bearers can be seen bringing the body to the stricken home. Nobody can look carefully into the picture without recognizing that, in the person of this rugged but fatherly miner, who is so eager to mitigate the grief of the bereaved woman, Mr. Longstaff has given us the news-breaker at his best....

But I have not yet told of the case on which I came nearer to success than on any other similar occasion. It was the one instance in which I was able, very largely, to dispense with words. We were just rising from tea one beautiful evening in the early summer when the telegraph boy rode up on his bicycle. I tore open the envelope and read: *'Please tell Mr. and Mrs. Millington that Stanley has been killed in action in France.'* Mr. and Mrs. Millington are among the nicest people I know; Stanley was their only boy. He was one of the most promising scholars and one of the finest athletes of his generation. His parents and his three young sisters were justly proud of him. I thought of the home—the walls covered with his portraits, the rooms adorned by the trophies he had won. Why should I be called upon to extinguish all its light and shatter all its happiness?

With a heavy heart I set out on my cruel mission, wondering at every step how I could temper to my poor friends the severity of the blow. When I came to the house—a pretty suburban home—I heard, issuing from within, the sounds of boisterous mirth. The girls were evidently having a romp before bedtime. My heart failed me; and I took a turn or two up and down the street before approaching the gate. Then I pulled myself together and braced myself for the ordeal. I rang the bell, and even its music seemed incongruous.

Mrs. Millington herself came to the door. She was full of smiles and cordial welcome. 'Was Mr. Millington in?' Mr. Millington was not in; but he would not be long; I was urged to come in and wait. I was inclined to go away and to return later; but I feared that such behavior might appear strange and lead to premature suspicion. Mrs. Millington took me into the drawing-room; we talked a little—a very little—about the weather and the health of our respective families; and then we lapsed into silence. A vague feeling crept over me that perhaps silence would do my sad work more gently and more gradually than speech. Except for an occasional word of a severely commonplace kind, nothing was said for some minutes. I knew that Mrs. Millington would slowly come to feel that this silence was not quite natural; I knew that it would very soon occur to her that I had not made my usual inquiries concerning Stanley; and I knew that when, in the silence, the first faint suspicion crossed her mind, she would reflect for a moment before she spoke.

Things happened exactly as I had foreseen. In the fading light of the summer evening, I watched the shadow creeping over her face—the reflection of the deeper shadow creeping over her heart. I saw her anxiety growing more acute as her suspicion deepened. Then, rising and coming towards me, she said quietly: 'You have come to bring us bad news?' There was no need for reply. I took her hand and led her back to her chair. She buried her face in her hands and the merciful relief of tears was richly ministered to her. It was the only case that I ever witnessed in which the news was really *broken*. It came to her little by little, and she was able to summon all the resources of her womanhood to meet it. I could not help contrasting her case with that of her husband and her daughters. In the nature of things, I had to break the news to them by means of words; it was crudely and clumsily done;

the strong man cried aloud in his anguish, and the grief of the sisters was a piteous thing to see.

Now why does silence break the news so much more skillfully than speech? The answer is obvious. Silence is the eloquence of Nature; and, in the art of breaking the news, Nature is incomparable. She has the most bewildering astonishments to impart; yet she contrives to communicate them so gradually and so slowly that, so far from shocking us, she scarcely awakens our sense of wonder....

Nature breaks the news to us very gently; she lays the burden, little by little, upon our shoulders; and the thing that once we dreaded as insupportable, we eventually endure with a smile.

F. W. Boreham, *Wisps of Wildfire* (London: The Epworth Press, 1924), 37-38, 44-47.

BROKEN REEDS

I have been on a visit to the Orient. And one memorable afternoon, when the sky was a vault of cloudless blue and all the earth was fair, I found myself wandering aimlessly but joyously among the soft green Syrian hills. I sat down on the side of a grassy knoll and feasted my eyes on the quiet beauty of this idyllic scene. Not many yards below me a little stream flowed gently past the foot of the sloping hillside and meandered through the silent valley. There was no laughter in its waters; they moved slowly and peacefully on. Reeds and rushes grew plentifully along its banks. All at once I realized that I was not alone. I heard first the bleating of sheep, and then, a little later, human footsteps. A shepherd came round the curve of the knoll, sauntering slowly, with his flock following at his heels. He did not notice me; his attention seemed to be fastened on the reeds flourishing beside the stream. When he reached them he began to look about, examining them with a critical eye. One, a tall one, was bent, and drooped towards him. The sheep may have broken it in browsing there the day before; or perhaps a gust of wind had caught it. Anyway, it was broken. With a rough hand he snatched at it; looked it up and down disdainfully; doubled it at the point at which it was damaged before; and tossed it out on to the gently moving waters. Then he cut for himself another reed, a sturdier one, without flaw or fault of any kind. And as he led his flock gently along the banks of the stream, watching the poor broken reed floating away on the sluggish current, he worked away with deft and practiced fingers, and out of the faultless reed he fashioned for himself a flute. And when it was finished he put it to his lips, and, lo, the sweet, clear music filled all that peaceful valley.

Harmony! It was a vision of *Harmony!*

When he paused to take breath and to look around upon his flock, I rose and approached him. Until then he had been unconscious of my presence. I sat sometimes talking with him and sometimes listening to the soft, sweet strains of his flute, until the approach of sunset reminded us that it was time to be moving. I walked with him up to the fold. The sheep appeared to resent my presence, and did not follow so closely at his heels as on their way down the valley earlier in the day. I watched him as he counted them and secured them for the night. And then he took me to his shepherd-hut some distance up the hillside. It was dusk by the time we reached it. He took down a lamp from the shelf and lit it. It was an odd little lamp, shaped like a tiny urn, and the wick protruded from the spout. It smoked horribly. He had gone to the back of the hut for some sticks with which to light his fire. When he returned and found the place reeking with the evil odor of the smoke, he was angry with the lamp, and, lighting another, he blew this one out and flung it unceremoniously back to the shelf. The second lamp burned beautifully; the fire blazed up; and all the room was bright....

After awhile the shepherd walked with me up the valley to my temporary home. It was a glorious starlit night: such a night as only the Orient knows. I bade him goodnight at the door; and we parted. He went back to his hut and to his fold. I, tired out, went straight to bed. And that night I dreamed.

I dreamed of the broken reed, crushed and crumpled in the shepherd's hands, that I had seen floating away on the stream.

And I dreamed of the lamp, the smoking lamp, extinguished so ruthlessly by the shepherd's hand, that I had seen thrown in disdain back to the shelf.

I remembered the words from Scripture pointing to the Messiah: 'He shall not cry, nor lift up, nor cause His voice to be heard in the street. A bruised reed shall he not break, and the smoking lamp shall he not quench ...'

And then I saw what it meant. The *shepherd's* way is the easy way. He snatches at the bruised reed, crushes it, and tosses it away on to the moving waters. And he takes another that has never been bruised, and from it he draws his melodies. He flings the smoking lamp back to the shelf and takes a new and faultless one, and from it he gets the light that fills his home with brightness. Anybody could do that, but the *Good Shepherd* of whom the prophet speaks takes the hard way. With infinite pity and infinite patience He works away at the bruised reed until from *it* He woos the eternal harmonies. With infinite pity and infinite patience He trims and cleans the smoking lamp until from *it* He draws the light that never was on sea or shore.

The bruised reed! The bruised reed represents the things that have never been of any use; the things that are marred in the making. From the bruised reed he gets the choicest harmony!

The smoking lamp! The smoking lamp represents the things that have been useful, but have lost the usefulness they had. Once luminous, they have become loathsome; once shining, they now smoke. From the smoking lamp he gets His clearest light!

From the bruised reed—*Harmony!*

From the smoking lamp—*Light!*

And *Harmony* and *Light,* as I saw from the shores of the uttermost star, are the two greatest things in the universe.

F. W. Boreham, *The Uttermost Star* (London: The Epworth Press, 1919), 22-26.

CATCHING THE TIDE

The Melbourne Art Gallery possesses, among its treasures, a painting by Arthur Boyd entitled 'Waiting for the Tide.' It represents a sheltered and tranquil cove in which a couple of boats are lying. The boat in the foreground is occupied by two men. It leans heavily over, showing that it is hard and fast upon the muddy bed of the little inlet.

Until the tide comes welling in, lifting and liberating it, its occupants are helpless. But their presence in the boat sufficiently indicates their determination to ply their oars and leave the bay the moment the waters rise.

Viewed superficially, the attitude of the two men seems to resemble the attitude of Mr. Micawber [in Charles Dickens' *David Copperfield*]. In the daytime Mr. Micawber mingles with the throng upon the city streets, hoping for something to turn up among the faces that he finds there. In the evening he throws himself into his chair, adjusts his spectacles and seizes his newspaper, just to see if anything turns up among the advertisements. All life is a lottery to him.

But between Mr. Micawber on the one hand, and the two boatmen on the other, there is, in reality, no ground for comparison. Mr. Micawber represents the wretchedness of wishful thinking; the boatmen represent the satisfaction of a well-based hope.

The tide stands for the stately dependabilities by which we are encompassed and surrounded. The masterly mechanism of the universe—the rising and the setting of the sun, the phases of the moon, the persistence in their orbits of the stars, the revolution of the earth, the cycle of the seasons, the round of the year—all this, like the ebbing and flowing of the tide, is amazingly reliable. It is this element of constancy that, in our friends, means infinitely more than good looks, agreeable behavior or outstanding ability.

In common with all the best things, the tide is leisurely. Like its kinsman, Old Father Thames, 'it never seems to hurry.' Like the men in Boyd's picture, we must wait its time. It soothes the brain and steadies the nerves and sweetens the soul to fasten one's eyes for awhile on these leisurely things. An oak tree takes just as long to grow in my garden as it took in the Garden of Eden. The tide ebbs and flows today exactly as it ebbed and flowed in the days of the Pharaohs.

Yet, although the tide does its work in a restful and leisurely way, it does it, and does it well. The world's best workers are those who never know the fret and fever of haste, yet who achieve their goals with meticulous certainty and exactitude. They always get there.

There is, according to Brutus, a tide in the affairs of men which, taken at the flood, leads on to fortune. As Shakespeare implies, and as Boyd's picture makes clear, the tide offers every person, sooner or later, the chance of escaping from the tiny cove of the *here* into the broad bosom of the *everywhere;* from the microscopic bay of Self to the infinite sea of Service. God suddenly confronts a person. The Savior, in infinite grace, presents Himself. Opportunity appears in some other form; and they are life's most enviable voyagers who, when the sublime moment actually arrives, are all alive and all alert, waiting, with oars in rowlocks, to greet the hour of destiny.

A person can no more hurry time along than these boat-men in the picture can hurry the tide. Life must be harmonized with, and harnessed to, the mighty forces operating around us. He alone is certain of happy days who, with open eyes and eager hands, stands ready to embrace the golden opportunities that every hour will offer.

F. W. Boreham, *The Tide Comes In* (London: The Epworth Press, 1958), 103-104.

CHRIST LAID HIS HAND ON ME

I possess documentary evidence to show that it was on November 28, 1887 that I went up to London to seek a situation there. I was then three months short of being seventeen....

The impact of London upon my boyish spirit was the greatest sensation that I have ever known. London took my breath away. It appalled me. I had never imagined such pushing, jostling multitudes. I remember standing in the heart of the world's metropolis, under the very shadow of St. Paul's, and shivering in the thick of the crowd at my own utter loneliness. Amid the hops and the clover and the orchards of my Kentish home, one could often shout to his heart's content and never a soul would hear him. Yet that was a delicious and tranquil loneliness—a loneliness that one loved and reveled in, but the loneliness of that immense and surging crowd seemed an intolerable affair.

And somehow I sensed something sinister in the atmosphere. Literature was surreptitiously slipped into my hand on the street; things were said to me by perfect strangers; and I detected on hoardings [billboards] and in shop windows indications of the existence of forces that seemed banded together for my undoing.

I was dazzled—and terrified. The glamour of London enthralled me: I dreaded lest I should have to leave it and return once more to my home. And yet I caught my breath in apprehension lest the mighty monster had magnetized me only that it might destroy me. I was like some tiny moth, basking in the brilliance of the glare, yet fearful that, sooner or later, its wings would be cruelly singed in the flame.

In those first days in London there fastened upon my mind a conviction that I needed Something or Someone—a Power outside myself to preserve me from contamination and to nerve me to live my life in London to some useful purpose. And it was then—and under the influence of that intense wistfulness—that the situation dramatically changed. Like Jacob's midnight struggle by the brook Jabbok, the transfiguring episode was marked by absolute solitude.

I cannot recall any sermon or book, any minister or missionary, any church or society, that played any part in that secret and spiritual adventure. I can only believe that, at that critical juncture, Christ laid His mighty hand upon me and claimed me as His own.

F. W. Boreham, *My Pilgrimage* (London: The Epworth Press, 1940), 59-60.

CIRCUMSTANCES HARD TO SWALLOW

'You will have to learn to *swallow faggots* [a bundle of sticks/branches] *crosswise!*' said the veteran to the raw recruit. The raw recruit, as it happens, was Charles Haddon Spurgeon; the veteran was an old Cambridgeshire minister to whom he had confided his intention of entering the ministry....

I am not sure that the expressive phrase will bear a very searching examination; like so many of our proverbs and epigrams, the saying must be judged, not by the actual words that it contains, but by the impression that it conveys. I see quite clearly what the good man means; and the speaker who can effectively communicate his meaning, whether by accurate or inaccurate terminology, is not to be despised. I have known people use the most exquisitely polished phrases and leave their hearers in a state of abject mystification....

Young Spurgeon was in no such perplexity as he left the old minister's house.... He meant, not that a minister must *swallow faggots crosswise,* but that he must acquire the habit of so turning with his tongue the faggots that are placed crosswise in his teeth, that he will be able to swallow them with the utmost ease.

What more natural than that he should allow his mind to play around those classical sentences that every minister so often ponders—the sentences in which the first great ministerial charge was uttered? *'Behold, I send you forth as sheep in the midst of wolves; be therefore as wise as serpents and harmless as doves,'* and so on.

'Well, well, Charles,' he said, 'so you are going to be a minister! You will have to learn to *swallow faggots crosswise.'*

It was excellent advice. A distensible gullet is an absolutely essential item in a ministerial outfit. I do not mean that a minister is called upon to perform greater gastronomic feats than other people. That may or may not be so; I do not know. Most people have at times to swallow extremely awkward things, and no person is the worse for a little elasticity in the region of the throat. The person who, on occasion, can gulp down a faggot or two, and smile as they descend into his dilatable interior, is likely to live to a hearty old age.

I have known many a man lose a night's rest through his inability to swallow something or other; but *Rogers on Reptiles* points out, with a good deal of perspicacity, that, after swallowing a creature greater than itself, a distended serpent will go away and sleep for an indefinite period. That is a fact in natural history which is worth the careful attention of all those unfortunate mortals who are troubled with chronic, or even occasional, insomnia.

The minister is not called upon to swallow more or bigger faggots than the butcher, the baker, or the candlestick-maker. It is as well that he should remind himself of this important circumstance when he finds himself wrestling with a particularly unsavory mouthful, or when the jagged edges of the faggot persist in sticking in his throat.

F. W. Boreham, *Wisps of Wildfire* (London: The Epworth Press, 1924), 88-95 (selected).

CLOSED DOORS OPENING CREATIVELY

As a young fellow in my teens, I went to London and was horribly lonely there. One wet evening, poking about the Strand, I noticed a crowd surging into Exeter Hall. Moved by curiosity, I followed and found that it was the annual missionary demonstration of the Methodist Church. I have forgotten everything else, but I can never forget the chairman's speech.

'I was born,' said Mr. W. E. Knight, of Newark, 'in a missionary atmosphere and I have lived in it ever since. As a boy my heart was touched by the story of the world's tragic need. I listened to such men as Gervase Smith, Morley Punshon, Richard Roberts, and others, and I resolved to lay my life upon the altar. I came up to London, offered myself as a candidate, and, to my speechless consternation, was rejected. I went to my little room, threw myself down beside my bed, and cried as though my heart would break. I felt that I was despised of men and forsaken of God.'

He told how, after remaining for some hours in this unspeakable misery, an idea suddenly seized his mind. Why not go into business and dedicate his commercial prosperity to missionary ends? He regarded it as a call, a challenge. He went into business, succeeded beyond his most sanguine dreams, gave liberally to mission funds, and had now been called to preside over this huge gathering in London.

'And to celebrate the occasion which means so much to me,' he said. 'I am laying on this table a check. The interest on this amount will maintain a missionary on the field, not only during my lifetime, but through all the years to come!'

F. W. Boreham, *Boulevards of Paradise* (London: The Epworth Press, 1944), 63.

COINCIDENCE AND MYSTERY

For a long time the scientist interpreted nature in one way, and the theologian interpreted the Bible in another. The inevitable discord led thoughtless people to suppose that, in some inexplicable way, a discrepancy existed between the natural and the religious view of things. Now everybody knows that the discrepancy—if indeed, there be one—is not between the things themselves, but between the faulty interpretations of those things. As those interpretations become more enlightened, more sympathetic and more intelligent, the gulf that divides them becomes small by degrees and beautifully less. They are like the lovers approaching [an agreed meeting place] from opposite directions. They draw nearer and nearer to each other. They must meet, and meet most happily, at last, because, in the essential nature of things, they have a tryst to keep.

Life is full of things that appear to be coincidences—things that are really trysts. Let me tell a story.

On a recent Saturday, a policeman came to the front door just before lunch. A man under arrest at the Melbourne Jail wished to see me at once. The constable gave me the man's name, but it conveyed nothing to me. My first impulse was to hurry away to the jail; and, indeed, the policeman urged this course upon me. On the other hand, an appetizing dinner was almost ready, and the cricket match at which I had expected to spend the afternoon was at a particularly exciting stage.

As I pondered the situation in which I found myself, an irresistible conviction settled down upon me that I should be wise to have my dinner in peace, to attend the cricket match to which I had looked forward, and then to go to the jail in the evening. The policeman protested that Saturday night would be the worst possible time at which to visit the Melbourne Jail; but the feeling in my mind would not be shaken off. Let me say in self-defense that I can recall no other case in which I put apparently selfish considerations before the clamant call of duty. But my mind was fixed. I ate my dinner and made my way to the cricket ground. In the pavilion I sat beside a man with whom I was acquainted many years ago in Tasmania.

'I don't know why I've come here to-day,' he said, 'I've never been here before, and I take very little interest in cricket!'

To my utter amazement, in the course of casual conversation, he mentioned the name of the man in the Melbourne Jail. I concealed my own intense interest in the case, but gently encouraged him to talk. In the course of half-an-hour I had all the facts of the case at my fingers' ends; and, when I went to the jail that night, I was able to deal with the man in a way that, but for my experience in the afternoon, would have been impossible! Now, why was my old Tasmanian friend so strongly moved to visit that particular cricket ground that afternoon? And why was I made to feel so deeply that I must go to the cricket-match before responding to the prisoner's call?

F. W. Boreham, *The Drums of Dawn* (London: The Epworth Press, 1933), 50-52.

COINCIDENCE, HISTORY AND MYSTERY

One of these days somebody will present us with a Philosophy of Coincidences, and when we have read it we shall recognize it as nothing more or less than a Philosophy of Twins.

Take a few cases at random. We all know that, on October 7, 1849 Edgar Allan Poe, the American poet, passed away; while on that very selfsame day, John Whitcombe Riley, another American poet, was born!

Again, on October 9, 1845, Renan put off his clerical habit and left the Roman Church; and on that selfsame day, Newman entered it! Readers of Macaulay will remember that, on the very day on which the elder Pitt made his last speech in the House of Commons, Burke made his first. And, later on, on the same day on which the younger Pitt first took his seat as Prime Minister, his supreme foe, Napoleon, was proclaimed as Emperor!

On February 12, 1809, Abraham Lincoln was born on one side of the Atlantic and Charles Darwin on the other. On another day, about ten years later Queen Victoria and Caroline Fox [well known English authoress of a diary who recorded memories of many distinguished people, such as John Stuart Mill, John Sterling and Thomas Carlyle] were simultaneously born! On the same day, in 1616, Shakespeare, the greatest English writer, and Cervantes, the greatest foreign writer, both passed away. And it has always struck me as a most impressive coincidence that, on the day on which the French mob tore the cross from Notre Dame and abjured Christianity, William Carey landed in India and claimed a new continent for Christ! Both events took place on November 1, 1793.

But, of all such twin-events, America can boast by far the most remarkable. Indeed, it may almost be recorded as a case of triplets. For, on July 4, 1826, the people of the United States celebrated the Jubilee of the Declaration of Independence. It happened that two of the great Independence Presidents—John Adams and Thomas Jefferson—were still living. Adams was ninety-one, Jefferson was eighty-three. It was decided to make the jubilee a festival in honor of these two veterans. From the Atlantic to the Pacific the names of Adams and Jefferson were that day toasted and acclaimed. And the two old men, how did they celebrate the great occasion? Both died on that auspicious day! Adams passed away at sunset, murmuring, 'Ah well, Jefferson still survives!' But therein he was mistaken, for his old comrade had crossed the bar at noon! The Jubilee of Independence, the death of Jefferson, and the death of Adams all took place on the very selfsame day!

But now let me lift the subject to a still loftier plane! I can never open the sacred records without discovering two distinct elements. I find the element of Prophecy and the element of History. But the striking thing is that the two run along precisely parallel lines. I find the prophets threatening Edom, Tyre and Babylon and Jerusalem with certain disasters as, one by one, overtaking the disobedient cities. I see at once that the Voice of Him that speaks in Prophecy is the Voice of Him whose hand directs the moving pageant of History. Prophecy and History are twins!

F. W. Boreham, *A Reel of Rainbow* (London: The Epworth Press, 1920), 127-129.

COMMUNION OF THE SAINTS

I am irresistibly reminded of that fine entry in Grant Duff's *Notes from a Diary*. An old priest was trudging home through the deep snow after early Mass in a tiny Irish chapel on the morning of All Saints' Day. A man stopped him to ask, with a suspicion of irony in his voice, how many had attended Mass on such a morning. A twinkle came to the eye of the little priest and his face literally shone. 'Millions!' he replied, 'millions! *millions!*'

He had been celebrating at Mass the fact that we are encompassed about by a countless cloud of witnesses! We do not need to wait for All Saints' Day to enter into the felicity of that uplifting thought. Those whom we have loved and lost awhile are never far away. For them the illusion of distance has been shattered for ever.

F. W. Boreham, *Boulevards of Paradise* (London: The Epworth Press, 1944), 59.

COMPLEMENTARY COMBINATIONS

In an essay on Swings and Roundabouts *F. W. Boreham claims:*

You must have both swings and roundabouts [merry-go-round].

A fine instance of this sort of thing occurred in the middle of the eighteenth century. We were at the crisis of our fate. Great Britain was at war on three continents. In Europe, in India, and in America things were going heavily against us. Disaster abroad led to confusion at home. Riots broke out everywhere, and the nation was for a moment entirely out of control. For eleven weeks England was without a responsible Ministry [Government]. And why? It was all a matter of roundabouts versus swings.

One crowd cried, *'Let Pitt be Minister!'*

The other crowd cried, *'Let Newcastle be Minister.'*

All England asked, *'Shall it be Pitt or Newcastle?'*

And then some genius inquired, *'Why not Pitt and Newcastle?'*

Exactly! Why ask whether it shall be swings *or* roundabouts? Why not swings *and* roundabouts? So England called Pitt and Newcastle together to save the nation.

'And thus it was found,' as Macaulay says, 'that these two men, so unlike in character, so lately mortal enemies, were necessary to each other. Newcastle had fallen in November for want of that public confidence which Pitt possessed and of that parliamentary support which Pitt was better qualified than any man of his time to give. Pitt had fallen in April, for want of that species of influence which Newcastle had passed his whole life in acquiring and hoarding. Neither of them had power enough to support himself. Each of them had power enough to overturn the other. Their union would be irresistible.'

They united; and the combination proved the salvation of the country. It is so silly to be always setting the swings against the roundabouts and the roundabouts against the swings.

F. W. Boreham, *The Other Side of the Hill* (London: Charles H. Kelly, 1917), 16-17.

COMPLEMENTARY GIFTS

Those who have studied carefully the story of the Reformation in Germany know how Luther and Melancthon toiled together in this way. Each seemed to supply what the other lacked, and neither was sure of the wisdom of his proposal until the sanction and approval of the other had been obtained.

We are told, concerning Charles Fox [great English orator and member of Parliament] and Sir James Macintosh [Scottish writer and philosopher] , that when Fox went to the desk and wrote, and Macintosh went to the platform and spoke, the cause they espoused seemed pitifully impotent. But when Macintosh took the pen and Fox the platform, they brought the country to their feet. The gifts of each exactly supplemented those of the other.

Huber, the celebrated naturalist, was blind. But he had the mental ability to think out his great works, were he only able to see the insects concerning which he wished to write. His wife, on the other hand, had not the power to think out the natural philosophy indicated by the wing of a fly or the head of a bee, but she had sight. And so they labored together, with what brilliant results the world very well knows.

F. W. Boreham, *The Whisper of God and other sermons* (London: Arthur H. Stockwell, 1902), 101.

COMPLIMENT OF CATFISH

I often take myself into a quiet corner and remind myself of my visit to the fish-pens or repeat to myself the famous tradition of the catfish. I find myself at times in a rebellious mood. Why is life so troubled, so agitated, so disturbed? If only I could be left alone! Why may I not fold my hands and be quiet? I am hunted up hill and down dale; I am driven from pillar to post. I have to work for my living—an irksome necessity. I often have to go out when I would rather stay in, and have to stay in when I would rather go out. I am the prey of antagonisms of many kinds. Life is full of irritations, annoyances, mortifications, and disappointments. I am not my own master. Like Paul, *I find a law that, when I would do good, evil is present with me; the good that I would I do not and the evil which I would not that I do.* Paul found it extremely exasperating, and so do I. If only I could live without work and without worry and without any of my present vexations! Why, oh why, must there always be a catfish in my well?

A catfish is an animated compliment. I do not suppose that a *Dictionary of Oceanography* or a *Cyclopaedia of Pisciculture* would define a catfish precisely in that way. But I prefer my own definition to that of the encyclopedia; it is more brief and it is quite as accurate. A catfish, I repeat, is an animated compliment. It is because the fisherman values his fish that he puts the catfish into the well to annoy them.

'I remember,' says Dr. James Stalker, 'I remember hearing a celebrated naturalist describe a species of jellyfish, which, he said, lives fixed to a rock from which it never stirs. It does not require to go in search of food, because in the decayed tissues of its own organism there grows a kind of seaweed on which it subsists. I thought I had never heard of any creature so comfortable. But the eminent naturalist who was describing it went on to say that it is one of the very lowest forms of animal life, and the extreme comfort which it enjoys is the badge of its degraded position.'

Now this seems to throw a little light on my own discontent. No fisherman would take any pains to preserve such worthless things. When the fisherman drops the hideous catfish into the well, it is his way of telling the shiny creatures that are already there of the high esteem in which he holds them.

F. W. Boreham, *Rubble and Roseleaves* (London: The Epworth Press, 1922), 203-205.

CONCENTRATING THE MIND WHEN PRAYING

When, as little more than a boy, I left my home at Tunbridge Wells and went to London, I fell under the influence of the Rev. C. Aubrey Price, of Clapham Park, an evangelical clergyman who exercised considerable authority in those days. I treasure some of his letters still. Our conversation one evening turned upon this very question. How, in moments dedicated to devotion, could I prevent my mind from wandering off to business, to pleasure, to the novel I was reading and to a thousand things beside?

'Take my advice,' he replied, sympathetically, laying his hand upon my shoulder, 'always pray *aloud!* It is very difficult to concentrate for long in silence. The mind is so accustomed to having thought communicated to it audibly that it feels lost without some such adventitious aid and saunters off on romantic excursions of its own. Moreover, the very exercise of composing sentences that express, as perfectly as it is possible for language to do, all that you wish to say, chains the mind to its task and keeps the faculties focused upon the business on hand.'

I owe a great deal to Mr. Aubrey Price for the counsel and inspiration that I received at his hands in those early days of my spiritual pilgrimage; but none of the wise words that fell from his lips upon my hungry ears have recurred to my mind more frequently than these. They are so true to actual experience. If I sit in a chair and ponder a theme in silence, my mind wanders repeatedly: if I discuss that theme aloud, my mind never wanders at all.

A few years later it was my good fortune to fall in with Dr. F. B. Meyer, of whose Saturday afternoon Bible class at Aldersgate Street I became a member. Dr. Meyer was then a comparatively young man—in the early forties—but he was the father of us all; and, had we been in very deed his sons, we could scarcely have loved him more. I really think that we lived for those Saturday afternoons. We counted the hours till they came; and, when they came, they never failed to minister to us such hope and faith and courage that we returned to our tasks with higher spirits and with braver hearts. With his unerring penetration into the real difficulties that presented themselves to our minds, he sensed this one, and, on several occasions, dealt with it.

'You will generally find,' he would say, 'that your thoughts are most inclined to wander when you are praying *for yourself.* The mind finds it difficult to fasten tenaciously upon things that are extremely familiar. It revolts and sets off in quest of something less prosaic. When, in praying about your own secret and personal affairs, you find your thoughts straying, drop that subject at once and begin praying for other people. The mental effort of envisaging your friend—his personality, his home, his circumstances, his needs—presents the mind with something concrete on which to work. You seem to see the familiar face, to hear the accents of his voice, and to enter into the secret struggles of his life. Thus furnished, the fancy feels less inclined to wander, and you find yourself praying for your friend with all your soul absorbed in the joy of intercession. And, quite possibly, the time that you spend in thinking of others, and laying their needs before the Throne of

Grace, will have brought the mental faculties to so rapt a state of application that you will find it easy to return to your earlier theme and to pray for yourself. And even if, at that point, you collapse a second time, you can comfort yourself with the reflection that the Lord turned the captivity of Job when he prayed for his friends.'

F. W. Boreham, *I Forgot To Say* (London: The Epworth Press, 1939), 80-81.

CONFRONTING OUR SHADOWS

On the eve of the poll at Bristol, when Edmund Burke rose to address a crowded and excited audience, a note was suddenly slipped into his hand telling him that the strain of the campaign had been too much for his opponent; he was dead.

Burke paused for a moment. Then, to a hushed assembly, he made the tragic announcement, and added, impressively, "What shadows we are and what shadows we pursue!"

F. W. Boreham, *Shadows on the Wall* (London: The Epworth Press, 1922), 231.

CONVALESCENCE

Convalescence has made so poignant an appeal to the fancy of eminent painters.

In the art gallery at Geelong [Australia] there is a picture entitled 'The Convalescent,' by Louis Pomey; in the Melbourne Gallery there is a canvas with the same title by Francis Tattegrain; in the Royal Academy not long ago Sir John Lavery, A.R.A., exhibited a fine study bearing the self-same title; and it would be easy to cite many others.

The patients portrayed in these handsome and striking pictures were discovering that there are periods of transition that are immensely more delectable than either the phase that they were leaving or the phase towards which they were advancing.

F. W. Boreham, *I Forgot To Say* (London: The Epworth Press, 1939), 104.

CONVICTION

The first [story] is from Sir James Stephen's *Essays in Ecclesiastical Biography*. The professor points out that William Wilberforce lived his parliamentary life as a contemporary of William Pitt, Edmund Burke, Charles James Fox, and Richard Brinsley Sheridan. Here was a galaxy of brilliance—the most polished and powerful orators who ever awoke the classic echoes of St. Stephen's!

Wilberforce's figure conveyed the inevitable impression of insignificance. Yet when he rose to address the Commons the House instantly crowded. Members held their breaths to listen. The little reformer spoke with an authority rarely wielded by the greatest masters. He was heard in a silence, and with a respect, which were never accorded to those illustrious rhetoric. And why? There is only one reason for it. Like Sir Galahad:

> His strength was as the strength of ten,
> Because his heart was pure.

The second of these companion pictures is from Sir Henry W. Lucy's *Sixty Years in the Wilderness*. In the last chapter of this fascinating book the author draws a striking contrast between John Bright and Benjamin Disraeli. 'Disraeli,' he says, 'lacked two qualities, failing which true eloquence is impossible: he was never quite in earnest, and he was not troubled by dominating conviction.' Now for the contrast. 'John Bright, perhaps the finest orator known to the House of Commons in the last half of the nineteenth century, was morally and politically the antithesis of Disraeli. To a public man this atmosphere of acknowledged sincerity and honest conviction is a mighty adjunct of power.'

F. W. Boreham, *The Luggage of Life* (London: Charles H. Kelly, 1912), 131-132.

CREATIVITY FROM DISAPPOINTMENT

At the age of twenty-one, Isaac Watts accompanied his father one day to a Nonconformist chapel at Southampton. In discussing the service on the way home, Isaac remarked that he had carefully examined the hymn-book and had found it very disappointing. There was not, he sweepingly declared, a decent hymn in the collection. Without an exception, they were all lacking in dignity and beauty.

'Then, my boy,' replied the philosophical father, who had come to realize, by this time, that his son's poetic impulses were incapable of restraint, 'the best thing that you can do is to write some better ones!'

On reaching home, Isaac sat down and called on his best powers to respond to his father's challenge. He wrote the first of his many wonderful songs.

F. W. Boreham, *A Late Lark Singing* (London: The Epworth Press, 1945), 31.

DARKNESS AND LIGHT

Strolling through the Art Gallery at Bendigo [Australia] … I was arrested by Mr. F. Boe's picture of 'The Midnight Sun.' It represents the crimson midnight as it is seen in the north of Norway. But as I stood admiring the picture it occurred to me that Norway has no monopoly of sunshine at midnight. The lurid spectacle, seen from those frozen fiords, is doubtless very wonderful; but it has its counterparts in other latitudes. Daylight and darkness do not depend upon the gyrations of the globes. I suppose there was a time when the sun ruled the day and the moon the night. If so, it was 'once upon a time,' when all the other wonderful things happened; but not now. In our era we are often enveloped in dense darkness at high noon, and bask in radiant sunshine at midnight. The sun and the moon have simply nothing at all to do with it. We determine daylight and darkness without consulting them. They look helplessly on.…

Now I have always felt that there is something cryptical about that suggestive record of the exodus of Judas from the Last Supper. 'He went out and it was night.'

There is some necessary and essential connection between moral dereliction and moral darkness. Treachery leads to twilight. 'He went out and it was night,' says John.

F. W. Boreham, *A Reel of Rainbow* (London: The Epworth Press, 1920), 133-134.

DEALING WITH THE FAULTS OF OTHERS

When Livingstone was asked how he contrived to treat the treachery and villainy of African natives and Arab traders with such infinite patience and extraordinary calm, he quietly remarked, "I have faults myself!"

His own sin, ever before him, gave him tender and charitable thoughts of others.

F. W. Boreham, *Mountains in the Mist* (London: Charles H. Kelly, 1914), 73.

DEATH IS A THOROUGHFARE

It was Victor Hugo who declared with splendid passion that, neither for youth nor for age, is a tomb a blind alley. He was himself old. 'But I feel,' he exclaimed, 'that I have not said a thousandth part of what is in me. When I go down to the grave, I can say, like so many others, "I have finished my day's work," but I cannot say, "I have finished my life." Another day's work will begin the next morning. *My tomb is not a blind alley,* it is a thoroughfare; it closes with the twilight to open with the dawn.' It is the only explanation of the incompleteness that we see everywhere. 'Truly,' Browning makes Paracelsus cry:

> Truly there needs another life to come! If this be
> all …
> And other life await us not—for one
> I say 'tis a poor cheat, a stupid bungle,
> A wretched failure. I, for one, protest
> Against it, and I hurl it back with scorn.

If that were so, we should all be caught in a blind alley. The Great Artist would have begun a picture which He had not the skill to finish. The Great Father would have given His children a promise which it was beyond His power to keep.

The New Testament contains a tragic story of a man who regarded the world in which he lived not as a means to an end, but as an end in itself. 'Soul,' he said, 'you have many goods laid up for many years! Take your ease; eat, drink, and be merry!' With his wealthy accumulation of goods he blocked the king's highway and turned it into a blind alley. The barricade that he had built stood at last between himself and heaven. He turned the highway into an alley and lost his soul in the process.

F. W. Boreham, *Wisps of Wildfire* (London: The Epworth Press, 1924), 76-77.

DECISIVE RESPONSE NEEDED

The evangelist D. L. Moody [whom F. W. Boreham heard on a number of occasions] made his appeal in his characteristic way. I never remember hearing him ask people, while heads were bowed, to raise a hand. Immediately at the conclusion of his address, while all eyes were wide open, he would say, 'Now, who will trust the Savior, here and now? If you will, stand up and say so! Spring to your feet and call out, *"I will!"* '

The response was sometimes like a clap of thunder. One evening, for example, there were in the congregation several rows of soldiers from Chelsea Barracks, wearing the brilliant scarlet uniforms that military men affected in those days. Mr. Moody concluded his address in the usual way: 'Now, then, who accepts this Savior tonight? Jump to your feet and cry, *"I will!"* '

And, among scores of others, numbers of the men in uniform stood instantly and shouted their decision. The effect was electrifying. It was this habit of Mr. Moody's that inspired the hymn that was so often sung at his meetings:

> And now, O Lord, give all with us today,
> The grace to join our song:
> And from the heart to gladly with us say:
> I WILL to Christ belong.
> I will! I will! I will! I will!
> I will, God helping me, I will, O Lord, be Thine!
> Thy precious blood was shed to purchase me—
> I will be wholly Thine!

'I love those *"I wills,"* ' Mr. Moody used to say.

At that extra meeting—the meeting for men only, sandwiched in between the afternoon and evening services—Mr. Moody made his familiar challenge. A storm of 'I wills' followed, and then the tramping of the feet of those who, desiring further enlightenment, made their way to the inquiry rooms. Mr. Moody then dismissed those thousands of men, and, half an hour later, was once more in the pulpit ready to grapple with a second evening congregation!

I doubt if any of the students of that day have ever shaken off, or would like to shake off, the impact upon their own plastic and impressionable minds of the rugged and commanding personality of Mr. Moody. It kindled a flame in the soul of every man that has burned steadily through all the years.

F. W. Boreham, *Cliffs of Opal*, (London: The Epworth Press, 1948), 60-61.

DELIGHT AND DESPAIR

Among the treasures in the Sydney Art Gallery is Sir Luke Fildes' famous painting entitled 'The Widower.' On the right-hand side of the picture sits the poor toiler, with his sick child on his knee. One overwhelming bereavement has already overtaken him, and another stares him in the face. His brow is clouded with uttermost sorrow and perplexity. He looks at his child and seems to say, 'If only *she* were here!' And on the left hand side of the picture are the younger children playing on the floor, laughing and crowing in their merriment. They are not old enough to understand; but their delight seems cruelly to mock his despair.

F. W. Boreham, *The Luggage of Life* (London: Charles H. Kelly, 1912), 142-143.

DEVELOPING A FAITH OF ONE'S OWN

There is, near the end of the brief Epistle of Jude, an arresting expression that always seems to me very striking. *'But ye, beloved,'* says the writer, *'building up yourselves on your most holy faith.'*

That is the only satisfactory way of building—to build on your own site. If I build my house on another person's piece of ground, it is sure to cause trouble sooner or later. Build your own character on your own faith, says the Apostle; and there is sound sense in the injunction. It is better for me to build a very modest little house of my own on a little bit of land that really belongs to me, than to build a palace on somebody else's soil. It is better for me to build up my character, very unpretentiously perhaps, on my own faith, than to erect a much more imposing structure on another person's creed.

In his *Priests and People in Ireland,* Mr. Michael J. F. McCarthy tells of a conversation he enjoyed with a typical Irish peasant.

> 'I want you to tell me,' said Mr. McCarthy, 'exactly what you believe!'
> 'I believe,' replied the Irishman, 'all that the Church believes!'
> 'Ah, just so,' exclaimed Mr. McCarthy, 'and what does the Church believe?'
> 'The Church believes,' replied the son of Erin, 'exactly what I believe!'
> 'I see!' responded Mr. McCarthy, 'and now I want you to tell me what it is that you and the Church both believe!'
> 'And it's strange that you should have asked that same question,' returned the Irishman, 'for me and the Church, we both believe the same thing!'

And that was as far as Mr. McCarthy could get. He was dealing with a person who carried a faith that was not really his own.

F. W. Boreham, *Boulevards of Paradise* (London: The Epworth Press, 1944), 47.

DEVELOPING THE SOUL

Frank Boreham was a good photographer and he processed his own photos. In this story he writes about the old style of developing and printing photographs:

The lure of the dark-room is indescribable. To a man who dabbles in photography, the dark-room is the witch's cavern and the magic grotto and the enchanted palace, all in one. To other eyes it may look dismal and bare. *He* knows better. He knows that the dark-room is alive with mystery and crowded with sensations. It is the haunt of a thousand thrills. It is the home of the most delicious surprises and of the most depressing disappointments! Smiles and sighs lurk in every crack and crevice of the gloomy place. He never knows what to expect next. A dark-room is one of the few places in which a person may become excited in silence and solitude. In the darkness the photographer forgets everything—even the darkness. The white plate is steeped in the fluid that is to woo from the picture that it so mysteriously conceals, and the operator holds his breath. Two pictures occupy his fancy—the vivid and variegated picture that, captivating his eye, led him to set up his camera, and the photograph in black and white that he so soon hopes to possess. Will the picture on the plate be the picture of his dreams? The enthusiasm that surged through his soul when he pressed the bulb rushes back upon him in an intensified form. As the dim and shadowy figures appear upon the plate, he can almost hear the beating of his own heart, and his hand trembles slightly as it grasps the dish.

I am merely recording an experience that has recently befallen me. I have been to Beechington with my camera. During my stay there, I took quite a number of photographs. Most of them, I knew, would prove the eeriest mediocrities— interesting only as domestic records. But one had stirred my very soul. It was a picture of the caves. Clambering over the reef, I saw them from a new angle, and was charmed with the opportunity that the scene presented. I determined to spare no pains in an endeavor to secure the picture that haunted my imagination. The gloomy recesses of the gigantic caverns; the massive boulders strewn about their yawning mouths; the great gaunt gums above; the breakers in the foreground and the towering peaks behind—all this made up an alluring combination of romantic features. If only I had the skill to do it justice! But it was difficult to judge the strength of the light and to gauge the exact exposure that the plate required. I took my time in focusing and arranging the camera. Nothing was likely to vanish and nothing was likely to intrude; there was every reason for acting leisurely. Watching the clouds, I selected with the greatest care the moment of exposure; and then, when all the conditions seemed ideal, I pressed the bulb. I am, however, only a novice, the veriest tyro [beginner or novice]. I am largely at the mercy of guess-work; and I could not, therefore, contemplate the result with any confidence. My uncertainty intensified my anxiety to get to the dark-room; and my eagerness to get to the dark-room added a fresh fever-ishness to my excitement when, in the dark-room, the critical moment came.

The critical moment is, of course, the moment at which the plate is removed from the developer. To my unbounded delight, I saw that my picture of the caves was a distinct success. More by good luck than by sound judgment, the exposure must have been perfect. As I bent over the developing-dish, I saw, first the bold outline, and then the microscopic detail, appear sharply and in vivid distinctness on the submerged plate. Every photographer knows the tense absorption of those anxious seconds.

Then comes the problem. When shall the negative be transferred to the fixing-bath? I am loath to remove it from the developer; another second or two may impart a finishing touch to the whole picture; the slightest impatience may rob the photograph of its chief charm. And yet, on the other hand, there comes a time at which the developing fluid begins to destroy its own work. The plate, left in this first dish, may be over-developed. The picture becomes blurred through remaining in the bath too long. He is a very skillful photographer who knows the precise second at which to arrest the process of development by plunging the plate into the chemicals that will fix for ever the impression it contains.

That crucial problem confronts us all. The soul and the sensitive plate are very much alike. Like the sensitive plate, the soul knows three really great moments—the moment at which it *receives* an impression, the moment at which it *develops* that impression, and the moment at which it *fixes* it.

Quite automatically, the soul receives impressions from everything to which it is exposed. Some of the impressions received are not worth developing; and some of those developed are not worth fixing.

But, every now and again, the soul enjoys an experience like my experience at the Beechington Caves. A particularly choice impression is received. But, unless it be most skillfully developed and most carefully fixed, the world at large will be none the better for it.

F. W. Boreham, *Wisps of Wildfire* (London: The Epworth Press, 1924), 250-254.

DIGNITY AMID INSULTS

In the days of the [New Zealand] Maori War some hostile natives resolved to insult Bishop Selwyn. They arranged to offer him a pig sty for his accommodation. The Bishop accepted; drove out the pigs; gathered some fern from the bush for his bed; and occupied his lowly residence with such charm and dignity that the Maoris exclaimed: "You cannot degrade that man!"

F. W. Boreham, *Mountains in the Mist* (London: Charles H. Kelly, 1914), 125.

DISCERNMENT AT THE CRICKET

Sheila had a problem. In a way, it really did not matter: there was no material difference in the length or easefulness or beauty of the two tracks. The point was that, if she took the road that led past Kirkland's farm, she would have to pass Jack Forsyth's place. Now Jack, I must explain, was the secretary of our Christian Endeavor Society and the captain of the Mosgiel Cricket Club. Without intending to intrude upon her maidenly privacy, Jack had been invading a good many of Sheila's dreams of late; and, although she had no suspicion of anything of the kind, her pretty face and handsome figure had lent a new loveliness to quite a number of Jack's. Some subtle magnetism had drawn Sheila and Jack a good deal together. Indeed, to sum up the situation in a single sentence, things between them had gone so far that Sheila felt—and rightly felt—that, if she gave him any further encouragement, Jack might justly feel that she had irrevocably committed herself.

To make matters worse, Sheila had undergone an experience on the previous day that had proved particularly baffling to heart and mind and faith. On the Saturday afternoon a cricket match was played between the Mosgiel Club under Jack's leadership and a strong team of city players from Dunedin. Moved by that local patriotism that is so marked a feature of small communities, everybody was desperately anxious that the local team should win. In company with several of the Bible Class girls, Sheila went—as did most of the townspeople—to see the fun. The contest proved more close and exciting than we had dared to hope. A quarter of an hour before stumps were drawn the position was that, with two wickets to fall, the city players needed seven runs to win. But the trouble was that their best bat—a man named Dennison, who had opened the innings and obtained from his own bat two-thirds of the score—was still at the wickets and was so maneuvering matters that the weaker batsmen at the tail-end of the team were getting scarcely any of the bowling. At this stage, however, with seven runs still needed, Dennison lost the strike, and the man at the other wicket had to face our left-hand bowler. Anxious to get a run in order to bring Dennison once more into play, he struck savagely at the ball, mis-hit it, and it soared to a terrific height above the head of mid-on, at which position Jack happened to be fielding. The excitement was intense: the whole match seemed for the moment to hang on the issue of that single catch. It was not an easy one to take, for the ball was spinning furiously in mid-air, and Jack was having to run under it with the ball coming over his shoulder.

It was only a matter of seconds, but to Sheila it seemed an eternity. 'If he catches it,' she said to herself, 'I'll let him see this evening that I care for him: if he misses it, I'll take it that it's not to be!' Whether Sheila was justified in submitting her destiny and Jack's to such a test is a question that need not now concern us. The thing that *does* concern us is that, with the ball falling towards Jack, she secretly invested the issue with fateful significance and breathlessly awaited the result.

Jack dropped the catch! Juggling with it for a second or two, he then let it slip through his hands to the ground. Observing out of the corner of his eye, however, that, while he fumbled with the ball, the batsmen were stealing a second run, he snatched it up, and, hurling it at lightning speed at the wicket, scattered the stumps, with Dennison, the champion, a yard outside his crease! The roar of the crowd was deafening. If Jack had taken the catch, the weaker batsman would have been out, and, in all probability, Dennison would quickly have scored the necessary runs. By dropping the catch, Jack had dismissed the sheet-anchor of the city team, and, since the remaining wicket fell in the same over, had won the match for Mosgiel!

Now how was Sheila to interpret this? It was as confusing as the stories she had read, in her schoolbooks … Beyond the shadow of a doubt, Jack dropped the catch. Literally interpreting her vow, she ought to drop him! But, by missing the catch, Jack had won the match, whereas, by taking it, he would have whelmed his team in defeat!

F. W. Boreham later tells of a conversation Sheila had with a friend: 'Mr. Doke [his mentor] would have called your tricks with the cricket ball … so much mumbo jumbo … You may depend upon it … that, in some perfectly simple and natural way, God will make your course clear.'

Sheila herself caught the vision of the Kindly Light and left forever the uncertain realm of elusive cricket balls …

F. W. Boreham, *The Drums of Dawn* (London: The Epworth Press, 1933), 12-14, 21-22

DISCERNMENT FORCES

I once heard Dr. A. T. Pierson advise the students never to leave one church for another unless they felt both a propelling and an attracting force at work. 'Do not go,' he said, 'unless you distinctly feel a hand pushing you out of your old sphere and distinctly see a finger beckoning you to the new one!' Was I conscious of these dual forces?

F. W. Boreham, *My Pilgrimage* (London: The Epworth Press, 1940), 176.

DISCOVERING THE POINT OF THE CHURCH

As I sat in the old church on Mount Ephraim [Tunbridge Wells, Kent], sometimes following the liturgy, sometimes listening to the sermon and sometimes dreaming of very different things, one problem perpetually assailed me. I cherished for the Church and all its teachings a veneration that almost amounted to awe; yet one thing puzzled me; I could see no utility in it all. I used to wonder what end was served by it. It seemed so hopelessly remote from real life and from the pleasures and pursuits of the week. I failed to detect any practical purpose in this aspect of things. I thought my father the very personification of everything that was upright, everything that was chivalrous, everything that was noble, unselfish and true; but it never occurred to me that there was any connection between his inflexible integrity on the one hand and his attachment to the sanctuary on the other.

I thought my mother the sweetest and most queenly woman of whom I had ever heard or read; but I never once imagined that her affection for these sacred and awful mysteries accounted in any measure for her charm. But, after a while, a thing happened that threw a new light upon everything.

In the dear old home that sheltered my earliest infancy there still hangs a framed text. It is only a plainly printed scrap of white paper, cut from the corner of a penny sheet-almanac; and yet, if something had to go, I fancy that the finest pictures in the house would be sacrificed to save it. It reads like this:

HITHERTO
HATH
THE
LORD
HELPED US

It occupies a place of honor in the room that was my mother's bedroom. It has been there for more than fifty years, but I remember, as though it were but yesterday, the day when it appeared there for the first time. We boys had a dim consciousness that things were going hardly with Father and Mother. *He* looked anxious and worried; *her* eyes were often red and swollen; both were unusually silent. Then one day the newly framed text made its appearance on the bedroom wall. We boys were only small, but it struck us as strange that this unpretentious scrap of white paper should have been thought worthy of such conspicuous promotion. Were there not hundreds of pretty cards lying about the home, any one of which would have made a much more tasty and beautiful adornment?

Yet, somehow, we felt that things were brighter. It was as if the weather had cleared up; the fog had lifted; drizzling rain had yielded to summer sunshine; Father and Mother were happier. One morning we mustered up courage to ask some explanation. Why had the plain little text been cut from the almanac in the kitchen and been honored with a frame in the bedroom? But it was never in the morning, amid the clatter and the bustle, that Mother opened her heart to us. We possessed our souls in patience until Sunday evening. It was in the flicker of the Sunday firelight that Mother told us all the secrets.

'You said the other morning, Mother, that you would tell us why you framed the paper text in the bedroom.'

'Well, I will. You know that Father and I had a crushing trouble and we feared a much heavier one. On Tuesday of last week I was feeling dreadfully worried. I do not know why I felt it so terribly just then, but I did. I had to drop my work, pick up the baby, and walk up and down the kitchen feeling that I could endure it all no longer. My burden was heavier than I could bear: it seemed to be killing me. In pacing up and down I paused for a second in front of the sheet-almanac on the wall. The only thing I saw was the text in the corner.

I felt as if it had been put there specially for me. It was as if someone had spoken the words. 'Hitherto hath the Lord helped us.' I was so overcome that I sat down and had a good cry; and then I began again with fresh heart and trust. When father came home I told him all about it, and he cut out the text with his penknife, had it framed, and hung it where you now see it.'

It was here that I made my discovery. Here was the long-lost secret. Here was the connection between religion on the one hand and real life on the other. I saw for the first time that there was a strong and subtle link between the services of the old gray church and the daily struggle in which my father and mother were so valiantly engaged. The discovery of that day took to itself all the elements of a great sensation. My eyes were opened; the whole world seemed changed. And among the big things of my little life the revelation of that memorable day stands out in bold and heroic relief.

F. W. Boreham, *My Pilgrimage* (London: The Epworth Press, 1940), 47-49.

DREAD OF DEATH

Louis the Fifteenth forbade any person to so much as mention death in his presence. He would allow no reference to it. Death had appeared to him like a lion that ought to be immediately faced; but he had fled from it. He sought to avoid all thought of it.... And yet, in spite of all his efforts, the dread of death was for ever upon him, and it became more terrible as the event itself drew near.

F. W. Boreham, *The Whisper of God and other sermons* (London: Arthur H. Stockwell, 1902), 65.

DREAMS AND DISCERNMENT

The dream may convince the dreamer; but it is of no evidential value to anybody but himself.

When Mr. Wesley returned from his fruitless visit to America, the ship anchored in the evening. In the roadstead lay another vessel just about to sail for America. Mr. Wesley learned that Mr. Whitefield was on board that vessel. He was very distressed; for he particularly desired to have Mr. Whitefield's company in England. Early next morning, he sent a messenger by a boat to the other ship. 'Tell Mr. Whitefield,' he said, 'that I have had a dream during the night and that it has been made clear to me that he is not to go to America!'

George Whitefield received the message and paced the deck for a moment or two in deep thought. 'Go back to Mr. Wesley,' he said to the messenger, 'and say that, if God had wished me to turn back, God would have given *me* the dream! Why should He send the dream to Mr. Wesley?' And he calmly went on with his tour.

F. W. Boreham, *A Late Lark Singing* (London: The Epworth Press, 1945), 189

DYING YOUNG

We have all felt the pathos of the snapped columns that are so often erected to commemorate lives that, broken suddenly, seemed sadly incomplete. From the waters of one of our Australian rivers—the Parramatta—there rises a tall but broken column to the memory of a young oarsman—Henry Ernest Searle—who, after winning the championship of the world, died at the age of twenty-one.

And, within walking distance of this quiet study of mine, is a broken column to which every year thousands of people pay pilgrimage. It marks the resting-place of Adam Lindsay Gordon, the poet of our vast Australian solitudes,

> "A shining soul with syllables of fire,
> Who sang the first great songs these lands can claim."

He was little more than a boy in years, and he was altogether a boy in spirit, when his light was suddenly extinguished. I select these two instances, almost at random, and because on these expressive monuments my own eyes have so often rested. The symbol is very common; and it is common for the simple reason that the poignant problem that it symbolizes is so common. Let Principal Fairbairn state it. 'Here,' he says, 'is a young man full of promise. He has been a bright and happy boy, the pride of his mother's heart, the light of his father's eye; he has been an earnest student, the joy of his tutors, the hope of his school and his college, raising high expectations even in the withered breast of his professor. He has been the center of a brilliant circle of friends, who talked with him, walked with him, disputed and argued with him concerning high things, ever stimulated by his brilliant thought and vivid speech. He comes to the threshold of life, with school and university behind him, high hopes and fair visions before him, and noble purposes looking out from his radiant face. And, just then, a fatal disease claims him as its own; and he dies, while people whose hearts are dry as summer dust linger on in what they call life.'

Every person who lets their memory roam for a minute among the old familiar faces of their school and college days will find it easy to fill out this general outline with personal detail.

In his *Life of Richard Jefferies,* who died at thirty-eight, Edward Thomas marvels that Jefferies was permitted to drop into his grave just as he was beginning to find himself and to see life whole.

And a later writer, singularly enough, has made a similar remark concerning Edward Thomas himself! 'What a mystery it is,' says Canon Ainger, in a letter to Mrs. Bowles concerning the death of her young brother, 'what a mystery it is that a life should be taken just when it has been receiving and was about to begin bearing fruit!' It is indeed! These gallant young souls were just getting into their stride when they found themselves confronted by an apparently impassable barrier. It really looks as if we have found a blind alley at last.

F. W. Boreham, *Wisps of Wildfire* (London: The Epworth Press, 1924), 71-73.

EFFECTIVE COMMUNICATION RELATES TO PEOPLE

Think of Thomas Chalmers. The most sensational discovery of his life was the discovery that for more than twelve years he had been preaching sermons at Kilmany that bore no relationship whatever to the actual lives of the people to whom he ministered. For more than twelve years the parish minister at Kilmany had been preaching to the Man in the Moon!

Then came the great awakening. Chalmers was seized by sudden illness. During his convalescence his mind underwent what he himself called a great revolution. He found the Savior, and entered into an experience of which he had previously never dreamed. It is difficult to read with dry eyes his own telling account of that great transformation. In due time he returned to his pulpit. The people were electrified. The minister was no longer preaching to the Man in the Moon; he was preaching to the people of Kilmany! And Kilmany was touched to tears in consequence.

'He would bend over the pulpit,' says an old hearer, 'and press us to take the gift as if he held it that moment in his hand and could not be satisfied till every one of us got possession of it!'

The effect was instantaneous. As long as Chalmers preached to the Man in the Moon, the Man in the Moon made not the slightest response; but when he preached to the people of Kilmany, Kilmany became a new village.

F. W. Boreham, *The Other Side of the Hill* (London: Charles H. Kelly, 1917), 91-92.

ESSENTIAL THINGS DO NOT CHANGE

Before I settled at my present church [in Armadale, Melbourne] I had the honor of holding two pastorates: one in New Zealand and one in Tasmania. In New Zealand no name is more honored than that of Bishop Selwyn; in Tasmania none is more cherished than that of Sir John Franklin. Now here is a striking and impressive coincidence! When young Selwyn landed in New Zealand, that country was the land of the Maori; and the Maori had the reputation of being the most ferocious of cannibals.

The youthful Bishop looked around upon a land of volcanic wonders and of the most unusual vegetation. When Sunday came, he conducted his very first service in the new land. Turning for a moment from the natives to his white companions, he exclaimed: 'A great change has taken place in the circumstances of our natural life; but no change which need affect our spiritual being. We have come to a land where not so much as a tree resembles those of our native country. All visible things are new and strange: but the things that are unseen remain the same.' And he took, as the text of that first sermon in New Zealand, the text from which, nearly a century later, Sir Ernest Shackleton drew such wealthy stores of inspiration: '*If I take the wings of the morning, and dwell in the uttermost parts of the sea, even there shall Thy hand lead me and Thy right hand shall hold me.*'

F. W. Boreham, *A Casket of Cameos*, (London: The Epworth Press, 1924), 37-38.

ETERNAL LAWS ARE UNCHANGING

The first men to land upon the moon will find themselves confronted by a huge notice-board [bearing the words]:

THOU SHALL NOT STEAL

At least, so Mr. Chesterton says. Perhaps he is not to be taken literally. It may be his whimsical way of saying that there are certain stately principles of conduct so fundamental, so inflexible and so penetrating that they stand, mandatory and imperative, in every world and in every age.

It is in his *Innocence of Father Brown* that Mr. Chesterton makes this excursion into astronomy; and it is into the lips of Father Brown himself that he slips the declaration about the signboard. The priest is arguing that, whatever fantastic conceptions you may form concerning the various orbs in the planetary system, Reason and Justice must be common to them all. Reason and Justice, he insists, grip the remotest and loneliest of the spheres.

'You can imagine,' he says, 'any mad botany or geology you please. Think of forests of adamant with leaves of brilliants! Think the moon is a blue moon, a single elephantine sapphire! But don't fancy that all that frantic astronomy would make the smallest difference to the reason and justice of conduct. On plains of opal, under cliffs cut out of pearl, you would still find a notice-board: *Thou shall not steal!*'

If this means anything, it means that our laws of property are graven in the eternal nature of things.

F. W. Boreham, *A Witch's Brewing* (London: The Epworth Press, 1932), 61-62.

EXPOSING PEOPLE TO STRUGGLE

Was it not Alfred Russel Wallace who tried to help an emperor-moth, and only harmed it by his ill-considered ministry?

He came upon the creature beating its wings and struggling wildly to force its passage through the narrow neck of its cocoon. He admired its fine proportions, eight inches from the tip of one wing to the tip of the other, and thought it a pity that so handsome a creature should be subjected to so severe an ordeal. He therefore took out his lancet and slit the cocoon. The moth came out at once; but its glorious colors never developed. The soaring wings never expanded. The indescribable hues and tints and shades that should have adorned them never appeared. The moth crept moodily about; drooped perceptibly; and presently died.

The furious struggle with the cocoon was Nature's wise way of developing the splendid wings and of sending the vital fluids pulsing through the frame until every particle blushed with their beauty. The naturalist had saved the little creature from the struggle, but had unintentionally ruined and slain it in the process.

F. W. Boreham, *Mushrooms on the Moor* (London: Charles H. Kelly, 1915), 135-136.

FACE OF GOD

One afternoon, I found that I was standing on the public pavement [sidewalk] outside a picture-framer's shop, and that my nearest neighbor was a small boy who was flattening his nose against the pane in his anxiety to inspect as closely as possible the treasures of art exposed in the window.

A moment later, an ill-kempt, coarse-looking woman shuffled up, seized his hand roughly, and proceeded to drag him away. He did his best to resist her violence, and, pointing to a delicately-executed sepia copy of one of Harold Copping's beautiful portrayals of the face of Jesus, he demanded: 'Who's that?'

'Oh, come on,' the woman cried, impatiently, giving another savage tug at the arm of her offspring, 'it's a portrait of Gawd, that's all!' And, his powers of resistance failing, she bore him triumphantly away.

'A Portrait of Gawd!' It sounded a trifle crude as she said it; but, reflecting on the incident during the moments of waiting that immediately followed, I was compelled to confess to myself that, all unconsciously, she had uttered a profound and sublime truth.

I seem to be gazing once more into those sad but beautiful eyes—the eyes that so completely captivated the small boy on the pavement. It is a study in thought-reading. When you come to think of it, thought-reading is the very essence of religion. Everything, in this world and in every other, depends upon a person's ability to read the mind of God. But the supreme vehicle for the revelation of thought is the face. If my friend particularly desires to penetrate my inmost thought and deepest emotion, he watches my countenance. I may frame my words to suit my purpose; but the lineaments of my face will probably betray my real pleasure or dissatisfaction in spite of myself. That is surely what Paul meant when he said that the ultimate revelation of the inmost thought of God was to be found in this thorn-crowned face so beautifully portrayed in the painting on which the small boy and I were gazing this afternoon….

No two faces are alike, and yet very few faces deviate very widely from the common standard. This is striking enough in its way; but there is something still more remarkable behind it. For the human face, wonderful as it is, is but the outward and visible symbol of something even more wonderful than itself. 'Strictly speaking,' says Victor Hugo, in his *Toilers of the Sea,* 'strictly speaking, the human face is a mask. The real person is that which is concealed behind it. The soul is the reality.' These thousands of faces at which one glances in his daily walk differ from one another for the simple reason that the souls behind them differ from one another. No two minds are duplicates. Each face is the outward expression of an individuality; and each individuality is absolutely unique.

It was this that led Ruskin to affirm that all the greatest painting in the world is the painting of the human face.... For if every face is the revelation of a personality, it follows that the face of Jesus is the most exquisite and most accurate revelation that has ever been given of the divine mind. I see now why the Most High, when He desired to reveal Himself to men, did so by means of the beauty and nobleness and pathos of a Face. I see now—or begin to see—what Paul means when he says that 'God, who commanded the light to shine out of the darkness has shined in our hearts to give the light of the knowledge of the glory of God in the face of Jesus Christ.' He means that the man who has once looked into the thorn-crowned face of Jesus has looked into the very heart of the Eternal.

F. W. Boreham, *Ships of Pearl* (London: The Epworth Press, 1935), 114-117.

FACING CLOSED DOORS

In our Mosgiel days my wife and I cherished a proud ambition. At first, and for some years, it was merely a dream, compounded of the stuff that dreams are made of; a rainbow-tinted thought; a wild flight of fancy. Then, with the years, it deepened into an actual hope; we talked of it as among the things that the future might conceivably hold in store for us; we made plans as to our behavior if it happened. Then the hope developed into a probability; and, all circumstances pointing steadily in one direction, the probability crystallized into a certainty. We set our hearts upon it.

The hour drew dear that was to decide our destiny. We were on holiday at the Nuggets. I walked four miles along the beach to the post office. The telegram was there! With trembling hand I tore it open. An unexpected development had taken place, and the gates of our Elysium were slammed in our faces! We spent the remainder of that holiday strolling amid scenes of the most bewitching loveliness with tears in our eyes and fierce rebellion in our hearts.

Yet, looking back upon it all after the passage of a quarter of a century, nothing on the horizon of the past stands out more clearly than the fact that, had our dream been realized and our desire granted, we should have missed the best all along the line. We can see now, as plainly as if it were written across the skies, that the opening of that door would have spoiled everything. It would have meant, to us, an irretrievable disaster.

F. W. Boreham, *The Fiery Crags* (London: The Epworth Press, 1928), 180-181.

Faith of a Scientist

The lecturer had vanished! A crowded gathering of distinguished scientists had been listening, spellbound, to the masterly expositions of Michael Faraday. For an hour he had held his brilliant audience enthralled as he had demonstrated the nature and properties of the magnet. And he had brought his lecture to a close with an experiment so novel, so bewildering and so triumphant that, for some time after he resumed his seat, the house rocked with enthusiastic applause. And then the Prince of Wales—afterwards King Edward the Seventh—rose to propose a motion of congratulation. The resolution, having been duly seconded, was carried with renewed thunders of applause. But the uproar was succeeded by a strange silence. The assembly waited for Faraday's reply; but the lecturer had vanished! What had become of him? Only two or three of his more intimate friends were in on the secret. They knew that the great chemist was something more than a great chemist; he was a great Christian. He was an elder of a little Sandemanian Church—a church that never boasted more than twenty members. The hour at which Faraday concluded his lecture was the hour of the week-night prayer-meeting. That meeting he never neglected. And, under cover of the cheering and applause, the lecturer had slipped out of the crowded hall and hurried off to the little meeting-house where two or three had met together to renew their fellowship with God.

In that one incident the man stands revealed. All the sublimities and all the simplicities of life met in his soul. The master of all the sciences, he kept in his breast the heart of a little child.

F. W. Boreham, *A Handful of Stars* (London: The Epworth Press, 1922), 178-179.

FAITH STARTING SMALL

A man must have a faith of his own. But what kind of a faith? How big a faith? The question reminds me of an episode in *The Cloister and the Hearth.* In the tenth chapter of that glorious novel, Charles Reade tells how Gerard, his hero, was imprisoned in the haunted tower of the Stadthouse at Tergou. All at once an arrow came hurtling through the tiny barred window high up in the cell. His first impression was that it was an attempt to assassinate him. But no other arrows came. He then crawled about on all fours trying to find the mysterious arrow. He found it, and found, attached to it, a skein of silk. Silk! How could silk save him? A sudden suspicion flashed into his mind. He felt that the hand of Margaret, his sweetheart, was behind the arrow. He lowered the silk from the window, and, when he drew it up again, a stout whip-cord was tied to it. He drew up the whipcord and it brought him a thicker cord. And, at the end of this, was a rope, and, by the rope, he escaped!

Let a man look round his cell. Is there no skein of fragile silk with which he may begin the process of salvation?

F. W. Boreham, *Boulevards of Paradise* (London: The Epworth Press, 1944), 48-49.

FAITHFUL SAYINGS

F. W. Boreham in writing about the biblical statement: "This is a faithful saying!" tells this story:

In the course of a recent tour through Western Australia, I was taken through the gold diggings. And, near Kanowna, I was shown the spot on which, years ago, there gathered one of the largest and most extraordinary congregations that ever assembled on this side of the world. It was whispered all over the diggings that an enormous nugget had been found and that Father Long, the local priest, had seen it and knew exactly where it was discovered. Morning, noon, and night the young priest was pestered by eager gold-hunters for information; but to one and all his lips were sealed. At last he consented to announce publicly the exact locality of the wonderful find.

At the hour fixed people came from far and near, some on horseback, some on camels, some in all kinds of conveyances, and thousands on foot. It was the largest gathering of diggers in the history of the gold fields. At the appointed time Father Long appeared, surveyed the great sea of bronzed and bearded faces, and then announced that the 'Sacred Nugget' had been found in the Lake Gwynne country.

In a moment the crowd had vanished! There was the wildest stampede for the territory to which the priest had pointed them. But as the days passed by, the disappointed seekers, in twos and threes, came dribbling wearily back. Not a glint of gold had been seen by any of them! And then the truth flashed upon them. The priest had been hoaxed! The 'Sacred Nugget' was a mass of common metal splashed with gold paint!

Father Long took the matter bitterly to heart; he went to bed a broken and humiliated man; and, a few months later, disconsolate, he died!

Boreham in his article on Hugh Latimer concludes: It was a great day in Hugh Latimer's life when he got among the 'faithful sayings' the sayings of which he was certain, the sayings that could never bring to any confiding hearer the heartbreak and disgust of disappointment.

F. W. Boreham, *A Bunch of Everlastings* (London: The Epworth Press, 1920), 61-62.

FEAR, FAITH AND DISBELIEF

In the biography of Bishop Westcott there is an affecting description of Dr. Westcott's visit to the deathbed of Bishop Lee, of Manchester. 'People quote various words of the Lord,' said the dying prelate to his distinguished visitor, 'people quote various words of the Lord as containing the sum of the gospel—the Lord's Prayer, the Sermon on the Mount, and the like; but to me the essence of the gospel is in simpler and shorter terms—*"Fear not; only believe."* '

And then, as he reflected a moment, the feeling swept over him that those words were not as simple as they seemed. He was frightened by the frailty of his faith. *"Only believe,"* he repeated, *"only believe,"* —ah, Westcott, mark that *"only."*

Tears filled his eyes. '*Only believe.*' But did he believe? And at last his soul found expression and consolation in the old, agonizing cry, '*Lord, I believe: help Thou mine unbelief.*'

F. W. Boreham, *The Other Side of the Hill* (London: Charles H. Kelly, 1917), 165.

FEELINGS ABOUT HOME

Rev. Alexander Connell, M.A., B.D., at Sefton Park Presbyterian Church, Liverpool said:

"I love at times to reflect on the three heads of discourse employed by an old Scottish divine of the Covenanting days. In preaching on the Prodigal Son, he divided his subject into these three parts. First, *Sick o' Hame!* Second, *Hameseick!* And third, *Hame!* That, I think, is just perfect."

F. W. Boreham, *The Prodigal* (London: The Epworth Press, 1941), 66.

FIND TIME FOR YOURSELF

Find time for Yourself! Feel it no shame at proper periods to be doing nothing. Make seasons for leisure and for recreation. Climb the hills; scour the valleys; row on the river; stroll along the beach. Cultivate the friendship of the fields and the ferns and the flowers. Laugh with the young folk and romp with little children. Be at your ease. Let the mind swing into an easy balance, a natural poise, an attitude of perfect repose. The restless soul, eternally doing something, never accomplishes anything. It is the person who can sometimes be at rest who produces the finest work in the long run. *Find time for Yourself!*

F. W. Boreham, *The Drums of Dawn* (London: The Epworth Press, 1933), 62.

FINDING A RESTING PLACE

As a boy, I came under the influence of a fine old clergyman—Canon Hoare, the rector of Holy Trinity, Tunbridge Wells—a man very highly esteemed in the South of England. I can see him now, tall, stately, and gray, my beautiful ideal of all that a minister should be.

In his study there hung a very beautiful and telling picture. It represented a shipwreck, a shipwreck from which one life was being saved. In confidential moments, Canon Hoare would tell the story of the picture. It seems that, years ago, a very wealthy man called to arrange with him about his burial place. The Canon walked round the churchyard with him and, after inspecting several possible positions, the gentleman at last selected the spot in which he wished his bones to rest.

This business completed, they paused for a second or two, listening to the birds, and then the Canon turned to his companion and said:

"Well, now; you have chosen a resting place for your body. Have you yet found a resting place for your soul?"

There was silence for a moment, and then, turning full upon the Canon, the gentleman exclaimed:

"You are the first person who ever asked me that question!"

It set him thinking. He sought and found the resting place, the only resting place, and he sent the Canon the picture as a token of his gratitude. He felt that his was the life that had been saved from shipwreck.

F. W. Boreham, *A Bunch of Everlastings* (London: The Epworth Press, 1920), 242-243.

FINISHING WELL

The joy of finishing and of finishing well! How passionately good people have coveted for themselves that ecstasy! I think of those pathetic entries in Livingstone's journal. 'Oh, to finish my work!' he writes again and again. He is haunted by the vision of the unseen waters, the fountains of the Nile. Will he live to discover them? 'Oh, to finish!' he cries; 'if only I could finish my work!'

I think of Henry Buckle, the author of the *History of Civilization*. He is overtaken by fever at Nazareth and dies at Damascus. In his delirium he raves continually about his book, his still unfinished book. 'Oh, to finish my book!' And with the words, 'My book! my book!' upon his burning lips, his spirit slips away.

I think of Henry Martyn sitting amid the delicious and fragrant shades of a Persian garden, weeping at having to leave the work that he seemed to have only just begun.

I think of Doré taking a sad farewell of his unfinished *Vale of Tears;* of Dickens tearing himself from the manuscript that he knew would never be completed; of Macaulay looking with wistful and longing eyes at the *History* and *The Armada* that must for ever stand as 'fragments'; and of a host besides. Life is often represented by a broken column in the churchyard. People long, but long in vain, for the priceless privilege of finishing their work.

The joy of finishing and of finishing well! There is no joy on earth comparable to this. Who is there that has not read a dozen times the immortal postscript that Gibbon added to his *Decline and Fall?* He describes the tumult of emotion with which, after twenty years of closest application, he wrote the last line of the last chapter of the last volume of his masterpiece. It was a glorious summer's night at Lausanne. 'After laying down my pen,' he says, 'I took several turns in a covered walk of acacias which commands a prospect of the country, the lake and the mountains. The air was temperate, the sky was serene, the silver orb of the moon was reflected from the waters, and all nature was silent.' It was the greatest moment of his life.

We recall, too, the similar experience of Sir Archibald Alison. 'As I approached the closing sentence of my *History of the Empire,*' he says, 'I went up to Mrs. Alison to call her down to witness the conclusion, and she saw the last words of the work written, and signed her name on the margin. It would be affectation to conceal the deep emotion that I felt at this event.'

Or think of the last hours of the Venerable Bede. Living away back in the early dawn of our English story—twelve centuries ago—the old man had set himself to translate the Gospel of John into our native speech. Cuthbert, one of his young disciples, has bequeathed to us the touching record. As the work approached completion, he says, death drew on apace. The aged scholar was racked with pain; sleep forsook him; he could scarcely breathe. The young man who wrote at his dictation implored him to desist. But he would not rest. They came at length to the final chapter; could he possibly live till it was done?

'And now, dear master,' exclaimed the young scribe trem-blingly, 'only one sentence remains! He read the words and the sinking man feebly recited the English equivalents.

'It is finished, dear master!' cried the youth excitedly.

'Ay, it is finished!' echoed the dying saint; 'lift me up, place me at that window of my cell at which I have so often prayed to God. Now glory be to the Father and to the Son and to the Holy Ghost!' And, with these triumphant words, the beautiful spirit passed to its rest and its reward.

The result is that Hudson Taylor became one of the most prodigious toilers of all time. So far from his trust in '*the Finished Work of Christ*' inclining him to indolence, he felt that he must toil most terribly to make so perfect a Savior known to the whole wide world.

There lies on my desk a Birthday Book which I very highly value. It was given me at the docks by Mr. Thomas Spurgeon as I was leaving England. If you open it at the twenty-first of May you will find these words: ' *"Simply to Thy Cross I cling" is but half of the Gospel. No one is really clinging to the Cross who is not at the same time faithfully following Christ and doing whatsoever He commands'*; and against those words of Dr. J. R. Miller's in my Birthday Book, you may see the autograph of *J. Hudson Taylor.* He was our guest at the Mosgiel Manse when he set his signature to those striking and significant sentences.

F. W. Boreham, *A Handful of Stars* (London: The Epworth Press, 1922), 103-105.

FIRING PEOPLE'S ENTHUSIASM

History is often made in slippers. Take the case of Sir Joseph Banks. The work that he did in slippers is one of the most extraordinary and unparalleled achievements in the story of the Empire. Joseph Banks accompanied Captain Cook as naturalist on those wonderful and epoch-making voyages that changed the face of the world.

But the work, even of the greatest navigators must, in the nature of things, be tantalizingly superficial. Cook skirted the coasts of immense continents, but had no time to explore them. Banks stood on the deck of the *Endeavour* and saw the shores of those vast but unknown lands pass, like a panorama, along the horizon, and he vowed that he would dedicate his energies to the work of inspiring young men with a passion for exploration. And most amazingly did he succeed in his self-imposed task.

In the days of his retirement, living in his quiet English home, he coaxed young men to his fireside, and, sitting there in his slippers, he told them of the vision of the unknown continents that haunted him sleeping and waking. Many of them went back to their homes and offices, smiling superciliously at the old man's enthusiasm. But on the minds of three of his listeners his story had the desired effect. He contrived to fire the fancy, one after the other, of three young men, who, as a result of those fireside conversations, wrote their names in letters indelible upon the world's broad scroll of fame. These three men were Mungo Park, Lachlan Macquarie, and John Franklin.

Mungo Park became, under Sir Joseph's influence, the pioneer of African exploration. He began the work that was afterwards completed by Burton, Speke, Livingstone, Stanley, and an army of dauntless and devoted pathfinders.

Lachlan Macquarie, also under Sir Joseph's influence, opened the gates of Australia, and converted a microscopic and insignificant settlement into a huge continental dominion. 'I would beg of you,' said Sir Joseph Banks to Colonel Macquarie, on the eve of his sailing for Australia, 'I would beg of you to go out with a strong resolve to open up the country and to discover and develop its resources.' Macquarie came, and, setting himself to the task that Sir Joseph had committed to his trust, the Blue Mountains were soon crossed and the incalculable possibilities of the continent revealed.

It was Sir Joseph Banks, too, who inspired Franklin with the idea of opening up the silent seas of the Far North. In 1818 he, being then seventy-five years of age, pleaded with the young naval officer to devote his life to the discovery of the North-West Passage. The nation being now at peace, he pleaded, some of the most daring and gallant young officers—men who had fought with Nelson at Copenhagen and Trafalgar—might now be commissioned to search for the long-dreamed-of waterway. The nation lent an ear to the old man's plea; young Franklin caught the contagion of the veteran's zeal, and, as a result, and after thirty years' of tireless search, the North-West Passage was discovered and sealed by the tragic and pathetic sacrifice of its discoverers.

Whenever I catch the thrill of African exploration; whenever I feel a glow of admiration as I contemplate the dauntless courage of our Australian pathfinders; whenever I read afresh that stirring record of suffering and adventure in the icy polar seas, I let my mind go one step farther back and I conjure up the image of a stately old gentleman, sitting with slippered feet by a comfortable English fireside. More often than we sometimes think, history is made in slippers.

F. W. Boreham, *The Uttermost Star* (London: The Epworth Press, 1919), 86-89.

FOLLOWING PUBLIC WORSHIP

In the porch of the little church near Hawarden Castle—the church in which [British Prime Minister] Mr. Gladstone bowed in worship every morning and in which he loved to read the lessons on Sunday—there is a notice which, I understand, was placed there at Mr. Gladstone's own suggestion. It lays down several simple rules for worship and closes with this admonition: 'Be quiet and thoughtful as you go. On your way home be careful of your talk *or the world will slip back into your heart.*'

F. W. Boreham, *A Late Lark Singing* (London: The Epworth Press, 1945), 90.

GETTING THE HEART RIGHT

You remember the old story of the conversation between Sir Walter Raleigh and his executioner. It is said that the executioner told his noble victim that he would find the scaffold more comfortable if he turned his head the other way.

Whereupon Sir Walter replied: "My friend, it matters little how the head lies so long as the heart is right!"

F. W. Boreham, *The Whisper of God and other sermons* (London: Arthur H. Stockwell, 1902), 109.

GIFT OF ABSENT-MINDEDNESS

I beheld the other afternoon a ridiculous spectacle. It was Speech Day at Haddington College. The orator who had been selected to do the honors of the occasion rose to address the pupils. Holding his pince-nez [glasses] breast-high in his left hand, tucking his right under his coat-tails, and looking wonderfully wise, he proceeded to impress upon his youthful auditors the astounding proposition that the secret of success is—Concentration! I could scarcely keep my seat. Only the severest self-restraint prevented me from springing to my feet and shouting to the entire assembled company that the secret of success is—Absence of Mind! Concentration indeed! What assumption could be more fallacious?

After I had cooled down and my wrath had subsided I forgave the little wiseacre on the ground that he was merely repeating what all the Speech Day orators have been saying from the time of Julius Caesar. Poor little man! He thought that, since all the other speakers said it, it must be the correct thing to say. It evidently never occurred to him that the thing that everybody says is the thing that ought most to be suspected.

'Concentrate!' he said. 'Whatever you have to do, apply to it all your powers of thought.' I wonder if it ever occurred to him that the most important things that he ever does, he does without even being conscious that he does them. Not only does he do them without thinking about them; but, as a fact, he could not do them as well if he *did* think about them. What can be more important to him than that his heart should beat, his lungs breathe, and his digestive organs fulfill their functions? But he does all these vital things without concentration! He does them while he reads, while he writes, while he sleeps! Indeed, he is doing them as he stands there before the pupils of Haddington College! While he raises his pince-nez, flicks the tails of his coat, and labors the theory that everything depends upon Concentration, he is doing the most necessary things that he ever does without any concentration at all! He is doing them in complete absence of mind! When he gets home, and, throwing himself into an armchair, rests after his strenuous and exhausting rhetorical effort, let the good little man concentrate upon the beating of his heart, upon the heaving of his lungs, upon the operation of his digestive organs! And he will discover that Concentration, so far from being the secret of success, is the secret of all kinds of trouble. As soon as he concentrates upon the beating of his heart, his heart beats irregularly and unnaturally; as soon as he concentrates upon the workings of his lungs, his breath comes rapidly and jerkily; as soon as he concentrates on his digestive organs, he becomes conscious of sensations that are designed to be subconscious. The happy man is the man who does not know that he possesses a liver. On all such physiological themes he is gloriously absent-minded....

All the world's greatest achievements were the result of magnificent absent-mindedness.

F. W. Boreham, *Home of the Echoes* (London: The Epworth Press, 1921), 91-93.

GIFT OF INQUISITIVENESS

Alfred Russel Wallace said of [Charles] Darwin that his whole character was reflected in the restless inquisitiveness of his boyhood. He demanded to know the '*how?*' and the '*why?*' and the '*what for?*' of everything; and he maintained his insatiable curiosity unabated to the end. It would have been one of the tragedies of civilization—a tragedy that would have been none the less calamitous because, in the nature of the case, it would have been unsuspected and unrecorded—if unsympathetic parents or unimaginative teachers had cured young Darwin of his penchant for interrogation.

F. W. Boreham, *Wisps of Wildfire* (London: The Epworth Press, 1924), 192-193.

GIFT OF THE DIVINE PRESENCE

In the consciousness of heavenly honor, the martyrs have welcomed earthly shame; in the knowledge of divine coronation, they have endured human crucifixion. 'Fear not,' they have heard a voice say to them, 'fear not, for when you pass through the waters, I will be with you; and through the rivers they shall not overflow you; when you walk through the fire you shall not be burned; and the flame shall not consume you.'

That is the passage marked in the Bible of Thomas Bilney, which may still be seen at Corpus Christi College, Cambridge. He marked it while he was awaiting the fiery ordeal amid which his radiant spirit subsequently took its flight. That promised presence has been vividly experienced by all who have endured hardship for the Savior's sake.

F. W. Boreham, *The Heavenly Octave* (London: The Epworth Press, 1935), 150.

GIFT UNSPEAKABLE

I one evening attended in Mosgiel the farewell service of an old minister. The good man was one of New Zealand's pioneers.... I can see at this moment the crowded church: I recall vividly his tall and massive form, his snowy hair, his rich

Scottish brogue. I can hear the eloquent and transparently sincere tributes paid to the old man by his elders, by his brother ministers and by the local authorities.

And then there came the climax of the great occasion—the moment at which the retiring veteran was to reply. What would he say in closing a ministry of nearly fifty years—the fifty years in which the entire settlement had sprung into being? He was to address people in whose hearts and homes he had been enthroned for a couple of generations. Greatly beloved and held in highest honor, he rose, stepped forward, leaned heavily upon the rail and looked into the faces of the congregation. But no words came. After a long struggle with himself, he resumed his seat, which happened to be next my own. The Chairman stepped across, begged him to take his time and then to try again. He rose a second time—with the same result. During a musical interlude, we gathered round to encourage and hearten him; but, when he again essayed the excruciating task, he was no more successful. It's no good; I can't do it! I heard him murmur under his breath as he finally abandoned the effort.

In some respects it was the most moving farewell which I have ever witnessed. He knew what he wanted to say: and he knew the language in which he wished to say it: but, in the crucial hour, his voice failed.

So that it comes to this. The gift of God is unspeakable because it transcends my powers of comprehension. But if I could comprehend it, I should be able to find no language in which to express it. And if I could comprehend it and could find such language, I should be so overwhelmed by the awe and the glory and the mystery and the wonder of it that my lips would refuse their office and my tongue would find speech impossible.

And even *if* I could comprehend it, and *if* I could find words to express it, and *if* I could command my powers of utterance, nobody would understand what I was saying. Like the things that Paul heard in Paradise, my hearers would be listening to unspeakable words—words that it is not lawful for a person to utter.

Thanks be to God for His unspeakable gift!

F. W. Boreham, *A Late Lark Singing* (London: The Epworth Press, 1945), 72-73.

GOD ABIDES

Two words the Muslim inscribes upon the tombstone of his friend. 'He remains.' He means that, let who will come and go, Allah abides. The love of God does not pass.

F. W. Boreham, *A Reel of Rainbow* (London: The Epworth Press, 1920), 179.

GOD IS LIGHT

God is light! Light is the source and sustenance of all life: the very plants wilt and die in the dark. Light is the source of all joy: the birds greet the dawn with a burst of blithest song. Light is the source of all beauty.

There is a loveliness, Richard Jefferies points out, that only light can impart. 'It reddens the cherry; it gilds the apple; it tints the rose; it ripens the wheat; it touches a woman's face with the golden-brown of ripe life—ripe as a plum. As the great painters of women's faces knew—Rubens, for instance—there is no other hue so beautiful as this human sunshine tint.' So that all life and all gladness and all beauty spring from light. Which is merely another way of saying that all life and all gladness and all beauty emanate from God; for *God is light and in Him is no darkness at all.*

F. W. Boreham, *I Forgot To Say* (London: The Epworth Press, 1939), 217.

GOD NOT HARD TO SWALLOW

On the other side of the Atlantic, Emerson told of two American senators who, each in his own way, spent twenty-five years in searching for evidence of the immortality of the soul. And Emerson marvels that they failed to notice that the impulse that prompted them to seek that evidence so patiently through all the years was in itself the strongest proof they could desire.

I like to watch the swallow turn its face to the ocean, and set fearlessly out over the waters. If I had no other proof of lands beyond the sea, the instinct of the swallow would satisfy me. 'Sir,' says Emerson grandly, 'I hold that God who keeps His word with the swallows and the fishes in all their migratory instincts will keep His word with Man!'

It was well and bravely spoken; and when my brain swims with the tiresome and tedious arguments of the schools, I shall think of the swallows, and shall pillow my tired head and weary heart on the great hope that their seaward flight affords me. 'Beautiful swallows!' Richard Jefferies fondly exclaims. 'Be tender to them, for they symbolize all that is best in Nature and all that is best in our own hearts.' They do indeed.

F. W. Boreham, *The Golden Milestone* (London: Charles H. Kelly, 1915), 44.

GOD'S ABIDING PRESENCE

I can see him now, as, stately and patriarchal, he walked up the desk-room of the old college to address us. As that impressive and striking figure appeared at the door, every student instinctively sprang to his feet and remained standing till the Grand Old Man was seated. I thought that I had never seen a face more beautiful, a figure more picturesque. A visitant from another world could scarcely have proved more arresting or awe-inspiring.

When it was announced that Dr. J. G. Paton, the veteran missionary to the New Hebrides, was coming to address the college, I expected to *hear* something thrilling and affecting; but, somehow, it did not occur to me that my *eyes* would be captivated as well. But, when the hero of my dreams appeared, a picture which I shall carry with me to my dying day was added to the gallery which my memory treasures. This was in London many years ago. I little thought that afternoon that the apostolic form before me would one day sleep in an Australian grave, and that my own home would stand within half an hour's journey of his lovely resting-place.

In preparation for the task to which I now address myself [writing an essay on Paton], I paid a pilgrimage to the Boroondara Cemetery [Kew, Melbourne] this afternoon, and read Dr. J. G. Paton's text bravely inscribed upon his tomb. It is not the kind of text that is usually engraved upon such monuments, but it is in every way appropriate to *him*. 'In his private conversation,' writes his son, the Rev. F. H. L. Paton, M.A., B.D., 'in his private conversation and in his public addresses, my father was constantly quoting the words, *Lo, I am with you always,* as the inspiration of his quietness and confidence in time of danger, and of his hope in the face of human impossibilities. So much was this realized by his family that we decided to inscribe that text upon his tomb in the Boroondara Cemetery. It seemed to all of us to sum up the essential element in his faith, and the supreme source of his courage and endurance.' *Lo, I am with you always* ...

F. W. Boreham, *A Casket of Cameos*, (London: The Epworth Press, 1924), 135-136.

GOOD MOURNING

The very brevity of the Bible's shortest text has given it an emphasis that has appealed to us all. *Jesus wept!* I have never in my life attended a funeral without pointing out that, since

He wept, there can be nothing weak or wicked or faithless in our human tears. He made us what we are—quivering bundles of emotion, creatures that cling fondly and tenaciously to one another. He made us what we are—made us in His own image. And, having made us what we are, and made us in His own image, He knows the wrench and the heartbreak. He sympathized; He understood; and so He wept. Is no work of grace effected by such tender tears? ...

In the middle of the nineteenth century a young minister visited Dundee. He was oppressed by the fact that, in spite of diligent study and conscientious labor, his work was not flourishing. He had been reading about Robert Murray M'Cheyne, and he felt that he should like to visit the scene of that extraordinary man's seraphic ministry. Mr. M'Cheyne had recently died at the age of thirty; yet, before dying, he had moved Scotland to its very depths. What was the secret of his amazing influence? The young minister came to St. Peter's. The old sexton who had served under M'Cheyne was still there. He reverently led the youthful inquirer into the vestry, and pointed to some of M'Cheyne's books still lying on the table.

'Sit down here,' said the sexton, motioning his visitor to the chair in which M'Cheyne had so often sat.

'Now, put your elbows on the table! That was the way Mr. M'Cheyne used to do!'

The visitor obeyed.

'Now, put your face in your hands!' The visitor did so.

'Now *let the tears flow!* That was the way Mr. M'Cheyne used to do!'

The sexton led his guest to the pulpit; and gave him a fresh series of instructions.

'Put your elbows down into the pulpit!' He put his elbows down.

'Now put your face in your hands!' He did so.

'Now let the tears flow! That was the way Mr. M'Cheyne used to do!'

Yes, *that* was the way; and those who today read the story of M'Cheyne's fruitful and abounding ministry will find in it the best possible illustration of the principle embedded in the second Beatitude.

F. W. Boreham, *The Heavenly Octave* (London: The Epworth Press, 1935), 37-38, 43-45.

GRACE OF GRATITUDE

Dr. Leslie F. Church, of London, once told me of three friends of his who, on a pouring wet day, attended a little church among the Yorkshire dales. The service was to be conducted by a local preacher who had fifteen miles to walk over the hills to the church.

'Is this man a great preacher?' asked one of the three as they trudged down the muddy lane.

'Oh, no,' replied one of his companions, 'he is no good at preaching, but he can pray; his prayers are a continuous torrent of thanksgiving!'

The visitors wondered what, on such a day, and with so scanty a congregation, could awaken the good man's gratitude. In due course the service began, as the little old man, drenched to the skin after his long walk over the moors, signaled to the people to bow their heads.

'Almighty God,' he cried with fervor, 'we thank you that it is not always as bad as this!'

Dr. Church's story reminds me of an old couple who, after having enjoyed a modest tea of fish and chips, knelt at their family altar and gave thanks to God that God had ransacked sea and land to provide their evening meal. Sea—the fish! Land—the chips! There is something very beautiful about the grace of gratitude.

F. W. Boreham, *Boulevards of Paradise* (London: The Epworth Press, 1944), 199.

Great Cloud of Witnesses

An old county cricketer had lost his sight. He was stone blind. And it was the grief of all his days that he could not see his own boy play the great game. The son became the crack bat of the school team, and used to lead his father to the ground. But, beyond hearing with inexpressible delight the comments of the crowd and his boy's play, he got small satisfaction from it.

One day he suddenly died. The following Saturday an important match was to be played. Other members of the team, who knew of the lad's affection for his blind father, took it for granted that their best bat would be absent. But, to their surprise, he strolled down in his flannels, and presented himself for play. And he batted that day as he had never done before. He snicked and cut and pulled and drove with magnificent audacity and judgment. His companions were bewildered. He rattled up a century in no time, and won the match with ease.

After the applause of the pavilion had died down, he turned to a comrade and asked, 'How did I play?'

'Never better; you outdid yourself. What did it all mean?'

'Why, you see,' said the young hero, '*it was the first time my father ever saw me bat!*'

F. W. Boreham, *The Other Side of the Hill* (London: Charles H. Kelly, 1917), 195-196.

Growing Desire for Rest

I have been reading Dr. C. W. Valentine's *Psychology of Beauty*. In his chapter on 'The Beauty of Color' he speaks of some remarkable experiments made by Mr. W. H. Winch. Mr. Winch tested two thousand London school children, and then a number of adults, as to their favorite colors. The results were most interesting, and may be briefly summarized.

With the tiny tots, red was an easy first, and green was nowhere! With the intermediates, blue was first, and green had improved its position. With the senior scholars, blue was still, and green had risen to second place. With adults, green was first, and blue had fallen to the second position. Now why this growing popularity of green as life wears on? Mr. Valentine thinks that it is because green is the restful color. The tiny children know no rapture but the ecstasy of movement; sitting still is torture unendurable; bedtime is greeted with sulks and tears; they have no love for green. But as life goes on, rest becomes less distasteful; then positively attractive; until, little by little, green comes into its own.

F. W. Boreham, *The Silver Shadow* (London: Charles H. Kelly, 1918), 29-30.

HAPPY ETERNITY!

'Gentlemen,' exclaimed old Rabbi Duncan to his students as he dismisses them at the end of the year's work, 'many will be wishing you a Happy New Year. Your old tutor wishes you a happy *Eternity!*'

F. W. Boreham, *A Bunch of Everlastings* (London: The Epworth Press, 1920), 252.

HARDSHIP AND CHALLENGE

We make an egregious blunder when we try to persuade people that the way to heaven is easy. The statement is false to fact in the first place; and, in the second, there is no responsive chord in human nature which will vibrate to that ignoble note. Hardship has a strange fascination for people.

Pizarro knew what he was doing when he traced his line on the sands of Panama, and cried: 'Comrades, on that side of the line are toil, hunger, nakedness, the drenching storm, desertion, and death; on this side ease and pleasure. Choose, every man! For my part, I go to the south.'

Garibaldi knew what he was doing when he exclaimed: 'Soldiers, what I offer you is fatigue, danger, struggle, and death; the chill of the cold night in the free air; the intolerable heat beneath the blazing sun; no lodgings, no munitions, no provisions, but forced marches, perilous watch-posts, and the continual struggle with the bayonet against strong batteries. Those who love freedom and their country may follow me.'

People love to be challenged and taunted and dared. Six thousand men eagerly volunteered to join Captain Scott's expedition to the South Pole. Some holding high and remunerative positions craved to be permitted to swab the decks of the *Terra Nova*. A captain in a crack cavalry regiment, with five clasps on his uniform, a hero of the South African war, counted it an honor to perform the most menial duties at a salary of a shilling a month.

Yes, Pizarro and Garibaldi, Peary and Scott knew what they were doing. They were obeying the surest instinct in the genius of leadership; for they were following Him who said: 'If any one will come after Me, let him deny himself, and take up his cross daily, and follow Me; for whosoever shall save his life shall lose it, but whosoever shall lose his life for My sake, the same shall save it.' On the road to Golgotha, the Savior challenged the daring among people, and the heroes of all the ages have in consequence trooped to His standard.

F. W. Boreham, *The Luggage of Life* (London: Charles H. Kelly, 1912), 228-229.

HARES AND TORTOISES

Recalling the story about the hare and the tortoise, history furnishes us with the records of some really brilliant hares.

If I were invited to name three of them, I should instance the cases of William Pitt, Lord Macaulay, and Charles Dickens. Pitt, although physically frail, took his university degree at seventeen, and became Prime Minister seven years later. Yet all his biographers agree that there is no evidence of intellectual development in the eventful years that followed.

In his *Life and Letters of Lord Macaulay,* Sir George Otto Trevelyan presents us with a similar picture. The first chapter is one of the most amusing, and one of the most amazing, records of youthful precocity ever penned. But, as Walter Bagehot, with his usual insight, has observed, there was no corresponding growth during his maturer years. 'His mind shows no trace of change. What he is, he was; and what he was, he is! He early attained a high development, but he has not increased it since. Years have come, but they have whispered little. His first speeches are as good as his last; his last no richer than his first. The events of twenty years have been full of valuable instruction on the events of twenty years ago, but they have not instructed him.'

It was much the same with Dickens. Dickens and Thackeray were contemporaries; they were born within a few months of each other. But Dickens was a hare; Thackeray a tortoise. Dickens was only five and twenty when he published *Pickwick Papers* and swept the world off its feet. The country was taken by storm. It was the greatest sensation that our literary history had experienced. From that moment his fame and position were assured. Thackeray, on the other hand, groped his way blindly among the intricate by-ways of London journalism. It took him ten years to feel his feet; the destiny to which he had been born dawned tardily upon him. Dickens had published *Pickwick Papers, Nicholas Nickleby, The Old Curiosity Shop, Barnaby Rudge, Martin Chuzzlewit,* and the *Christmas Stories* before, in giving *Vanity Fair* to the world, Thackeray announced the rise of another first class English novelist.

Pitt, Macaulay, and Dickens were essentially hares. They ran swiftly and stopped suddenly. Still, they covered a vast stretch of ground before their progress became arrested. The fact that they now sleep together in Westminster Abbey shows that they each earned the gratitude of the ages for having traveled so far in the course of a brilliant dash. Their lightning fleetness carried them to a point at which it was possible for them to render services to their country that their country can never forget.

But enough of this! In order to adopt a more conciliatory tone towards one whose diverting fables beguiled and instructed my infancy, let me confess that it would certainly have been better if the hare had kept going. Similarly, it would have been better if Pitt and Macaulay and Dickens had kept growing. I don't know why they stopped.

I have been reading several volumes of Sir William Osler's lectures to medical students. I find that Sir William, too, is puzzled as to why hares stop. In season and out of season, he urges his young doctors to keep learning. Do anything, he says, to keep your brain fresh! Go back to the university classroom or the hospital ward; take up new studies or new hobbies; adopt any precaution against an arrested intellectual progress! He begs old doctors to keep in touch with young students. And, in his lecture on 'Basset,' he commends the old doctors of France who mingle their white locks with the boys who are just beginning, and pursue their profession to the end with the passionate ardor of youth. On almost every page Sir William Osler warns doctors against settling down to a stereotyped order of things. 'Keep going!' he cries, again and again, and 'Keep going!'

When is the hare most in danger of stopping? In his able criticism of Voltaire, Lord Morley speaks of the thirty-third year as 'that earlier climacteric when the men with vision feel conscious of a past and reflectively mark its shadow.' It is then, Lord Morley thinks, that a person is most in danger of burying his ideals and ambitions.

Sir William Osler is discreetly silent as to the exact period at which such a crisis may be expected. But in several of the lectures he significantly reminds his students that when, in 1616, William Harvey announced his notable discovery concerning the circulation of the blood, no doctor over forty was found willing to accept his conclusions. In the same way, Koch and Lister found their brilliant and epoch-making discoveries acclaimed almost exclusively by the younger men. In the *physical* realm, growth is not a matter of volition; in the *intellectual* realm, it is.

Mark Pattison used to say that he owed all his achievements to his resolute refusal to stop growing. 'I am an old man now,' he writes, 'and my story is a story of ceaseless development.' In the fable, the hare, by his pitiful lack of persistence, lost the advantages which his fleetness of foot had secured to him. Let the hare emulate the stubborn persistence of the tortoise, and all the prizes must of necessity be his!

[The apostle] Paul devoted an entire epistle to the hares. 'You ran well,' he says sorrowfully to the Galatians, 'what stopped you?'

That is the question. Why do the hares stop? There is no reason why the Kingdom of Heaven should be the monopoly of the slow-witted and slow-footed. It opens its gates to the tortoises, but it calls also for the hares. Let them come—the smart, the clever, the dashing, the athletic, the brilliant—let them all come! Many a fleet young hare, with his eyes turned wistfully towards the Kingdom of Heaven, has been deterred from starting by the memory of other hares who, as Paul says, *did run well, but stopped.*

'I am afraid,' they say, 'that I, too, should stop. I could never keep it up. I should only make myself a reproach and a byword. I should be like the people to whom Paul wrote. I should be like the hare in the story!'

But it need not be; that is the point; it need not be. There is no reason why the hare should not be as persistent as the tortoise. Pliable was Bunyan's Hare. He set out for the Celestial City with a fleet foot—but stopped! People like Paul and Bunyan see few tragedies in life comparable in pathos to the arrest of the hares. Paul and Bunyan knew no joy like the joy of seeing people set out with eager feet for the Kingdom of Heaven; they knew no sorrow like the sorrow of seeing people abandon so sublime a quest.

F. W. Boreham, *The Fiery Crags* (London: The Epworth Press, 1928), 128-137 (selected).

HAZARDING EVERYTHING

When [Horatio] Nelson was a small boy he conceived the idea of entering the Navy. Then, one day, his mind became filled with doubts. No powerful interests lay behind him; no social influence could be enlisted on his behalf; what chance had he of promotion and distinction? He pulled himself together and looked his doubts in the face. 'I love England,' he said to himself, 'and I believe that I can best serve England in the Navy. I will serve her just because I love her, and leave promotion to chance!'

He entered the Navy and won such dazzling distinction that we still speak of him as 'the greatest sailor since the world began.' There came a day, just before Trafalgar, when—to employ *one* of those revealing verbs on the leaden casket—he had to *hazard* everything. 'Here goes!' he cried; 'if I succeed, I shall have a tomb in Westminster Abbey; if I fail, I shall be burned in effigy on every village green!' And, a little later—to employ the *second* of those revealing verbs on [his] leaden casket—he *gave* everything! And his glorious death has been the pride of the Navy, and of the nation, ever since.

F. W. Boreham, *The Fiery Crags* (London: The Epworth Press, 1928), 157.

HE LEADS ME

In so microscopic a fragment of Scripture as the twenty-third Psalm, one would scarcely expect to find a repetition. Yet, even within that small compass, one phrase occurs twice. He leads me! He leads me beside the still waters.... He leads me in the paths of righteousness for His name's sake. The repetition is significant.

In January, 1895, at the close of my college course, I found myself on the deck of a steamer that was to bear me away from everything that was familiar to a land in which everything would be strange. I felt terribly lonely, almost frightened. Just before the ship cast off at the docks, Mr. Thomas Spurgeon, who had a few months earlier succeeded his father, sent me a message. It was a text: "He that has mercy on them shall lead them." And, looking back across the years, I joyously and confidently confess that no promise ever made has been more faithfully and constantly fulfilled than that one.

At two most crucial points Christianity fearlessly challenges experiment and bravely dares a test. The first is in the matter of Prayer; the second is in the matter of Guidance.

F. W. Boreham, *In Pastures Green* (London: The Epworth Press, 1954), 23.

HE LIVES AND STRENGTHENS

Martin Luther's house is entered by a richly-carved portal. On either side is a stone seat, and, over the seat, a canopy. On the one canopy you see a portrait of Luther; on the other his arms are engraved. Round the arms are the five letters

V.I.V.I.T.—He lives! They reflect Luther's exultant faith in the living presence and ultimate triumph of his risen Lord.

On the opposite canopy, round the portrait, is this text: *In returning and rest shall ye be saved; in quietness and in confidence shall be your strength.* 'Those words,' Luther used to say, 'were an exceeding comfort to me.'

F. W. Boreham, *A Faggot of Torches* (London: The Epworth Press, 1926), 125.

HEROISM THEN AND NOW

A story ... occurs in the life of Wendell Phillips, the heroic conqueror of slavery. They had been sitting by the fire, the old hero of a hundred fights on one side of the hearth, and a young friend on the other. The younger man never understood how that memorable evening slipped so swiftly away. Memory had flushed the cheeks of the veteran abolitionist; the heroic days of the long ago came rushing back upon him; his tongue was unloosed; and 'the old man eloquent' completely lost himself in the thrilling recital. The youth sat enthralled. At last he recognized, with a start, that the evening was gone. He rose to leave.

'Mr. Phillips,' he said, as he took the old man's hand, 'if I had lived in your time, I think I should have been heroic too!'

The veteran, who had accompanied his young visitor to the door, was roused. He pointed down the street, and drew the attention of his companion to the glaring saloons and to all the flaunting indications of audacious vice. His voice was tremulous with indignation.

'Young man,' he said, 'you *are* living in my time, and in God's time! Be sure of this: No person could have been heroic *then* who is not heroic *now*. Goodnight!'

F. W. Boreham, *The Other Side of the Hill* (London: Charles H. Kelly, 1917), 192-193.

HIGH ART OF FORGETTING

Many years ago I visited an old man on his deathbed. He was a man whom nobody liked—hard, sullen, taciturn and dour. If you met him on the street and wished him Good-day, he would keep his eyes straight in front of him, grunt sulkily and pass on. He lived in a tumble-down old hut away back in the bush; he spoke to nobody; and he made it perfectly plain that he wished nobody to speak to him. Even the children shunned him. Some said that he was a hermit; some that he was a woman-hater; some that he was a miser; some that he was a fugitive from justice, a man with a guilty secret. But they were all wrong.

The simple truth was that, in his youth, a companion had done him a grievous injury. 'I'll remember it' he had hissed, in a gust of passionate resentment, 'I'll remember it to my dying day!' And he did. But when his dying day actually came, he realized that the rankling memory of that youthful wrong had soured and darkened his whole life.

'I've gone over it by myself every morning,' he moaned, as he lay gasping in his comfortless shanty, 'and I've thought of it every night. I've cursed him a hundred times each day. I see now,' he added brokenly, a suspicion of moisture glistening in his eye, 'I see now that my curses have eaten out my soul: they've been like gall on my tongue and gravel in my teeth. My hate has hurt nobody but myself. But, God knows, it's turned my life into hell!'

It was true. The man at whom he had spat out his venomous maledictions, having done all that a man could do to atone for the suffering that he had thoughtlessly caused, had dismissed the matter from his mind a generation back. Upon *him* my gnarled old friend's bitterness had produced little or no effect. It was the man who cherished the sinister memory who suffered most. It shadowed his life: it lent a new terror to death: it expelled every trace of brightness and excluded every ray of hope: and, at last, a grim and ghostly companion, it lay down with him in his chill and cheerless grave.

There is such a thing as the high art of forgetting. It is a divine art. The most astounding thing that the Bible tells us about God is that, remembering all that He wishes to remember, He forgets all that He wishes to forget. Even God declines to carry *everything* in His memory. He sternly refuses to harbor any recollection of the transgressions that He has once forgiven. *Their sins and iniquities will He remember no more.*

F. W. Boreham, *The Drums of Dawn* (London: The Epworth Press, 1933), 77-78.

HOLDING SANCTUARY IN YOUR HEART

It is a great thing—a very great thing—to have been died for.

On the last page of his book Dickens tells us what Sydney Carton would have seen and said if, on the scaffold, it had been given him to read the future.

'I see,' he would have exclaimed, 'I see the lives for which I lay down my life—peaceful, useful, prosperous and happy—in that England which I shall see no more. I see her with a child upon her bosom who bears my name. I see that I hold *a sanctuary in all their hearts,* and in the hearts of their descendants, generations hence. I see her, an old woman, weeping for me on the anniversary of this day. I see her and her husband, their course done, lying side by side in their last earthly bed; and I know that each was not more honored and held sacred in the other's soul than I was in the souls of both!'

'I see that I hold *a sanctuary in all their hearts!*'—it is a lovely phrase.

It is a great thing—a very great thing—to have been died for!

F. W. Boreham, *A Handful of Stars* (London: The Epworth Press, 1922), 54-55.

HOMING INSTINCT

That homing instinct, which our dearest homes leave still unsatisfied, is not only the strongest of all our cravings, it is the truest. It is the one passion that grows more intense as all others weaken and pass away. 'Sir,' said Emerson finely, 'I hold that God, who keeps His word with the birds in all their homing and migratory instincts, will keep His word with Man!' That witness is grandly true. The homing instinct means *HOME!*

F. W. Boreham, *The Passing of John Broadbanks* (London: The Epworth Press, 1936), 216.

HOPE'S RESOLVE

And it would certainly be pleasant to discuss the profound significance of the familiar painting by G. F. Watts. In most of our homes there hang copies of the famous picture in which Hope is portrayed as a female figure seated upon the globe, bending fondly over her broken harp. The light is dim and uncertain; but she is blind to the gloom, for her eyes are bandaged. Only one string of the harp remains; but to that single string she applies her skillful fingers, a look of infinite wistfulness and expectancy lighting up her gentle face. One string remains: and, that being so, she bravely resolves to flood the world with melody.

F. W. Boreham, *The Three Half-Moons* (London: The Epworth Press, 1929), 85.

HUMANS A BUNDLE OF CONTRADICTIONS

When Dr. Burroughs, Bishop of Ripon, was here in Australia, he told a story of a small boy who had been drafted in at the last moment to fill a vacant place at a fashionable dinner party—the sort at which the menu offers a choice for nearly every course. Hardly had he settled down when a problem confronted him on which his previous experience threw no light. In a low, compelling voice, the waiter put the alternatives to him: 'Thick or clear?' Playing for safety, our young friend answered '*Both!*'

What the waiter did is not related; perhaps he brought a mixture; but it really does not matter. The thing that does matter is that in saying '*Both!*' that boy described himself and every other human being. No boy is altogether thick or altogether clear; altogether kind or altogether cruel; altogether good or altogether bad. He is *both!* He [and all of us!] is an everlasting anachronism, an animated ambiguity, a bundle of contradictions; and he is all this for the simple reason that, first and last, and through and through, he is so essentially *a boy.*

F. W. Boreham, *The Fiery Crags* (London: The Epworth Press, 1928), 15-16.

HUNGER FOR THE WORLD

The aching hunger of the human heart for the whole wide world! It is a positively fearsome thing. Many illustrations rush to memory, but the most clear and the most classical is that of David Livingstone. What a day that was when, after his long seclusion in the forests of Central Africa, he was at last found by Stanley! Let Stanley himself tell the great story:

'The doctor asked me to tell him the news. "No, doctor," said I, "read your home letters first; you must be impatient for them!"

' "Ah," said Livingstone, "I have waited for years for letters. I can wait a few hours longer. No, tell me general news: *how's the world getting on?*" '

And then, buried in that African jungle, the two men sat for hours while the one told the other of the completion of the great Pacific railroad, of Grant's election to the Presidency, of the realization of electric cables, of the Franco-German war, of the siege of Paris, of the Cretan rebellion, of the sensational developments in Egypt, of the Spanish revolution which had driven Isabella from the throne, of the assassination of General Prim, and of a hundred other historic transformations. Even as Stanley told the story, Livingstone became a changed man. Fresh tides of vitality rushed into his frame; his appetite strangely returned to him; his haggard face simply shone with the glow of human enthusiasm. "You have brought me new life! You have brought me new life! You have brought me new life," he repeated again, and again, and again.

What did it all mean? It meant this. The heart of a person cries out for the world, the whole wide world; and it is starved if you confine it to the African forest or the Australian bush.

F. W. Boreham, *Mountains in the Mist* (London: Charles H. Kelly, 1914), 14-15.

I HOLD AND AM HELD

F. W. Boreham writes: I am the son of a college [Spurgeon's] that has, for its crest a cross grasped by a hand. The motto beneath it reads: *Et teneo et teneor—I hold and am held.*

The only things worth holding are the things that we cannot let go.

F. W. Boreham, *Wisps of Wildfire* (London: The Epworth Press, 1924), 248.

I KNOW WHOM I HAVE BELIEVED

The text—"I know whom I have believed, and am persuaded that He is able to keep that which I have committed to Him against that day"—is an ill-used text. It is frequently misquoted.

It occurred one day in the course of a theological lesson over which Rabbi Duncan was presiding.

'Repeat that passage!' said the Rabbi to the student who had just spoken.

'I know in whom I have ...'

'My dear sir,' interrupted the Rabbi, 'you must never let even a preposition come between you and your Savior!'

And when Dr. Alexander, of Princeton, was dying, a friend endeavored to fortify his faith by reciting some of the most familiar passages and promises. Presently he ventured upon the words 'I know in whom I have believed, and ...'

But the sick man raised his hand.

'No, no,' exclaimed the dying Principal, 'it is not "I know *in* whom" but "I know *whom*"; I cannot have even the little word "in" between me and Christ. *I know whom I have believed, and am persuaded that He is able to keep that which I have committed unto Him against that day!*'

F. W. Boreham, *A Handful of Stars* (London: The Epworth Press, 1922), 184-185.

IADOM

I heard a gentleman one evening telling, on the radio, of his experience in a great munitions factory. He said that, as he approached the factory, the first thing that impressed him was a word painted in huge white letters on the gate. It was the word IADOM. It puzzled him, but he thought no more of it until he discovered that, inside, the same word appeared on every wall and over every window.

'Iadom!' he said to himself. 'What can it mean? I'm a university man and ought to know; yet, frankly, I don't!' And just because he felt he ought to know, and didn't, he was too proud to ask.

When his tour of inspection was complete, the manager
bade him farewell and asked a young typist who stood near to
attend him to his car. On the way across the yard she chatted
to him of what he had seen, and then abruptly exclaimed:

'You noticed our motto, of course!'

'No,' he answered a trifle shamefacedly.

'I suppose you know what it means?' He had not the heart
to deceive her, so confessed his ignorance.

'Oh,' she replied with a smile, 'it's quite simple. The letters stand for: *It All Depends On Me!*'

F. W. Boreham, *Boulevards of Paradise* (London: The Epworth Press,
1944), 66-67.

IF

If! If! If! Small as the word is, it fills a large place in our
vocabulary; yet nobody seems to know how it got there....

Which of our great historians, for example, has been able
to do his work to his own satisfaction without calling in its
aid? The *ifs* of history are innumerable. I can only select a
few at random.

If, says Gibbon, if, at the battle of Tours, the Saracen host
had been triumphant, the Arabian fleet might have sailed without a naval combat into the mouth of the Thames, Muslim
doctors might now be teaching the doctrines of the Koran in
the quadrangles of Oxford, and the pulpits of England might
be demonstrating to a circumcised people the sanctity of the
revelation of Mohammed!

If, says Macaulay, *if* Elizabeth's successors had inherited
her wisdom with her crown, Charles the First might have died
of old age and James the Second would never have seen St.
Germains. In that event Queen Victoria and her illustrious sons
would never have come within sight of the British throne.

If, says Buckle, *if* the north of Scotland had been fertile and the south barren, instead of the reverse, the north would have been the populous area, border warfare and southern aggression would have been unknown, and the entire history of Europe would have been different.

If, says Goldwin Smith, *if a* bullet had entered the brain of Cromwell or of William the Third in the first battle that either of them fought, or *if* Gustavus had not fallen at Lutzen, the whole course of world history would have been changed!

If, says Mr. Sydney Low, *if a* careless nurse had allowed Julius Caesar to die of whooping-cough in his cradle; *if* Alexander the Great had not done himself too well when he dined at Babylon; *if* the pistol which Robert Clive snapped at his own head had not misfired, what a different story our text-books would have had to tell! And *if,* Mr. Low adds, *if a* fair wind had blown down the English Channel during the last week of July 1588, a Cardinal Archbishop of London might now be preaching from the pulpit of St. Paul's.

If, says Dr. Fitchett, in his *Deeds that Won the Empire, if* Napoleon had succeeded at Trafalgar, the fate of the world would have been changed; and Toronto, Cape Town, Melbourne, Sydney, and Auckland might have been ruled by French prefects!

And, to take yet one more example, let me cite the question that Lord Rosebery propounded to the graduates of Glasgow University. *If,* he asked, *if,* instead of accepting a peerage, the elder Pitt had declined it, what would have become of the British Empire? *If* that had happened, Lord Rosebery says, the passage of the Reform Bill would have been materially hastened; Pitt, by remaining in the Lower House, would have been able to bring the King to reason; the break with America would have been averted; the map of the United States would be painted red; an American city would have become the seat of the British Government; and a perpetual procession

of tourists and pilgrims would now be crossing the Atlantic
from west to east to visit London and other famous shrines
intimately associated with the earlier history of the Empire!

If! If! If! In each of these instances the *if* introduces a flight
of fancy; but it is a valuable flight of fancy. It may be said
that life's truest wisdom lies in making the most of things *as
they are.* And that contention is indisputably sound. But it
often happens that we can only appraise things *as they are* at
their proper value by comparing—or contrasting—them with;
another set of things that *might have been.* It is good to
make the most of health; but no man can justly estimate the
value of his health except by reflecting on the conditions that
would have encompassed him if an accident which he nar-
rowly escaped had deprived him of his powers, or *if* a disease
by which he was once threatened had obtained a deadly grip
of his vital organs.

It is at this point that we immortals differ radically and
essentially from the brute creation. The beasts of the field
never contrast their present comfort with a less desirable set
of conditions that might have been, nor with a still more perfect set of conditions that may yet await them. They never
say *if.* Herein lies their stolidity. No man in his senses would
envy them this quality. Man is infinitely superior. He can say
if. His power of uttering that magic monosyllable enables him
to set due store on the privileges that he today enjoys, and to
aspire towards an ideal that he cherishes for tomorrow. *If,* he
says, things had gone otherwise than they did at such-and-
such a juncture, the felicities of today could never have been.
And *if,* he adds, I adopt such-and-such a course, or acquire
such-and-such a habit, I may enter upon a still ampler prosperity. And so, by means of his *ifs,* he forges his way towards
the grandeur of his destiny.

But there is more in it than this. Take the *ifs* of the historians by way of illustration. Nobody can read those formidable

ifs—*if* Napoleon had won the battle of Waterloo; *if* the Armada had been triumphant; and so on—without feeling that there is some stupendous force working through the episodes of history. The great events on which the lives of people and nations hang are not determined by the twists of chance or by the freaks of fate. Whenever I come upon the word *if* in any of our historical classics, I think of a story which, possessing its ludicrous aspect, has also its profounder implications.

It is said that, when railways were first introduced into Ireland, two countrymen from a remote village came to one of the towns and visited the railway station to see the new wonder. After awhile, an express rushed past the platform and vanished with a roar into a tunnel a few hundred yards away. The two men, utterly unaccustomed to such a spectacle, stared at each other in dumb amazement. When at length they had recovered in some measure from their astonishment, and had regained their voices, the one exclaimed solemnly to the other, 'Pat, what a terrible smash there would have been *if* the train had missed that hole!'

If the train had missed the tunnel! *If* Britain had been defeated at Trafalgar! *If* the Saracens had been victorious at Tours! But the Irishmen had failed to notice the vital significance of the *rails*. There were forces at work guiding the train to the tunnel. And, in exactly the same way, there are tremendous forces at work directing the impressive pageant of events. Nations do not rise and fall by chance. Battles are not decided by the big battalions. Like the stars in their orbits, the mighty movements of men are marshaled and directed. The chariots of history are not running wild, the reins trailing loosely over the horses' backs. They are driven, firmly driven; skillfully driven; and driven by a divine hand. Philip of Macedon, the chroniclers tell us, received an insulting letter from one of his numerous enemies. 'If,' it said, *'if* I enter your city, I will slay, kill, and lay waste everything and everybody in it.' Philip read the letter, smiled, and contemptuously tore it to pieces. He was careful, however, not to destroy the first word—the word *if.* The scrap of paper containing that word he returned to his boastful foe. We may do pretty much the same with the *ifs* of the historians.

I like to think that Jesus came into the world to free it from the tyranny of some of its *ifs. 'If,'* exclaimed Socrates, as he prepared to drink the hemlock, *'if* death be a removal to another place, and *if* what is said of the dead be true, then those who live there are thenceforth immortal, *if* at least what we have taught be true. But the hour has now come. I go to die; you to live; but which of us is destined to a happier being is concealed from every one except from God!' And so, with his mouth full of *ifs,* and an awful *perhaps* clutching at his throat, the most lovable of the ancients went down among the shadows. The Light of the World had not yet shone; Paul had not yet uttered his tremendous affirmations: *We know; we know: we know!*

And yet, like Doubt, Faith has its *ifs.*... In the eighteenth century, John Berridge, the Vicar of Everton, was considered one of the most eccentric and remarkable preachers in England. One of his most famous sermons was a sermon on the word *If.* 'My brethren,' he used to say, 'we will dub *If* an officer, and call him "Sergeant If," and regard him as the watchman or guard attending on the doctrine of perseverance. Sergeant *If,* you will notice, is low in stature, but he is lofty in significance—a very valiant guard, though a monosyllable.' And so on; it is all very quaint and fantastic.

I have sometimes thought of following good old Mr. Berridge's example. Why not preach on *If?* I have not yet made up my mind as to the text. There are so many. *'If* any one will come after Me, let him take up his cross and follow Me'; or, *'If* any one be in Christ, he is a new creation'; or, 'What shall it profit a man *if* he gain the whole world and lose his own soul?'; or, 'How shall we escape *if* we neglect so great salvation?' But, although I have not decided on the text with which I shall begin, I know the story with which I shall close. I shall tell of old Edwin Rushworth, who, having been a skeptic all his life, resolved to read for an hour a day the book that he had so long derided.

'Wife,' he said, as he looked up from his first perusal, '*if* this book is right, we are all wrong!' He continued his readings for another week.

'Wife,' he exclaimed, at the end of that time, '*if* this book is right, we are lost!' He went on reading with more avidity than ever.

'Wife,' he said earnestly, a few nights later, 'if this book is right, we may be saved!'

And they were! And, in entering the Kingdom of God, they left all their *ifs* behind them.

F. W. Boreham, *The Fiery Crags* (London: The Epworth Press, 1928), 58-67 (selected).

IF I COULD HAVE MY MINISTRY ALL OVER AGAIN

"If I could have my ministry all over again," F. W. Boreham writes at the age of eighty-six, after writing more than fifty-five books, penning over 3,000 editorials and preaching countless sermons over a span of almost seventy years. What ever would he want to do differently?

Dr. Boreham continues: "If I could have my ministry over again, I would talk more about God. Not about God's works or God's ways, God's power or God's bounty. But about God's very self—God's omnipresence, God's omniscience, God's omnipotence; God's unutterable goodness, God's ineffable holiness, God's splendor, God's glory, God's love. For if I could make people very sure of God, they would soon hurry to that divine Savior who is able to save to the uttermost those who come to God by Him.

F. W. Boreham, *The Tide Comes In* (London: The Epworth Press, 1958), 60.

IGNORANCE AND PASSION TO KNOW

It was Thomas Huxley who gave us the word *agnostic*—'one who does not know.' But, when Huxley described himself as an agnostic, he did not mean that, not knowing, he did not want to know. He longed for knowledge as blind people long for light. When he heard a person tell, in simple phraseology but with profound conviction, of their own personal experience of the Savior's grace, Huxley—apparently the most unemotional of people—would say, with moist eyes and a catch in his breath, that he would gladly give his right hand to possess a similar serene conviction. Here we have ignorance—is he not the prince of agnostics?—but ignorance illumined by a passionate craving for knowledge.

F. W. Boreham, *Cliffs of Opal*, (London: The Epworth Press, 1948), 97.

ILLUMINATION FROM UNEXPECTED DIRECTIONS

Mark Twain, in one of his frolics, tells how he and his companions toiled all night up the slopes of one of the mountains of Switzerland in order to see the sunrise from the summit. That gorgeous spectacle was numbered among the wonders of the world. Arrived at the pinnacle, heated with their climb, they soon found themselves shivering in the piercing cold of that bleak and snow-capped height. They wrapped themselves up as snugly as they could, huddled together under the shelter of a huge rock, and settled down to await the glory that had brought them to so inhospitable a spot. After an unconscionable period spent in this cramped and comfortless situation, it appeared to them that, although the sun had not risen, the daylight was becoming more and more pronounced. They started up to investigate the mystery. To their horror they discovered that they had been sitting with their faces to the West; and, over the back of the boulders that had sheltered them from the cold wind, the sun was well up in the sky!

I thought this very droll when I first came across it, and laughed as lustily as anybody else. But I have today moderated my judgement.

F. W. Boreham goes on to say that in reading A Boswell of Baghdad *by Mr. E. V. Lucas he came across this statement:* 'My friend,' says Buri Taj Al-Muluk, 'approached from the West, riding a gray horse, and I exclaimed: "Glory to the Almighty, the sun has risen in the West!" ' It was this that brought back to my mind the passage in Mark Twain at which I laughed so heartily long years ago.

"Glory to the Almighty, the sun has risen in the West!" It is a characteristically Oriental way of describing the coming of a friend at an unlikely moment, or from an unexpected direction.

F. W. Boreham, *Home of the Echoes* (London: The Epworth Press, 1921), 97-99.

IMPORTANCE OF PLAY

Friedrich Froebel and the Baroness Marenholz-Bulow were laughed to scorn when, as the pioneers of the kindergarten system, they affirmed that play is really the most vital element in the culture of the child. 'Play is not trivial,' declared Froebel; 'it is highly serious and of deep significance.' Cultivate and foster it, O mother! Protect and guide it, O father!

This novel philosophy was at first met with a snigger of contempt and a shout of derision; but the world that ridiculed soon began to reflect; and the result of its reflection is that the kindergarten system has become one of the established commonplaces of education the wide world over.

F. W. Boreham, *The Fiery Crags* (London: The Epworth Press, 1928), 93-94.

IN QUIETNESS IS STRENGTH

Mr. Harold Begbie once gave us a striking little novel entitled *Racket and Rest*. It is a story of two women: one of them is the wife of the hero; the other is his mother. The wife represents *racket;* the mother represents *rest*.

Dolly, the wife, leaving her husband and child, pursues a hectic career upon the stage. Her life is one wild flutter of excitement. And, all through the book, the gentle old lady in the background murmurs her message of rest. After some years, Dolly is suddenly seized with ear trouble. An operation leaves her stone deaf. She returns, chastened by suffering, to her husband's home. His constancy is the wonder of all her days. She finds her child, Dorothea, grown into a tall and graceful girl. Shortly afterwards the old lady lies down to die. Dolly feels that she cannot bear to let the tranquil spirit go without learning the secret of her restful and beautiful life. She begs her, since she herself cannot hear, to write it down. The dying woman, with radiant peace, takes a pencil and tablet which rest on a table at her side, and scrawls the words: *In returning and rest shall you be saved: in quietness and in confidence shall be your strength.* That sums up everything.

F. W. Boreham, *The Passing of John Broadbanks* (London: The Epworth Press, 1936), 21.

IN THE BEGINNING GOD

'In the beginning, God!' God is the one inescapable fact of the universe. No interpretation of the first chapter of Genesis can exclude God. If you believe that, some thousands of years ago, a Voice said: 'Let there be light—and land—and sea—and stars!' It was *God's* Voice that echoed through the corridors of space and caused these things to be. And if you believe that, myriad millions of ages ago, in some protoplasmic slime, something twitched and started the age-long process of evolution, it must have been *God's* divine finger that electrified that microscopic germ, and *God's* divine hand that folded up all that afterwards unfolded.

You know how Darwin himself closes the book that launched upon a startled world the evolutionary controversy. 'There is grandeur,' he says, 'in this view of life, with its several powers, having been originally breathed by the Creator into a few forms or into one.'

'By the Creator!' mark you. No theory can exclude *God.* 'In the beginning God.'

F. W. Boreham, *Boulevards of Paradise* (London: The Epworth Press, 1944), 69.

INFLUENCE OF PICTURES

Henry Drummond used to tell of a Cambridge undergraduate whose sweetheart visited his room. She found its walls covered with pictures of actresses and racehorses. She said nothing, but, on his birthday, presented him with a picture of Christ's Thorn-Crowned Face.

A year later she again called on him at Cambridge. The Thorn-Crowned Face hung over the fireplace; and the other walls were adorned with charming landscapes and reproductions of famous paintings. He caught her glancing at her gift.

'It's made a great difference to the room,' he said, 'and, what's more, it's made a great difference *in* me!'

That is a way our pictures have. They insist on ruling everything and everybody.

F. W. Boreham, *Rubble and Roseleaves* (London: The Epworth Press, 1922), 234-235.

INSPIRED BY SACRIFICE

It is an equally fine thing for a man, with his life all before him, to accept a sacred charge from dying lips.

A thought like this was surely surging in the mind of Abraham Lincoln when he dedicated the battlefield of Gettysburg as a place of public burial. 'We cannot dedicate, we cannot consecrate, we cannot hallow this ground,' he said. 'The brave men who struggled here have consecrated it far beyond our power to add or detract. It is for us, the living, rather to be dedicated to the unfinished work which they who fought here have thus far so nobly advanced. It is rather for us to be here dedicated to the great task remaining before us, that from these honored dead we may take increased devotion to that cause for which they gave the last full measure of devotion. Let us here highly resolve that these dead shall not have died in vain.'

F. W. Boreham, *The Other Side of the Hill* (London: Charles H. Kelly, 1917), 53.

INSTINCT OF IMMORTALITY

And what of the greatest of all our migratory instincts—the instinct of immortality? For, after all, immortality is an instinct and not an argument. A few may think that they can prove it. But there are millions who, unable to *prove* it, nevertheless feel it.

Look at the inscriptions on the monuments of antiquity, to be seen at such places as the British Museum. Here are grotesque representations, thousands of years old, of the soul, in the form of a bird, departing from the prostrate body; of the heart being weighed at the judgment of Osiris; and of many similar scenes depicting the fates and fortunes of men and women in the afterlife. Why did the Arab bury the horse with his master? Why did the African bury the slaves with their chief? Why did the South Sea Islander bury a bevy of wives with their king? Why did the Maori bury some weapons with the warrior? Nothing can be more intensely impressive than the unanimity with which earnest people in all ages have sensed a life beyond the grave. Whether you turn to the manuscript of the learned sage or to the customs of the most savage barbarian, you are driven to the conclusion that when Almighty God, amid the glistening dews of creation's early morning, stooped over Adam's prostrate clay and breathed into his nostrils the breath of life, God at the same time whispered to the conscious instincts of man's unsullied spirit a radiant promise of immortality.

F. W. Boreham, *A Late Lark Singing* (London: The Epworth Press, 1945), 138.

INSTINCT OF LOVE

The earliest political speech that I remember reading was a speech about a kiss, and I have read no parliamentary oration since which has moved me as much. It was the speech in which Mr. Gladstone announced to the House of Commons the death of the Princess Alice. He described the little boy tossing in the delirium of diphtheria, his mother, the Princess, watching ceaselessly beside his bed. Mr. Gladstone told the House how the doctors had warned Her Royal Highness on no account to inhale the child's poisoned breath; how she had laid her cool hand for a moment on the fevered brow; how the child, recognizing his mother, had thrown up his arms and cried 'Kiss me, Mamma, kiss me!' and how the instinct of motherhood had proved stronger than the instinct of self-preservation. The lips of mother and child met; and the Princess paid the penalty with her life. I was only a small boy at the time; but the incident made me feel that royalty was very human; and I think that my allegiance to the throne gathered to itself that day an element of kinship by which it was substantially enriched.

F. W. Boreham, *The Crystal Pointers* (London: The Epworth Press, 1925), 250.

INSTINCT OF THE CONFESSIONAL

We were sitting round the fire, and I was reading aloud—a favorite amusement of ours. We were suddenly interrupted by the ringing of the front door bell.

'You are wanted. It's a young woman; she says she won't come in. I think she's crying.'

I went to the door, and at first thought that our visitor had fled. But she was standing a step or two along the verandah, out of the light of the hall lamp. It was a miserable night, black as ink, with a high wind that was occasionally laden with sleet. I begged her to come in; but in vain. At last, with a thought, evidently, for myself, she faltered in this resolve of hers.

'Are you sure that all the blinds are down?' she asked.

I excused myself that I might make sure. Opening the study door, I lit the gas, saw to the blinds, and returned to bring her in. She slipped in furtively, as though pursued. I motioned her to the armchair; she threw herself into it, and, burying her face in her hands, burst into a tempest of tears.

I need not record the story that, on recovering her voice, she unfolded to me. It has been written, very sternly and sometimes very tenderly thousands of times since our little race began. At length she rose to go.

'But why,' I asked, 'did you come to *me?* Have we met before?'

'No,' she replied, 'but I just had to speak at last. I felt that I had kept it to myself long enough and that, unless I told it all to somebody, I should lose my reason or die!'

With the contrite and tearful confession that she made to me as she sat in the arm-chair I am not now concerned. Of that nothing will induce me to write. But this second confession, made up on her feet while preparing to leave, struck as being intensely significant.

'I just had to speak.... I had kept it to myself long enough.... Unless I told it all to somebody, I should die!'

In those artless words she expressed a deep and inexpressible human instinct—the Instinct of the Confessional.

F. W. Boreham, *A Reel of Rainbow* (London: The Epworth Press, 1920), 46-47.

JESUS THE PRETENDER

Jesus Himself *pretended* on occasions. He behaved towards the Syro-Phoenician woman as though He had no sympathy with her in her distress. He saw the disciples in trouble on the lake; and, walking on the water, He made as though He would have passed them by. When, after journeying with two of His disciples to Emmaus, He reached the door of their home, He made as though He would have gone farther! 'He made as though!' 'He made as though!' 'He made as though!' The feints of Deity!

F. W. Boreham, *Rubble and Roseleaves* (London: The Epworth Press, 1922), 131.

JOHNSON'S RESOLVE

It has often struck me as an impressive coincidence that it was when Dr. Johnson [Samuel Johnson—one of England's greatest literary figures] was approaching his fiftieth birthday … that he discovered a significance in Saturday that, until then, had eluded him. He felt, as we all feel on Saturdays, that the time had come to clear up, to put things in their places and to overtake neglected tasks. And this is the entry he makes in his Journal:

"Having lived, not without an habitual reverence for the Sabbath, yet without that attention to its religious duties which Christianity requires—I resolve henceforth—*First,* to rise early on Sabbath morning, and, in order to do that, to go to sleep early on Saturday night. *Second,* to use some more than ordinary devotion as soon as I rise. *Third,* to examine into the tenor of my life, and particularly the last week, and to mark my advances in religion, or my recessions from it. *Fourth,* to read the Scriptures methodically, with such helps as are at hand. *Fifth,* to go to church twice. *Sixth,* to read books of divinity, either speculative or practical. *Seventh,* to instruct my family. *Eighth,* to wear off by meditation any worldly soil contracted in the week."

The significance of this heroic record lies in the resolve that Saturday, so far from unfitting him for Sunday, shall lead up to it as a stately avenue leads up to a noble entrance-hall. "I resolve to go to sleep early on Saturday night."

F. W. Boreham, *Rubble and Roseleaves* (London: The Epworth Press, 1922), 154-155.

JOURNEY INTO LOVE

'I was staying with a party of friends at a country house during my visit to England in 1884,' says Mr. Moody. 'On Sunday evening, as we sat around the fire, they asked me to read and explain some portion of Scripture. Being tired after the services of the day, I told them to ask Henry Drummond, who was one of the party. After some urging, he drew a small Testament from his hip pocket, opened it at the *thirteenth chapter of First Corinthians,* and began to speak on the subject of Love. It seemed to me that I had never heard anything so beautiful, and I determined never to rest until I had brought Henry Drummond to America to deliver that address.'

'Some men,' Mr. Moody adds, writing many years later, 'some men take an occasional journey into the *thirteenth of First Corinthians;* but Henry Drummond was a man who lived there constantly, appropriating its blessings and exemplifying its teachings.'

Henry Drummond repeated that fireside talk all over the world. He could not help it. He was brimming over with its theme. He talked about Paul's Great Hymn of Love in all the principal cities of England and America, and afterwards in Africa, in China, in Japan, and in the South Sea Islands—everywhere! He delivered that address within a few hundred yards of this Australian study of mine. In 1889 it was published. Its sale was phenomenal. Within six months, 185,000 copies were bought up. Since then it has been issued by the million and translated into every European and into many Asiatic languages. When it was translated into German it commanded a greater sale than any German publication of that year. The book brought its astonished author an avalanche of correspondence from all over the world. He had struck a chord that vibrated in every human soul. For the world is dying for love; and Henry Drummond knew it.

'The real secret of his charm,' says Sir William Robertson Nicoll, 'lay in his passionate devotion to Jesus Christ.' Henry Drummond really loved his Lord; loved Him naturally, intensely, increasingly.

F. W. Boreham, *A Temple of Topaz* (London: The Epworth Press, 1928), 97-99

JOY AFTER SORROW

Dr. A. M. Fairbairn paints three pictures. The *first is* the picture of a blithe young soul, full of laughter, full of sunshine, full of song. Go to this glad, lightsome spirit and say, *Blessed are they that mourn!* The words will seem like the incomprehensible speech of some weird and distant world: the countenance will take on an expression of amazement and incredulity.

The *second* picture depicts a man who has been tortured by grief and crushed by heavy losses. His spirit writhes in the dust. Sorrow has soured and embittered him. His soul is in revolt. Go to him and say, *Blessed are they that mourn!* The words will mock his suffering; they will act like brine on smarting wounds; to him *blessedness* and *mourning* are not only sharply antagonistic; they are hopelessly irreconcilable.

The *third* picture presents to our gaze one who has known the joyousness of the first and the bitterness of the second. 'There has been love and less; vigorous youth or sweet maidenhood lies far behind; the hour of grief with its dull stupor is overpast; calm has come and the nature has emerged from its sorrows richer, more conscious of the infinite within and its kinship with the infinite without.' In this case the words that seem so incredible to the sunlit soul in the *first* picture, and so cruelly incomprehensible to the rebellious spirit in the *second,* have been interpreted by the tense realities of an abysmal and illuminating experience. The eyes, cleansed by weeping, have obtained a clearer vision of life's profound mystery and beneficent discipline. The subject of this *third* picture knows the secret of the mourner's blessedness.

That is precisely the Master's meaning. We love the cloudless hours; yet we love still more the days when snowy clouds fleck the sky—clouds that, irradiated by the westering sun, become a gorgeous pageant of topaz and gold. We love the summer sunshine; yet we love the sweetness of the garden after rain. We love the exquisite rapture of Spring; yet, but for winter-time, we should never know the beauty of the crocus. We like the course of true love to run smooth; yet sweethearts tell us that there is a delicious ecstasy in making-up. Health is never so precious as when it returns to us after the long agony of fever and of pain. In the same way, we love the sorrowless and tearless days; and yet life teaches us to love the days when, our souls having been bowed down in deep humiliation, and our cheeks made the channels of scalding tears, the tender benediction of the mourner's beatitude has stolen into our hearts.

F. W. Boreham, *The Heavenly Octave* (London: The Epworth Press, 1935), 28-31.

JOY OF IGNORANCE

Where ignorance is bliss, 'tis folly to be wise. Although Gray's famous epigram has been quoted so frequently that it has become hackneyed and threadbare, and quoted so authoritatively that it has sounded like the voice of the ultimate wisdom, nobody has ever taken the trouble to tell us with scientific accuracy and limpid precision under what exact circumstances ignorance is preferable to knowledge.

Lady Bracknell, in *The Importance of Being Earnest,* is wholeheartedly with Gray. Realizing that Jack Worthing's courtship of her daughter Gwendolin threatens to become quite a serious affair, her ladyship determines to put the ambitious young suitor through his paces. Notebook in hand, she proceeds to interrogate him. Having inquired as to his parentage and prospects, she approaches the matter of education.

'I have always been of opinion,' she condescendingly explains, 'that a person who desires to get married should know either everything or nothing. What do you know?'

Jack hesitates. 'I know nothing!' he at length stammers out.

'I am pleased to hear it,' replies Lady Bracknell. 'I do not approve of anything that tampers with natural ignorance. Ignorance is like a delicate exotic fruit: touch it and the bloom is gone!'

F. W. Boreham, *Cliffs of Opal*, (London: The Epworth Press, 1948), 92.

JUSTICE AND MERCY

I remember once chatting for an hour or so with a Tasmanian friend of mine, a Jewish rabbi.

'Do you know,' he asked abruptly, 'the essential difference between our preaching and yours?' I asked him to answer his own question.

'Well,' he continued, 'the difference is that you have a great deal to say about the mercy of God, but you seldom preach about God's justice; we, on the other hand, say less about God's mercy, but we constantly emphasize God's justice; and we stress the thought because we hold that the greater includes the less; God's mercy is but one phase of God's justice.'

F. W. Boreham, *Boulevards of Paradise* (London: The Epworth Press, 1944), 121.

KEEPING SHORT ACCOUNTS

In my London days I was a member of Dr. Meyer's Saturday afternoon Bible class. I have often wondered how any minister would get on nowadays who attempted to run a Bible class for young men on Saturday afternoons! But Dr. Meyer did it, and, every Saturday, some hundreds of young fellows flocked to him at Aldersgate Street. I seem to see him now as he sat on his high stool at his table below us—for the seats sloped up from him to the back of the building—pouring out to us the treasures of his deep experience. Every now and again, becoming moved or excited by his theme, he would leave the stool and, pacing to and fro with eyes sparkling and hands gesticulating, would exclaim: 'Oh, my brothers, I want you always to remember *this!*' And then he would lay down some vital principle of Christian life and service—a principle that, falling from *his lips,* was unforgettable.

And one of those principles—I must have heard him enunciate it at least a dozen times—was this: 'Oh, my brothers,' he would say, 'I do want you to remember this: Keep short accounts with God!'

Keep short accounts with God! Do not let the arrears mount up! Do not carry anything forward from today to tomorrow! You have lost your temper? Some ugly thought has swept across the pure screen of your fancy? You failed, when the guidance was clear, to follow the gleam? Get the whole thing settled up at once! If we confess, He is faithful and just to forgive! Keep short accounts with God!

F. W. Boreham, *I Forgot To Say* (London: The Epworth Press, 1939), 116-117.

KEEPING TORCH OF FAITH BURNING

Among the minor sensations of the nineteenth century were the thrillers of Guy Thorne. His most dynamic and explosive production, *When It Was Dark,* was proclaimed as the most daring and original novel of the period, and enjoyed the distinction of being glowingly commended by the Bishop of London from the pulpit of Westminster Abbey.

It tells how Constantine Schuabe, a millionaire, loathing Christianity with a venomous hatred, resolves, at any cost, to destroy it. Discovering that Professor Sir Robert Llewellyn, the most brilliant antiquarian and archaeologist of his day, is leading a double life and is up to his ears in debt, Schuabe cultivates his acquaintance, lends him fourteen thousand pounds, and, shortly afterwards, demands repayment under penalty of having the whole vile story of Llewellyn's private life exposed.

While Llewellyn is groveling at the feet of the plutocrat, begging for time, Schuabe startles him by remarking that it would be easy for him to wipe out the debt and become a wealthy man. How?

Schuabe tells Llewellyn that he must, on the excuse of ill-health, get a year's leave from the British Museum; he must then go to Palestine and discover that the record of the Resurrection is just a pious fraud.

'Backed by your unimpeachable reputation,' Schuabe tells him, 'your verdict will be readily accepted, and Christianity will be an exploded myth.' What could be more simple?

A few months later the world learns with speechless amazement that a new cave has been unearthed in the Holy Land. It contains a slab inscribed: *'I, Joseph of Arimathea, took the body of Jesus from the tomb and hid it in this place.'* On a ledge near by, a slight mould is spread, probably all that remains of a decomposed body.

The announcement creates a sensation such as the nation has never previously known. Llewellyn's name carries weight. Press, Parliament and people are alike dumbfounded. Stocks and shares collapse. With the decline of public confidence, commerce is reduced to stagnation and industry is paralyzed. Bankruptcy and unemployment become the order of the day. Depression reigns everywhere.

Those whose religion is of the formal, superficial kind, abandon it: the bubble has burst; they feel ashamed of their own gullibility. But there are others. All over the country there are thousands of simple souls whose personal experience of the Savior's transforming grace has been so vivid, so profound and so convincing, that the tidal wave of unbelief fails to affect them. Drunkards who have been delivered from the tyranny of their old enslavement, women who have been lifted from a career of shame to a life of purity and sweetness, worldly men and women who have found their way, by means of the Cross, into avenues of devoted and unselfish service—how can this sensation in the newspapers affect *them?* They are bewildered by the new development. But they know their Savior too well to be influenced by any such inexplicable happenings. And so they keep the torch of faith burning brightly in churches and chapels all over the land until the gigantic fraud is exposed and the multitudes return shamefacedly to the faith that, during the dreadful crisis, they had repudiated.

F. W. Boreham, *The Gospel of Uncle Tom's Cabin* (London: The Epworth Press, 1956), 25-27.

Kindness to Animals

We all know that, in the days of the Caesars, spectators commented like connoisseurs on the varying expressions of agony portrayed on the countenances of dying gladiators; soldiers played at dice at the scene of a crucifixion; women stepped among the miserable victims of a Roman holiday, laughing and jesting at their doleful plight. And what could be more terrible than the shrieks of laughter with which a Spanish audience will watch the gored horses, staggering in agony, being led from the bull-ring? The reflections suggested by such recollections are not pleasant.

The Russian Litany contains a beautiful petition 'for those, O Lord, the humble beasts, who with us bear the burden and heat of the day, and offer their guileless lives for the well-being of us all, we supplicate Your great tenderness of heart.'

No form of religion is quite satisfactory that does not find room within the scope of its sympathies for the lowliest phases of life that live and move and have their being about us.

F. W. Boreham, *The Ivory Spires* (London: The Epworth Press, 1934), 123.

LEAP YEAR CHALLENGES

The twenty-ninth of February! It is a great day; at least, it is a great day for some people. It is a very great day for my little friend, Beryl Burleigh, who suffered the misfortune to be born on that rarely recurring date. Beryl is in excellent company, if that is any consolation to her. Among many other distinguished people, I find that John Whitgift, a very celebrated Archbishop of Canterbury, and John Byrom, who composed our National Anthem and some of our best known hymns, shared with Beryl the distinction of enjoying a birthday only once in four years. In the careers of all of these famous men there was a time when they went to bed with sad thoughts on the night of the twenty-eighth of February, and woke up with still sadder ones on the morning of the first of March. They felt like children who, after waiting for fully an hour at a railway station for the train that is to take them to the sea-side, watch it rush through without stopping: they turn away nursing a bitter disappointment. If the reflection that she is not alone in her misfortune fails to comfort Beryl, I can scarcely expect her to find balm for her wounds in the thought that, badly off as she is, others are still worse!

I once married a couple on the twenty-ninth of February; and I shall never forget the lugubrious expressions that overspread their countenances when one of the guests—more mathematical than discreet—asked them when they proposed to celebrate their Silver and Golden Weddings. The twenty-ninth of February comes, at best, only once in four years; not always then. And, since neither twenty-five nor fifty are divisible by four, the only hope that my bride and bridegroom could cherish was the hope of celebrating their Diamond Wedding sixty years hence on such a scale as would atone for the omission of the Silver and Golden ones.

Miss Priscilla Pettigrew was born, as everybody knows, on February the twenty-ninth, 1764. She celebrated her *eighth* birthday in 1796; but she had to wait until 1804 for her *ninth!* Those who were born on the twenty-ninth of February any time during the nineteenth century, and who lived to the dawn of the twentieth, suffered a similar deprivation when the year 1900 broke upon them. But those who come into the world on any twenty-ninth of February *this* century are safe! For the year 2000 will behave handsomely by them! If they wish to go eight years without a birthday they must contrive, by hook or by crook, to live until the year 2100 comes round.

The fact is that the twenty-ninth of February is a piece of chronological padding. It represents all those things in life that are extras and makeweights. Are not *two* sparrows sold for a farthing? Are not *five* sparrows sold for two farthings? The fifth sparrow is the extra; the makeweight; a something thrown in. By such extras life is incalculably enriched.

F. W. Boreham, *The Blue Flame* (London: The Epworth Press, 1930), 263, 265, 270-271.

LET THE THIRSTY COME

I have somewhere read that, out in the solitudes of the great dusty desert, when a caravan is in peril of perishing for want of water, they give one camel its head and let him go. The fine instincts of the animal will lead him unerringly to the refreshing spring. As soon as he is but a speck on the horizon, one of the Arabs mounts his camel and sets off in the direction that the liberated animal has taken.

When, in his turn, he is scarcely distinguishable, another Arab mounts and follows. When the loose camel discovers water, the first Arab turns and waves to the second; the second to the third, and so on, until all the members of the party are gathered at the satisfying spring. As each man sees the beckoning hand, he turns and beckons to the man behind him. He that sees, signals; he that hears, utters.

It is the law of the life everlasting…. "Let the one that is thirsty come."

F. W. Boreham, *A Handful of Stars* (London: The Epworth Press, 1922), 42-43.

LIBERATING SYMBOLISM

Think of the tragedy of slavery. The whip in the white man's hand was the badge of the black man's degradation. The crack of the whip, as it resounded across the cotton plantations, was not so much the proclamation of the white man's cruelty as the proclamation of the white man's pride. The whip in his hand made him feel like a king; and he yielded to the temptation to which those kings yielded who degenerated into tyrants. But the abuse of the whip was the whip's undoing. It gave the abolitionists an argument by which they were able to awaken the indignation of the country. The white man with the whip in his hand lorded it over his ebony brethren; and what happened?

Look at this! We are in Jamaica! It is the early gray of the morning of August 1, 1838—the day on which emancipation came into force. William Knibb is conducting a funeral service; and, as the ornately carved and beautifully polished coffin is lowered into the grave, the doxology rises from ten thousand throats! What does it mean? Never before, surely, had the lowering of a coffin been accompanied by the singing of the doxology! But this coffin contains *a whip!* The slaves are burying the insignia of their bondage. The episode is almost allegorical in its intense significance. The whip was man's first symbol of power, of dominion, of authority; but, so surely as that power is abused, a swift nemesis and a crushing humiliation must inevitably overtake it.

F. W. Boreham, *The Nest of Spears* (London: The Epworth Press, 1927), 27-28.

LIFE'S CRISES

A painting by Mr. Frank Dicksee, R.A., in the Victorian Art Gallery [Melbourne] is entitled *The Crisis*. It is a picture that grows upon you. I felt its poignant and resistless pathos when I first saw it many years ago; I felt it still more today. One never tires of gazing into the haggard face of the anxious husband as, with his chin resting on the palm of his right hand and the thumb embedded in his cheek, he sits by the bedside of his unconscious wife. As she lies there, propped up with pillows, her thin, worn hands lying stretched out on the white sheet, her wan, pinched face is turned away from him. We are impressed by the contrast between the pitiless indifference of her unconsciousness and the strained intentness with which all his soul is focused upon her. Life is trembling in the balance. The catching of a breath may end it. A single flutter of the tired heart may decide the fearful issue. One finds himself pausing before the painting as though in hope that, even while he waits, the sickness will take a more favorable turn and the agonizing suspense be relieved....

Thomas Huxley has a striking sentence to the effect that 'there is always a Cape Horn in every one's life.' ... Thomas Huxley had his long voyage across lonely seas before he sighted his Cape Horn. Eighty years ago he was appointed assistant-surgeon of the *Rattlesnake*—a leaky and worm-eaten old battleship engaged on survey work in these Australian waters. In Sydney the young doctor fell in love with Miss Henrietta Heathorn, for whom, as his son and biographer afterwards said, 'he was to serve longer and harder than Jacob thought to serve for Rachel.'

Huxley returned to England, but everything went against him. Year succeeded year, but the prospect of marriage seemed as remote as ever. He thought of his fair Australian sweetheart ripening into mature womanhood under other stars; but promotion studiously avoided him. 'A man of science,' he snarled bitterly, 'may earn distinction, but not bread.' At length, in 1855, after a weary wait of eight long years, Miss Heathorn joined him in England. She was very ill; the doctors were summoned; and they told Huxley that she could not live six months. 'Ah, well,' he replied, 'six months or no, she is going to be my wife!' And he married her.

She lived to be nearly ninety, surviving her husband by nearly twenty years. For forty years, as her son proudly says, she was his constant help and stay; in his struggles ready to counsel; in adversity ready to comfort; the critic whose judgment he valued above that of any, and whose praise he most desired to win. It was thus that Thomas Huxley, after long tossing upon desolate waters, doubled Cape Horn, and turned his prow to the sunshine.

In one or other form, life's supremest crisis comes to all of us.

F. W. Boreham, *A Tuft of Comet's Hair* (London: The Epworth Press, 1926), 101-102, 107, 111-112.

LIFE'S CRITICAL MOMENTS

Andrew Duncannon joined the church late in life, and nurses day and night a bitter regret. When he was scarcely more than a boy he heard Mr. Moody in London. 'I shall never forget that night,' Andrew was saying, 'Mr. Moody preached on *"Seek ye first the kingdom of God and His righteousness, and all these things shall be added unto you."*

'It seemed to me as if the gates of the kingdom of God stood wide open before me, and heaven and earth were both urging me to enter. I really meant at that moment to have done so. But somehow I allowed the occasion to slip by; I drifted out with the crowd; and it was nearly fifty years afterwards before I became a Christian. God is very pitiful,' he said, with evident emotion, 'God is very pitiful and of wondrous mercy; but life can never be what it might have been if I had done what I meant to have done that night!' Andrew was simply feeling, as I have so often felt, that the person who knows how to recognize life's critical moments when they come, and to fix his impressions on their arrival, is a very skillful photographer indeed.

F. W. Boreham, *Wisps of Wildfire* (London: The Epworth Press, 1924), 260-261.

LINKING OF LIFE

Near to one of the great English universities is a bluff that commands a magnificent outlook across the charming country stretching away and away to the distant sunlit hills. On the summit of the bluff is a stone seat. And on the back of the rough stone bench is carved this legend:

TO THOSE WHO SHALL SIT HERE
REJOICING,
AND TO THOSE WHO SHALL SIT HERE
LAMENTING;
GREETING AND SYMPATHY!
SO HAVE WE DONE IN OUR TIME.

Here are students whose faces are flushed with success, and students whose lips quiver with the bitterness of failure, both of whom feel that in their hours of exaltation and of humiliation they must span the terrible gulf that separates them from similar students yet unborn. And, by means of this rough stone bench upon the bluff, they fling a bridge across the chasm of time, and put themselves into communication with students who shall pass their examinations, and students who shall fail their examinations, long after the moss and the mildew have gathered about their own tombstones.

F. W. Boreham, *Mountains in the Mist* (London: Charles H. Kelly, 1914), 115.

LIVING THE WORD

A padre was leaning over a dying soldier. 'Let me read a few words to you!' he said taking out his pocket Testament. 'Oh, I'm thirsty!' complained the soldier, and the chaplain rose and brought him water. 'Now may I read?' asked the padre. 'No,' replied the soldier, 'I'm cold!' The chaplain took off his own coat and wrapped it round the man. 'I'll read a word or two now!' said the minister. 'I'm too tired!' moaned the man. 'Well,' answered the padre, 'pillow your head on my lap and try to get some sleep!'

The man closed his eyes and lay still for awhile; but he soon opened them again. 'Look here, padre,' he exclaimed, 'if there's anything in that book of yours that will make one person behave towards another as you've behaved towards me, for God's sake read it!'

F. W. Boreham, *A Late Lark Singing* (London: The Epworth Press, 1945), 161.

LIVING UP TO A NAME

In describing the striking experiences through which he passed on being made a free man, Booker T. Washington, the slave who carved his way to statesmanship, tells us that his greatest difficulty lay in regard to a name. Slaves have no names; no authentic genealogy; no family history; no ancestral traditions. They have, therefore, nothing to live up to. Mr. Booker Washington himself invented his own name. 'More than once,' he says 'I tried to picture myself in the position of a boy or man with an honored and distinguished ancestry. As it is, I have no idea who my grandmother was. The very fact that the white boy is conscious that, if he fails, he will disgrace the whole family record is of tremendous value in helping him to resist temptations. And the fact that the individual has behind him a proud family history serves as a stimulus to help him to overcome obstacles when striving for success.'

Every student of biography knows how frequently people have been restrained from doing evil, or inspired to lofty achievement, by the honor in which a cherished memory has compelled them to hold the names they are allowed to bear.

Every student knows the story of the Grecian coward whose name was Alexander. His cowardice seemed the more contemptible because of his distinguished name; and his commander, Alexander the Great, ordered him either to change his name or to prove himself brave.

F. W. Boreham, *Mushrooms on the Moor* (London: Charles H. Kelly, 1915), 248-249.

LIVING UP TO EXPECTATIONS

The dazzling genius of Horatio Nelson was never displayed to greater advantage than in his immortal signal at Trafalgar. 'Mr. Pasco,' he said, as he stepped on to the poop [deck] of the *Victory* and addressed the signal-lieutenant, 'Mr. Pasco, I wish to give a fillip [to rouse, excite] to the whole fleet.' And how did he compass his end? He did it by presenting every man with a great expectation! 'England expects that every man this day will do his duty!'

'England expects!' At the *first* of those two words, every sailor in the fleet saw, in sudden fancy, the old home circle; at the *second* he saw a look of fond and wistful expectancy mantle those familiar features; and he vowed that their hope should not be disappointed.

F. W. Boreham, *Shadows on the Wall* (London: The Epworth Press, 1922), 20.

LONELINESS OF THE CROWD

I shall never forget the day when, at the age of sixteen, I left home and found my way up to the roar and din of London. I had never seen such crowds anywhere else, jostling and pushing for every inch of pavement. And yet I remember standing that day in the heart of the world's metropolis, under the very shadow of St. Paul's, and shivering in the thick of the crowd at my own utter loneliness.

Amid the hops and the clover and the orchards of my Kentish home one could often shout to his heart's content, and never a soul would hear him. Yet that was a delicious and tranquil loneliness that one loved and reveled in, but the loneliness of that awful surging crowd seemed an intolerable thing.

F. W. Boreham, *The Whisper of God and other sermons* (London: Arthur H. Stockwell, 1902), 137.

LOOKING OUT FROM OURSELVES

A man may look within himself, but he does not find himself by looking within. He much more often finds himself by looking away.

The story of Diehl, the artist, comes to mind. During his childhood his mother was greatly troubled about him. He was evidently a prodigy; he was always talking about his artistic feelings and his artistic tastes. Occasionally, but only occasionally, he set to work. Sir Frederick Leighton was consulted, and soon saw how the land lay. He invited the boy to his studio to inspect his own paintings and to tell which of them pleased him most. 'I like these figure sketches,' the lad replied; 'but why do you hang those landscapes? I do not think they are worth much!' Sir Frederick *took* the criticism patiently. He saw that the boy had been thinking too much of the artist *within* and too little of the beauty *without*.

'By hook or by crook,' he said to Mrs. Diehl, 'send him to Italy! Let him see snow-capped mountains and pine-clad valleys; let him see the isles of the Adriatic and the waterways of Venice; let him catch the beauty and romance of other times and other climes!'

The parents accepted the advice; the boy went abroad; he forgot the artist *within* him in contemplating the grandeur *around* him; and on his return, he, still only seventeen, sent pictures which adorned the Royal Academy.

It is good to look out—and around—and away. We find ourselves by looking away from ourselves.

F. W. Boreham, *Home of the Echoes* (London: The Epworth Press, 1921), 179-180.

LOSING PERSPECTIVE

In one of her cleverest novels, Lucas Malet—the pen name of Charles Kingsley's brilliant daughter—describes with terrific power and rare insight the painting of a celebrated artist. The picture is entitled 'The Fool.' It represents a cloudless evening sky, the primrose tints fading, first into an olive green, and then into the softest blue. In the foreground is a garden path, set about by a row of tall hollyhocks. Nearby, leaning against the crumbling cottage wall, reclines a full-grown man, whose dull eyes are majestic in the depth of their pent-up incommunicable sorrow. He is tenderly nursing an old broken-limbed Dutch doll! This man is capable of love and worship, of joy and anguish; yet, while the vast universe of richest beauty woos his heart, he squanders all his sublime powers upon a cast-off toy!

The Church exists to set the splendor of life's vital issues before people's eyes in such an alluring guise that, while the baubles of folly shall seem to them like broken dolls, the path of wisdom, glowing beneath a primrose-tinted sky, shall seem set about with hollyhocks and roses....

It is woefully easy to view things in a false perspective, mistaking planets for pebbles and regarding molehills as mountains. This man talked flippantly enough about days and months and years, and carefully prepared for them, but when eternity suddenly burst upon him it took his breath away. He had never conceived of its splendor: had given no thought to its demands: was lamentably unprepared for its tests and tasks.

F. W. Boreham, *I Forgot To Say* (London: The Epworth Press, 1939), 177.

LOVING THOSE WHO DESPISE YOU

In George Fox's Journal the Quaker tells a great story of the Ulverston [England] riots of 1682. 'The man in the leathern breeches' had been preaching with his wonted plainness and fervor. The crowd set upon him and beat him with holly bushes and hedge stakes till he was insensible. On his recovering consciousness, a rough lout rushed at him and struck him so savage a blow on the arm that the limb fell useless to his side and he could not lift it. There were many who feared that he would never be able to use it again.

'But,' Fox says in his Journal, 'I looked at it in the love of God, for I was in the love of God to them that had persecuted me!'

'*I looked at it in the love of God!*' says the Quaker, and it is wonderful how fair the most repulsive faces may appear if only we can contrive to see them through that divine and wondrous medium. That is the highest form of chivalry, but there is certainly nothing instinctive about it.

F. W. Boreham, *The Golden Milestone* (London: Charles H. Kelly, 1915), 76-77.

LUMIERE FOR DISTINCTION

A French proverb, which Dumas uses as the title of one of the chapters of his *Three Musketeers,* affirms that, at night, all cats are gray. The aphorism is obviously designed to emphasize the principle that it is the primary prerogative of light to enable us to distinguish between things that differ.

F. W. Boreham, *Arrows of Desire* (London: The Epworth Press, 1951), 9.

LURE OF THE NEW

We have an infinite capacity for growing tired of things. It is one of the noblest traits of our humanity; it is the hallmark of our grandeur.

Watch for a moment the antics of this baby playing on the nursery floor! He has just survived the wild excitements of a birthday, and as you glance around his playroom you will see at once that he has sharply divided all his possessions into two distinct classes. There, in the corner, are the old toys of which he has grown tired; and here, in the middle of the room, are the new ones of which he hasn't.

In a few weeks Christmas-time will come; Santa Claus will bring a fresh supply of wonders; and these birthday presents that are today invested with all the charm of novelty will then be added to the pile of fallen idols. He will weary of them; and what then? Shall we blame him, chide him, scold him? Shall we call him fickle, volatile, inconstant? Shall we take away the new treasures in order to compel him to play with the old? Do it at your peril—*and at his!*

If you are half as wise as he is, you will smile at his merriment and then return to the sitting-room rejoicing that, up there in the nursery, you have seen a man in the making! You have seen a man moved by all the traditional instincts of the race! For, in preferring the new toys to the old ones, this baby of yours is but expressing, with all a child's simplicity and all a child's candor, one of the deepest and most fundamental laws of our humanity. They may call him inconstant who will; it is always easy to call people names. They may scold him who must. Those who, destitute of all imagination and all heart, care to remove from him the new toys of which he is so proud will, as a result of this painful discipline, cure him in time of his preference for things which are bright and fresh and new. But let them have a care lest, in curing him of this, they rob him of the *glory* of his manhood and reduce him to the level of the beasts that perish!

For here, in the nursery, with the old toys relegated to the corner and the new ones holding pride of place in the middle of the room, one sees reflected, as in a mirror, the history of the ages. Man has made his way from savagery to civilization by the simple process of growing tired of his toys.

F. W. Boreham, *Shadows on the Wall* (London: The Epworth Press, 1922), 246-247.

Luther's Great Discovery

In the Convent Library at Erfurt [Germany], we are shown an exceedingly famous and beautiful picture. It represents Luther as a young monk of four and twenty, poring in the early morning over a copy of the Scriptures to which a bit of broken chain is hanging. The dawn is stealing through the open lattice, illumining both the open Bible and the eager face of its reader. And on the page that the young monk so intently studies are to be seen the words: 'The just shall live by faith.' These, then, are the words that made the world all over again.

And now, leaving the Convent Library at Erfurt, let us visit another library, the Library of Rudolstadt! For here, in a glass case, we shall discover a manuscript that will fascinate us. It is a letter in the handwriting of Dr. Paul Luther, the reformer's youngest son. 'In the year 1544,' we read, 'my late dearest father, in the presence of us all, narrated the whole story of his journey to Rome. He acknowledged with great joy that, in that city, through the Spirit of Jesus Christ, he had come to the knowledge of the truth of the everlasting gospel. It happened in this way. As he repeated his prayers on the Lateran staircase, the words of the Prophet Habakkuk came suddenly to his mind: "The just shall live by faith."

Thereupon he ceased his prayers, returned to Wittenberg, and took this as the chief foundation of all his doctrine.' 'The just shall live by faith!'

The picture in the one library, and the manuscript in the other, have told us all that we desire to know.

F. W. Boreham, *A Bunch of Everlastings* (London: The Epworth Press, 1920), 22-23.

MAGNANIMITY IN FORGIVENESS

[British Prime Minister] Gladstone was at the time Chancellor of the Exchequer. He sent down to the Treasury office one day for a sheaf of statistics on which he based his budget proposals. Now it happened that, in compiling the statistics, the clerk had made a mistake that vitally affected the entire situation. The blunder was only discovered after Mr. Gladstone had elaborated his proposals and made his budget speech in the House of Commons. The [news]papers immediately exposed the fallacy, and for a moment the Chancellor was overwhelmed with embarrassment. He was made to appear ridiculous before the entire nation.

He sent down to the Treasury for the clerk to come to him at once. The clerk duly arrived, trembling with apprehension, and expecting instant dismissal. He began to stammer out his apologies, and his entreaty for forgiveness. Mr. Gladstone stopped him. 'I sent for you,' he said, 'because I could imagine the torture of your feelings. You have been for many years dealing with the bewildering intricacies of the national accounts, and you have done your work with such conscientious exactness that this is your first mistake. It was because of your splendid record that I did not trouble to verify your calculations. I have sent for you to compliment you on that record and to set you at your ease.' ...

If the New Testament means anything, it means that a person who can forgive with such gallantry and chivalry is a very great Christian indeed.

F. W. Boreham, *The Other Side of the Hill* (London: Charles H. Kelly, 1917), 241-242.

MAINTAINING SENSITIVITY

Ulysses Androvaldus remarks that a dove is so afraid of a hawk that one feather of that bird will paralyse all its powers. I have seen a horse thrown into paroxysms of terror on scenting the beasts in a passing menagerie. Most of us learn to treat with equanimity the things that we should hate and dread. It is a great art to preserve one's capacity for emotion unblunted to the end.

F. W. Boreham, *The Heavenly Octave* (London: The Epworth Press, 1935), 35.

MARTYRS MORE ALIVE THAN EVER

A prayer meeting was being held by [some Afro-American] people in one of the Southern States. 'O Lord,' exclaimed the leader, in the course of his prayer, 'we bless you for the glorious company of the Apostles!' 'Glory be to God!' shouted a devout old woman at the back of the hall.

'And we bless you,' the leader continued, 'for the goodly fellowship of the prophets!' 'Glory be to God!' the old woman cried again.

'And we bless you,' the good man went on, 'for the noble army of martyrs!' 'Glory be to God!' called the enthusiastic woman a third time. 'But,' proceeded the leader, adopting a more subdued tone, 'but they're all dead, O Lord, they're all dead!' 'Glory be to God, *that's a lie!*' shouted the old woman, and the interjection was greeted with a thunder of 'Hallelujahs.'

F. W. Boreham, *Boulevards of Paradise* (London: The Epworth Press, 1944), 142.

MATTER OF TEMPERAMENT

In the days in which I made up my mind to be a minister, I fell under the influence of the Rev. James Douglas, M.A., of Brixton, a most devout and scholarly man. He often took me for a walk on Clapham Common, and said things to me that I have never forgotten.

"When you are a minister," he said one day, as we sat under the shelter of a giant oak, "when you are a minister, you will find, wherever you go, that there are a certain number of people whom you are not fitted to influence. It is largely a matter of personality and temperament. Don't break your heart over it. Satisfy your conscience that you have done your duty by them, and then leave it at that!"

It was wise counsel.

F. W. Boreham, *Rubble and Roseleaves* (London: The Epworth Press, 1922), 48.

MEETING A GREAT CHALLENGE

George Selwyn became the first Bishop of New Zealand. His energy was inexhaustible. One would have thought that a country like New Zealand, a thousand miles long, would have been big enough to satisfy the consecrated ambition of any reasonable person. But it was not big enough for Selwyn.

In drawing up the Letters Patent for his antipodean episcopate, the Crown solicitors made an astounding and egregious blunder. Although Selwyn noticed it, he whispered not a word. The area under the new bishop's authority should have been defined as lying between latitude 39 *south* and latitude 50 *south*. But, by an incredible slip, it was actually defined as including all territories between latitude 34 *north* and latitude 50 *south!*

Selwyn chuckled to himself, for he saw that this definition would make him Bishop of the entire Pacific and would afford him the opportunity of visiting and evangelizing all the scattered islands of that immense ocean!

Later on, during a period of disturbance and turmoil in New Zealand, in which his work was brought practically to a standstill, he determined to avail himself of the privileges conferred upon him by the clerical error. He would attempt the evangelization of all the coral reefs and cannibal islands of the tropical seas! He recognized, of course, that it would be absurd for him to undertake missionary work, in the ordinary sense, among these countless groups. It would take years to acquire the languages, understand the customs, and overcome the prejudices of the islanders. He determined to resort to strategy. The individual must become the key to the situation. He took a boy from *this* island and a boy from *that* one; he persuaded them to accompany him to New Zealand; and then he bent all his energies to winning them for Christ. Afterwards he returned each of these neophites to his native island to evangelize his own people. In this *way* the Pacific was soon dotted with active evangelistic agencies, and the colorful archipelagoes of the South Seas soon heard, from men of their own blood and language, the words of life eternal.

F. W. Boreham, *Cliffs of Opal*, (London: The Epworth Press, 1948), 48-49.

MEMORABLE MONUMENT

I have a photograph of a monument in Westminster Abbey. It is the only monument to a pair of brothers to be found there. The brothers thus memorialized are, of course, the brothers Wesley. At the top are the two names, with the dates of their births and deaths. In the center is a plaque representing their two faces; with, beneath it, John's triumphant death-bed boast: 'The best of all is, God is with us!' And, at the foot, is a bas-relief, depicting John preaching to a motley multitude in the open-air, with the inscription: 'I look upon all the world as my parish.'

F. W. Boreham, *A Late Lark Singing* (London: The Epworth Press, 1945), 100.

MIMIC OR ORIGINAL

For the [Australian] lyre-bird is an ape, as most birds are. Indeed, other birds are more apish than he, for, while he confines his performance to the songs that he steals from the repertoire of his feathered neighbors, they, some of them, attempt to mimic such of the beasts as have won their admiration. Even the ostrich, the largest of all birds sets a bad example in this particular. The ostriches that dwell among the great African solitudes are as silent as the veldt over which they roam. But the ostriches that live in the vicinity of lions soon acquire a leonine roar. The huge bird admires the terrifying sound emitted by the king of beasts, and, in his feeble way, does his best to ape it.

The jay tries hard at times to bleat like a lamb, and to neigh like a horse. The bunting copies the call of the pipit; the greenfinches steal the notes of the yellow-hammers; and the starling impersonates the cuckoo. Even the nightingale is guilty of occasional plagiarism. Like the lyre-bird down by the creek, he is an ape; so are the magpies and parrots that we frightened from the fences as we came along. So are we all.

Yes, so are we all—humans especially. We are the greatest apes on the planet. Our poorer relatives of the brute creation owe a good deal of their sagacity to instinct; but for some inscrutable reason we learn very little at that school. We owe almost everything to our cleverness as mimics.

As soon as we open our eyes we begin to imitate every gesture that attracts our attention. A child apes everything he sees. You take him for a drive, and for the next week he plays at horses from morning to night; everybody, from his baby sister up to his grandmother, has to go into harness at his behest. You take him in a railway train, and for a week afterwards all the chairs are drawn up as railway carriages, while he is himself the engine, puffing and screaming without a moment's intermission.

As Professor Drummond has pointed out, the very language that we speak is frankly an imitation. The child calls the cow a moo-moo; the dog a bow-wow; the duck a quack-quack; the rooster a cock-a-doodle-doo; the clock a tick-tick; the train a puff-puff; and the rest. His father is scarcely any better. He talks of the hum of the bee; the click of the gate; the whir of machinery; the chirp of the grasshopper; the twitter of the sparrow; the hiss of the snake; the boom of cannon; the roar of thunder; the tramp of armies; and so on. We imitate everything.

Here and there you will find a man who plumes himself on his originality …

F. W. Boreham, *A Reel of Rainbow* (London: The Epworth Press, 1920), 181-183.

MIXTURE OF GOOD AND EVIL

In his *Reminiscences,* Sir Henry Hawkins tells of a woman whom he once defended. She was so utterly abandoned and depraved that she had undertaken to assist her husband and son in murdering a servant-girl. While the two men committed the revolting crime, the woman held down the victim. And yet, when the issue of the trial was trembling in the balance, this same woman came forward with an astounding proposition. 'If the trial goes on,' she said, 'we may all three get off, or we may all three be hanged. I wish to place my husband and my boy beyond the pale of so terrible a risk.' And then she pleaded that she might be sent to the gallows, and that, with her execution, justice might be satisfied!

'Here,' as Sir Henry says, 'was a strange mingling of evil and good—of diabolical cruelty and noble self-sacrifice—in one breast! I leave others to work out this problem of human nature.'

F. W. Boreham, *The Other Side of the Hill* (London: Charles H. Kelly, 1917), 163.

MONUMENT IN WORK

St. Paul's—Christopher Wren's masterpiece—took thirty-five years in building. With what pathetic pride and tenderness the old architect watched it grow! Amid the decay of his physical and intellectual powers, he insisted on being carried down to the city every now and again that, with his fast-dimming eyes, he might actually see the fulfillment of his magnificent dream. Happily, he lived to see it finished. He was nearly eighty. Thirteen years later, his noble cathedral extended to him the hospitality of sepulcher. He who, today, enters St. Paul's from the north, reads over the doorway the historic inscription: 'Beneath is buried Christopher Wren, architect of this church and city, who lived more than ninety years, not for himself, but for the public good. Reader, if thou seekest his monument, look around!'

We may leave it at that. As long as London stands, and as long as English history is read with patriotic pride, his will be one of the names that must always be mentioned with affectionate homage and reverent gratitude.

F. W. Boreham, *The Drums of Dawn* (London: The Epworth Press, 1933), 213.

MORE HEAVENS THAN ONE

My home is adorned by a picture of which I am particularly fond. It is by A. Kemp Tebby and is entitled 'More Heavens than One.' It represents two women, both young, and beautiful. The first is seated in the front room of her cottage: the door stands open to the village street. A baby sleeps serenely in a plain wooden cradle. A little girl—a tiny toddler of two or three—is perched upon the edge of the table. The mother is sitting near her, holding her securely, and gazing into the child's eyes with a look of infinite rapture and pride. While she, transported with maternal ecstasy, is thus lost to all the world, a tall nun passes the cottage and glances, with eyes of unutterable wistfulness, at the charming picture framed by the open door. There are, she feels, *more heavens than one.*

F. W. Boreham, *I Forgot To Say* (London: The Epworth Press, 1939), 24-25.

MOTIVATING MUSIC

Johann Sebastian Bach was an intensely devout man and his great religious masterpieces were the natural outpourings of his inmost soul. 'Deep down in his great heart,' we read in the

Little Chronicle, 'he always carried his Lord Crucified, and his noblest music is his secret cry for a clearer vision of the risen Christ. In his lullaby in the *Christmas Cantata* he could write music tender enough for the Babe of Bethlehem; in the Crucifixion of his *Great Mass* he could find strains grand enough for the Savior of Calvary. At the end of his earlier scores he always inscribed the letters S.D.G.—*To God be the glory!*' It mirrored the motive of the man.

F. W. Boreham, *Dreams at Sunset* (London: The Epworth Press, 1954), 87-88.

MY AUTOBIOGRAPHY

Very few of the people who have written autobiographies have realized the sacramental character of their task. Between a biography and an autobiography there is a fundamental distinction. An autobiography should be far more than a self-written biography. An autobiography should be an epic of spiritual portraiture—a faithful record of the soul's secret pilgrimage. An autobiography should reveal things of which a biographer knows nothing. A biographer views the temple of his hero's personality from the outer court; the autobiographer views it from the inmost shrine. A biography is eventual—a record of events; an autobiography is psychic—a seismograph of the soul. The pivotal passages of life are all essentially spiritual. The subtle processes of education—both in and out of school—are spiritual processes; the choice of a vocation is a poignant spiritual crisis; the surge of sex, the capture of the affections and the phenomenon of mating are all of them spiritual experiences; and it goes without saying that the dawn of faith is spiritual. These are the things that we have a right to expect in an autobiography. The man is in the confessional, and, having voluntarily entered it, he is under obligation to bare his inmost soul....

The trouble about the *important* things is that they are not the distinctive things. And, when I open a man's autobiography, it is the distinctive things that I want—the things that, differentiating him from the common mass of men, lifted him out of the ruck.

F. W. Boreham, *Ships of Pearl* (London: The Epworth Press, 1935), 37-38, 40.

My Shepherd

I knew a padre—the Rev. J. A. Gault, O.B.E.—who did a wonderful work in France during the First World War. It was his custom, when men were going into the firing-line, to get them to repeat with him the opening clause of the Shepherd Psalm, ticking it off on the fingers of their left hands.

The little finger represented the word *The;* the next finger, *Lord;* the middle finger, *is;* the index finger, *my;* and the thumb, *Shepherd.* He called it his *Five-finger Exercise.* Every man was asked to mark the palm of his hand with an indelible pencil to remind him of the text, and special stress was laid on the index *finger—my* Shepherd—the finger that spoke of the personal appropriation of the shepherdly care.

After the battle of Bullecourt, one of Mr Gault's young fellows was found, quite dead, grasping firmly with his right hand the *index finger* of his left.

'Don't say *your;* say *my!*' pleaded the puzzled mother. But the tiny tot did not understand.

But Mr Gault's young soldier understood. And, with an innumerable host of saints and heroes and martyrs, he rejoiced that he had a place peculiarly his own in the heart of the Good Shepherd, and clung to that sweet faith in perfect serenity to the last.

F. W. Boreham, *In Pastures Green* (London: The Epworth Press, 1954), 14.

NAMING OUR DISAPPOINTMENTS

Hamilton Hume was the first of that gallant band of 'over-landers' of whose splendid exploits Australians are so justly proud. He it was who led the first pathfinders from Sydney to Melbourne. In the course of that tedious and historic pilgrim-age, there were two great and memorable moments, one of exultation and one of depression.

The first was when Hume, on ahead of the party, sud-denly stopped, waved his hat in boyish glee and came run-ning back to announce to his comrades his discovery of the Murray [River].

The other was when, exhausted and famished, they sighted the mountains that we know as the Hume Range. The party were worn out, and begged to be allowed to give up and return. Hume pointed to a mountain ahead of them. "From that summit," he assured them, "we shall see the ocean, and shall go back and tell of our success!" The mountain was climbed; "but when, after a desperate struggle, they reached the top, nothing met their eyes but miles and miles of ridges and gullies covered with trees"; they named it 'Mount Dis-appointment' and, to their everlasting credit, pressed on and safely reached their goal.

F. W. Boreham, *Mountains in the Mist* (London: Charles H. Kelly, 1914), 254-255.

NATURE OF COVETOUSNESS

In his lecture on *The Valley of Diamonds,* John Ruskin dis-cusses the nature of covetousness. What is covetousness? Wherein does it differ from the legitimate desire for wealth? Up to a certain point the desire for riches is admirable. It develops intellectual alertness in the individual, and, in the aggregate, builds up our national prosperity. If nobody

wished to be rich, the resources of the country would never
be exploited. Why should people trouble to clear the bush or
sink mines or erect factories or cultivate farms? Apart from
the lure of wealth, we should be a people of sluggish wit and
savage habits. Viewed in this light, the desire for wealth is not
only pardonable; it is admirable.

At what point, then, does it curdle into covetousness and
threaten our undoing? Ruskin draws the line sharply. The
desire for wealth is good, he argues, as long as we have some
use for the riches that we acquire; it deteriorates into mere
covetousness as soon as we crave to possess it for the sheer
sake of possessing it and apart from any use to which we propose to put it. 'Fix your desire on anything useless,' he says,
'and all the pride and folly of your heart will mix with that
desire; and you will become at last wholly inhuman, a mere,
ugly lump of stomach and suckers, like a cuttlefish.'

F. W. Boreham, *Boulevards of Paradise* (London: The Epworth Press,
1944), 132-133.

NEED FOR MOTHERING

We *all* need mothering. It is one of the essential facts of our
make-up. One of the finest pictures in the Sydney Art Gallery is 'The Widower,' by Sir Luke Fildes, R.A. It represents
a laborer who, at the close of the day, has come home to his
motherless children. One of them is sick. And there he sits,
with the peevish child on his knee, and a look of utter help-
lessness on his face! The little ones sadly need mothering;
but, alas, there is no one to mother them.

One of the finest pictures in the Melbourne Art Gallery
is 'The Mitherless Bairn,' by Mr. Thomas Faed, R.A. These
pathetic paintings eloquently express the plight into which
we should all have been plunged if there had been nothing
motherly in God. Fatherliness is very fine and very beautiful;

but it does not cover all the ground. If God had been just a Father—'*Our Father, which art in heaven*'—we should all have been like the little children in the paintings. We should all have been motherless bairns.

F. W. Boreham, *The Fiery Crags* (London: The Epworth Press, 1928), 114.

NEGLECT

Professor Drummond tells of fish that have dwelt so long in dark submarine caverns that their eyes have become sightless.

The same stern law ordains that the man who habitually views the world through the optics of others shall eventually possess no vision of his own.

F. W. Boreham, *When the Swans Fly High* (London: The Epworth Press, 1931), 255.

NEVER IN A HURRY

I once attended a farewell meeting tendered to a minister who, after a remarkably fruitful and prosperous pastorate extending over more than twenty years, was laying down his charge.

I have forgotten all that they said. But I distinctly remember the utterance of a man, who, towards the close of the meeting, craved the chairman's permission to add a single sentence.

'I have met Mr. Falkland nearly every day of my life for twenty years,' he said, 'and I have never yet seen him in a hurry!'

Mr. Falkland told me afterwards that he treasured that tribute as the highest of the compliments paid to him at the meeting.

F. W. Boreham, *The Uttermost Star* (London: The Epworth Press, 1919), 172-173.

New Directions out of Difficulties

In his biography of the poet [John Milton], Mark Pattison tells us that, at the age of forty-three, blindness fell upon Milton like the sentence of death, and he fancied for awhile that he had reached the end of everything. His only gleam of comfort lay in the fact that he had written, during his last year of eyesight, a pamphlet on the Civil War! 'He could not foresee,' his biographer remarks, 'that in less than ten years his pamphlet would be merged in the obsolete mass of civil war tracts, and only be mentioned because it had been written by the author of *Paradise Lost*.'

The new day dawned with the coming of the darkness. Before his blindness, Milton wrote political pamphlets; only that and nothing more! In his sightlessness he developed an imagination which, for sublimity and splendor, has never been surpassed. The dawn rose out of the sunset.

F. W. Boreham, *Home of the Echoes* (London: The Epworth Press, 1921), 102-103.

No Books Without Readers

O you that read! I have a friend, a comrade, a kindred soul whose sympathetic cooperation and trusty help it imperatively behooves me to acknowledge. He is virtually the author of these books, since, but for him, not one of them would have been written. His smile has been my sunshine; his praise my music; his wise and honest criticism my clear and guiding star. His very existence has been an inspiration, calling out all that was best in me. His patience has been inexhaustible; his kindness the wonder of my days. Yet, strangely enough, I should not know him if I met him on the street. But *you* know him! For, every morning, thou see his face in the mirror!

F. W. Boreham, *A Tuft of Comet's Hair* (London: The Epworth Press, 1926), 7.

NO CHANGE FOR ME

We grow to things, like the ivy to the wall.

Richard Jefferies was once asked why he walked the same road every day. The question startled him, and he could not immediately answer it. It had never occurred to him that he *had* adhered so closely to the same path.

'Not till years afterwards,' he says, 'was I able to see why I went the same round and why I did not care for change. I do not want change; I want the same old and loved things. I want the same wild flowers, the same trees, the same soft ash-green. I want the same turtle-doves, the same blackbirds, the same colored yellowhammer, singing, so long as there is light enough to cast a shadow on the dial the same old song! And I want them all in the same places! Let me see the idle shadows resting on the white dust; let me hear the bumble-bees, and stay to look down on the dandelion disc; let me see the chaffinch with a feather in her bill! No change for me! Let me see the same things on the same road, keeping the same succession year by year!'

F. W. Boreham, *The Uttermost Star* (London: The Epworth Press, 1919), 118-119.

NO ROOM

In his *Les Miserables,* Victor Hugo tells the story of the dire distress of Jean Valjean, the ex-galley slave. He was driven out of one inn and then out of another. At last he took his knapsack and stick and went away. As he strode off, some boys who had followed him from the Cross of Colbas, and seemed to have been waiting for him, threw stones at him. He turned savagely, and threatened them with his stick, and the boys dispersed like a flock of birds. He passed in front of the prison, and pulled the iron bell-handle; a wicket [gate] was opened.

'Mr. Jailer,' he said, as he humbly doffed his cap, 'would you be kind enough to open the door and give me a night's lodging!'

A voice answered, 'A prison is not an inn; get yourself arrested, and then I will open the door.'

As he did not know the streets, he wandered about without purpose. He thus reached the prefecture and then the seminary. It occurred to him that, if the influence of the Church were what it should be, the people beneath its sway would have shown more pity to an outcast like himself. At that moment he passed into Cathedral Square. The great dome towered above him. The resentment of his soul reached its climax in a striking gesture. He looked up bitterly and *shook his fist at the church.* Victor Hugo probably meant the incident to stand as an allegorical representation of the greatest tragedy in the religious experience of his country.

F. W. Boreham, *Wisps of Wildfire* (London: The Epworth Press, 1924), 135-136.

No Short Cuts

One Wednesday morning, the postman handed me a letter from Brian Gray. Brian was born just after I settled at Mosgiel. During my twelve years there, I got to know him well and became very fond of him. He writes for advice. 'I have made up my mind,' he says, 'to enter the ministry. But, as you know, I am twenty-eight. If I go to college in the ordinary way, the course will occupy several years, and I shall be thirty-two or thirty-three before I shall be ready for ordination. For some months, however, I have been preaching on Sundays at Lower Redfern. Mr. Clifford, the secretary, took me home to supper with him last Sunday night and told me that he thought the Church would be willing to call me to the pastorate straight away; and he pointed out that, if I approved myself in the work, I might in a few years' time be able to secure full ministerial status without the necessity of passing through college. What do you think?'

I wrote to Brian urging him most strongly to seek a college education. I recognize his temptation. He is tempted to enter the ministry quickly [like opening a door] without turning the handle. It is often done; but it is seldom done without subsequent regrets. When Brian has been ten or twenty years in the ministry he will find the strain of it so great, and the perplexities so baffling, that he will never forgive himself for having neglected any opportunity of equipping himself for such pressing and solemn ordeals.

We are all prone to forget that our duty in life is, not only to do the right thing, but to do the right thing *in the right way.* We must not only enter the right room, but we must enter it by turning the handle. We are too keen on short cuts and royal roads.

F. W. Boreham, *A Tuft of Comet's Hair* (London: The Epworth Press, 1926), 245-246.

NOT TOO LATE

At the battle of Marengo, on June 14th, 1800, when the Austrians, under Melas, faced the French, under Napoleon, a messenger rode up to the Emperor at three o'clock in the afternoon, and said: "It is lost, sire; all is lost!"

"Very well," said Napoleon, "but there is plenty of time to win it all back again before the sun goes down!" And at six o'clock the French victory was complete!

F. W. Boreham, *The Whisper of God and other sermons* (London: Arthur H. Stockwell, 1902), 97.

ONE BOOK

It all comes back to that pathetic entry in Lockhart's diary at Abbotsford. 'He [Sir Walter Scott] then desired to be wheeled through his rooms in the bath-chair. We moved him leisurely for an hour or more up and down the hall and the great library....

'Next morning he desired to be drawn into the library and placed by the central window that he might look down upon the Tweed. Here he expressed a wish that I should read to him. I asked, from what book. He said, "Need you ask? There is but one!" I chose the fourteenth chapter of St. John's Gospel.' He listened with mild devotion, and, when Lockhart had finished reading of the Father's house and the many mansions, he said, "That is a great comfort!" The juxtaposition of phrases is arresting: 'In the great library'—'there is *but one book!*'

F. W. Boreham, *The Luggage of Life* (London: Charles H. Kelly, 1912), 44-45.

ONE SIZE FITS ALL?

Drawing was a perfect bugbear to me. I entered for it because the classes were available and because Gilbert Finch was joining them. But it was useless. I took courses in freehand, model drawing, geometry and all the rest; but, although the lessons awoke a certain languid interest in me, and although the subjects seemed more easy than many of those that led to successful examinations, I failed deplorably every time.

The admonition afforded by this shameful collapse should have saved me from a humiliation that followed a few years later; but only wise men learn from experience. I had undertaken to lecture in a small country chapel on 'Robert Moffat.' It occurred to me that a picture of the missionary would greatly assist the effect of the lecture. But nowhere could I find one. In the biography that I had so carefully studied there was a small engraving; but this was too insignificant to be of use.

Then came a brain-wave! Why not draw a life-size portrait from this tiny one? I bought the parchment; set to work; and, not to put too fine a point upon it, was more than pleased with the result. On the day of the lecture I took my masterpiece to the chapel and hung it above the pulpit. I liked the look of it, and, before leaving the building, I again surveyed it with pride from the porch. Then, emerging on to the village green, I chanced to encounter a young lady in whose aesthetic and artistic taste I had implicit confidence. I explained the reason for my visit to the chapel at that unusual hour and begged her to return and inspect my handiwork. A few minutes later, we were standing side by side in the aisle, examining the sketch over the pulpit.

Greatly daring, I asked her opinion.

'It should,' she observed thoughtfully, 'be a very valuable picture!'

This completely took my breath away. I had fondly hoped that, with characteristic courtesy—and charity—she might perhaps say that it would answer its purpose; but 'a very valuable picture!' I had never dreamed of so dazzling a bouquet.

'And may I ask,' I resumed, in the moment of my elation, 'why you think it so valuable?'

'Well, you see,' she replied, with a charming smile, 'you happen this evening to be lecturing on Robert Moffatt. But, in days to come, you may find yourself lecturing on other men; and *that*,' she continued, glancing at my picture, 'would fit any conceivable occasion!'

I felt that no punishment could be too severe for a young lady who could be guilty of such cold-blooded cruelty. So, later on, I married her. But that is another story.

F. W. Boreham, *My Pilgrimage* (London: The Epworth Press, 1940), 37-39.

ONE'S CONDITION AFFECTS ONE'S VISION

I knew two men in New Zealand—Norman Findlay and Eric Williams. Each decided to spend his holiday in the wild, romantic country around the slopes of Mount Earnslaw. 'Well, and how did you enjoy it?' I asked Norman, a few months later. 'The most desolate district I have ever seen,' he replied gloomily, 'a perfect wilderness!'

A couple of days later I met Eric, and asked the same question.

'A glorious place,' he exclaimed, with enthusiasm, 'a perfect paradise. New beauties break upon you everywhere!'

I found out afterwards that, while staying at Earnslaw, Norman was waiting impatiently for the results of his final University examination, about which he was justified—as the event proved—in being extremely apprehensive. Eric, on the other hand, went there for his honeymoon.

It makes all the difference. Take, for example, the Highlands of Scotland. Today they are numbered among the scenic grandeurs of Europe. People gladly journey hundreds of miles that they may gaze with awe upon those great, silent hills, all draped in their mantle of brown heath and shaggy wood. The descriptions of visitors are couched in a vocabulary that simply glows with the fervor of unbounded admiration.

But it was not always so. Captain Burt, the first Englishman to visit that awe-inspiring region, described those towering peaks as 'monstrous excrescences.' Their deformity, he said, was such that the most sterile plains seemed lovely by comparison! Oliver Goldsmith, too, after exploring Highland scenes which today swarm with enraptured tourists, ridiculed it all as 'an unfruitful country, its hills all brown with heath, and its valleys scarcely able to feed a rabbit!'

Or go to Italy. When Thomas Gray, the author of the *Elegy*, looked upon Italy from Mount Cenis—a landscape that, for loveliness, stands almost unrivalled in the world—he wrote to his friend, Benjamin West, that 'its horrors were accompanied with too much danger to give one time to reflect upon their beauties.'

Now why this thusness? Has Scotland changed? Has Italy changed? Of course not. The change is in the emotions of those who gaze upon these unchanging things. When Burt and Goldsmith visited the Highlands of Scotland, traveling had not been made as safe as now it is; and their minds were terrorized by a thousand apprehensions. The same sense of fear peeps out of Gray's letter to West. As Macaulay says, 'A traveler is not likely to be thrown into ecstasies by the abruptness of a precipice from which he is in imminent danger of being hurled; by the boiling waves of a torrent which suddenly swirls away his baggage and forces him to run for his life; by the gloomy grandeur of a pass where he finds a corpse which marauders have just stripped and mangled; or by the screams of those eagles whose next meal may probably be on his own eyes.'…

But the difference was not in the scenes upon which they gazed. The difference was within. The horror, the terror, and the beauty lurked within the souls of the respective visitors.

F. W. Boreham, *A Reel of Rainbow* (London: The Epworth Press, 1920), 137-139.

PAIN AND LAUGHTER

A ministerial friend of mine was recently traveling in the far east of Australia. On his return he penned a most picturesque account of the wilds and wonders of the Queensland bush. And, in the process of his cinematographic description of a glorious motor ride, he includes this realistic and characteristic touch:

"In the heart of the bush," he says, "we came upon a tragedy that must often be enacted among the animal dwellers of the great solitude—a kangaroo, a mother, unable to resist the pangs and pains thrust upon her by her destiny, lay dead upon the roadside, and above, on a branch of a tree, stood a pair of laughing-jackasses [kookaburras], guffawing their loudest, as if life knew no tragedy and no pain."

Here, then, is a painting, skillfully finished, before which we may profitably pause. And the charm of it—as of all great pictures—is that it is so true to life. The laughing kookaburra and the dead kangaroo.

F. W. Boreham, *The Luggage of Life* (London: Charles H. Kelly, 1912), 140-141.

PASSION

I was shown a most interesting letter…. It was the letter of an accomplished pianist concerning music and musicians. The writer lives, moves, and has her being in a world which, I blush to confess, I have never invaded. A message from Mars could not have possessed greater novelty. But let me hasten to the point. The writer speaks of her acquaintance with a certain eminent pianist whose recitals crowd the most spacious auditoriums in Europe with ecstatic admirers. But, our correspondent goes on to say, there is just one thing lacking. This brilliant pianist is a lonely, taciturn man, and a certain coldness and aloofness steal into his play.

And then the writer of our letter mentions the name of a lady pianist. That name is a household word in musical circles the wide world over; and the writer says that, to her personal knowledge, this illustrious lady one day laid her hand on the shoulder of the brilliant young performer, and said: "Will you let me tell you, my boy, that your playing lacks one thing. So far you have missed the greatest thing in the world. And, unless you fall in love, there will always be a certain cold perfection about your music. Unless you come to love another human being passionately and unselfishly, you will never touch human hearts as deeply as you might."

F. W. Boreham, *The Luggage of Life* (London: Charles H. Kelly, 1912), 105-106.

PEACE AT LAST

After his splendid and triumphant warfare against slavery, William Wilberforce lay dying. His Quaker friend, J. J. Gurney, went to see him. The aged warrior was very frail and very feeble. He was swathed in flannels, and at the point of death. "But," says Gurney, "he unfolded his own experience to me in a highly interesting manner. He told me that the text on which he was then most prone to dwell, and from which he was deriving peculiar comfort, was this:

"Be careful for nothing; and the peace of God which passes all understanding shall keep your hearts and minds through Christ Jesus." While his frail nature was at the point of collapse, and his mortal tabernacle seemed ready to be dissolved, this peace was his blessed and abundant portion.

F. W. Boreham, *Mountains in the Mist* (London: Charles H. Kelly, 1914), 149-150.

PEOPLE WITH TWO FACES

Samuel Creggan is no frolic of my fancy—nor of any other man's. Samuel Creggan is a real character, or at least he was. Indeed, he is the original on whom one of our greatest pieces of fiction has been founded. It was he who suggested to Robert Louis Stevenson the conception of *Dr. Jekyll and Mr. Hyde*. 'I was in Stevenson's company,' Mr. Charles H.

E. Brookfield tells us, in his *Random Reminiscences,* 'I was in Stevenson's company at the moment that he conceived the germ of the idea.'

He was inveighing against a man named *Samuel Creggan* with whom he had done business, and with whose methods he was dissatisfied. 'He's a man who trades on the *Samuel,*' Stevenson declared in his rather finiking, musical Scotch voice. 'He receives you with *Samuel's* smile on his face; with the gesture of *Samuel* he invites you to a chair; with *Samuel's* eyes cast down in self-depreciation he tells you how well satisfied his clients have always been with his dealings; but every now and again you catch a glimpse of the *Creggan* peeping out like a white ferret; *Creggan's* the real man; *Samuel's* only superficial.' So much by way of introducing *Samuel Creggan.*

F. W. Boreham, *The Other Side of the Hill* (London: Charles H. Kelly, 1917), 161-162.

PERFUMED BY SWEET FRAGRANCE

I remember to have read of a Valley of Roses. It is so extensive, and the lovely odors hang so heavily about the beauteous vale, that the traveler who passes through it carries the perfume on his person for days afterwards, and people look knowingly at each other as he enters the room.

A Persian fable says: One day a wanderer found a piece of clay that was so redolent of sweet perfume. Its odor scented all the room. 'What is this?' was the quick demand to the salesperson, 'Is it some gem from Samarcand? Or spikenard rare in rich disguise? Or some other costly merchandise? Where does the sweet fragrance come from?'

The salesperson said, 'This is an ordinary piece of clay. Before it was being formed it was sitting near a rose.'

F. W. Boreham, *The Other Side of the Hill* (London: Charles H. Kelly, 1917), 270-271.

PILGRIM OR GIPSY?

There is all the difference in the world between a pilgrim and a gipsy. One of the most interesting words in our vocabulary is the verb *to saunter.* It comes from *Sainte Terre*—the Holy Land.

In medieval ages, when the crusades were at the height of their popularity, idle people roved about the country begging for money to help them to go *á la Sainte Terre* to rescue the sacred soil from the hand of the infidel. But they never went. And when they were seen still drifting about England, they were called in derision *'sainte-terrers'*—*saunterers!* They pretended to be pilgrims, and were only gipsies after all!

There is a vast difference. A *pilgrim* is going somewhere and he is eager that others should go with him. A *gipsy* is going nowhere, and he has no prospect to offer a companion.

F. W. Boreham, *The Passing of John Broadbanks* (London: The Epworth Press, 1936), 179-180.

POCKET EDITIONS

An acorn is a wonderful thing; it is a pocket edition of a forest. Space is a wonderful thing; it is the tabloid of infinity. Time is a wonderful thing; it is the tabloid of eternity. The Bible is a wonderful thing; it is a pocket edition of the thought of God. A baby is a wonderful thing; it is a pocket edition of everything. And more even than any of these, the Christian life is a wonderful thing. And its real wonder arises from the fact that it is a pocket edition of the highest life of all. A Christian life is the reproduction of the stately idyll of the four Gospels, just as this neat little pocket edition on my desk is a representation of the three bulky volumes at the public library.

F. W. Boreham, *The Crystal Pointers* (London: The Epworth Press, 1925), 217.

Pointers

Cruising, some years ago, across the Southern Ocean, we encountered ice in latitudes in which, at that time of the year, ice is seldom seen. For some hours we were entirely surrounded by it. A few of us, gathered in the stern after dusk, were amusing ourselves by speculating, in an amateurish kind of way, as to the points of the compass and the bearings of the ship. The problem was suddenly solved. Piercing the gloom about us, two bright points of light gleamed over the virgin shoulder of one of the bergs, looking as cold and glassy as the ice itself.

'The Pointers!' exclaimed one member of the party, pointing to them; and, surely enough, in a few moments, the Southern Cross itself burst upon our view, looking, in those seas, particularly splendid.

Everybody in these Austral lands knows the Pointers. Strictly speaking, they are no part of the Southern Cross; but they point to it: and the one who catches sight of them looks wistfully for the glittering Cross itself.

Somehow, this experience of years ago rushes back upon my mind as I lift my pen from these pages. The papers that I have written possess no value or importance of their own; but they point to things that no man can afford to miss: *that* is their only glory.

F. W. Boreham, *The Crystal Pointers* (London: The Epworth Press, 1925), 7-8.

Poking the Fire

Sir William Osler, one of the most eminent Professors of Medicine that our generation has seen, has delivered lectures to his Oxford students that should be read by all kinds and conditions of people. Again and again he shows how fond we all are of poking the fire. There is really nothing to be done, yet we fidgety mortals must do something! It may not be a case for drugs, yet we are unhappy if the doctor leaves without ordering us to swallow something nasty! 'Human beings,' he says, 'have an inborn craving for medicine. Heroic dosing for several generations has given his tissues a thirst: for drugs. The desire to take medicine is one feature which distinguishes man, the animal, from his fellow creatures. It is really one of the most serious difficulties with which we doctors have to contend. Even in minor ailments, which would yield to dieting or to simple home remedies, the doctor's visit is not thought to be complete without the prescription!'

Indeed, Sir William, in another lecture, avers that the doctor's visit itself is often a matter of poking the fire. There is nothing to be done; the doctor cannot help the person in any way; but the talk with his physician soothes and reassures him! He has poked the fire; he feels that, at any rate, he has done something. The phenomenon is very common.

F. W. Boreham, *A Reel of Rainbow* (London: The Epworth Press, 1920), 113-114.

PORTRAYING THE HABAKKUK VISION

There is on record a conversation between Daniel Webster and some of his illustrious compeers. Somebody raised the question as to which was the finest passage in the Bible. One argued for the Creation story, another for the Sermon on the Mount, and a third for the description of the redeemed in the book of Revelation. But Webster slowly quoted those exquisite verses from one of the minor prophets: "Although the fig tree shall not blossom, neither shall fruit be in the vines; the labor of the olive shall fail, and the fields shall yield no meat; the flock shall be cut off from the fold, and there shall be no herd in the stalls: yet I will rejoice in the Lord, I will joy in the God of my salvation."

"I am amazed," said Webster, "that no talented artist has seen there a subject for a masterpiece—the prophet Habakkuk sitting in the midst of his dreadful desolation, still praising God and rejoicing in his unseen Savior!"

F. W. Boreham, *Mountains in the Mist* (London: Charles H. Kelly, 1914), 147, and F. W. Boreham, *A Handful of Stars* (London: The Epworth Press, 1922), 138.

POSSIBILITIES

The possibilities of tea are simply infinite. By means of tea, Charles Simeon changed the face of the world. For fifty-four years he gave a tea-party every Friday evening; he invited the undergraduates of Cambridge University to his table; and statesmen like Macaulay and Wilberforce and Sir James Stephen have told us that, by means of those tea-parties, Charles Simeon did more for the evangelization of the world than any man of his generation. Hundreds of men left that modest tea-table and went forth to dispel the darkness of continents....

Dr. Johnson once thundered, 'Do you not recognize that religion has its social side! Have you never read that of olden time men saw God and did eat and drink? Are you not aware that religious service consists in common friendship and mutual helpfulness? Can you not see, Sir, that, to minister effectively to each other, men must know each other? Would you have the members of your congregation to come silently in, and to steal silently out, aloof, distant, remote—isolated units, strangers to each other? Is that your idea? A rope of sand, Sir!' the doctor roars, bringing his huge hand down on the table with a terrific bang. 'A rope of sand, I tell you! No, Sir, bring out the tea-pot! Get them together! Let them eat together and drink together! Let them chatter and gossip and talk! Yes, Sir, let them talk! And what will make them talk like tea, Sir? Tell me that—what will unloose their tongues like a good cup of steaming, fragrant tea? Be thankful for tea, I tell you, and the more you use your tea-pot the better!'

F. W. Boreham, *The Crystal Pointers* (London: The Epworth Press, 1925), 126, 129-130.

POWER OF PERSONAL INVITATION

Dr. Alexander Whyte loved to tell of a commercial traveler named Rigby who, when in Edinburgh, used to stay at the Waverley Hotel, and, on Sunday, always made his way to St. George's [Church]. The man could not preach and found it difficult even to discuss spiritual themes with others. But before leaving the hotel for the church he always looked around for somebody whom he could invite to accompany him. One morning, on approaching a man with this invitation, he received something very like a rebuff. The stranger at first refused, but finally consented, and was so moved by the service that he asked Mr. Rigby to go with him again in the evening. That night, at St. George's, he found Christ. Next morning, in the course of his business, Mr. Rigby chanced to pass the home of Dr. Alexander Whyte. Acting on a sudden impulse, he made up his mind to call and tell Dr. Whyte of his experience on the Sunday. Dr. Whyte was deeply moved. 'I thought,' he said, 'that last night's sermon fell very flat, and I have been feeling very depressed about it. But what did you say your name was?' Mr. Rigby repeated it.

'Why,' exclaimed Dr. Whyte in delight, 'you are the man I've been looking for for years!' He then went to his study, and returned carrying a bundle of letters, from which he read such extracts as these: 'I was spending a weekend in Edinburgh some weeks ago, and a fellow commercial [traveler] called Rigby invited me to accompany him to St. George's.

The message of that service changed my life.' 'I am a young man, and the other day I came to hear you preach, at the invitation of a man called Rigby, and in that service I decided to dedicate my life to Christ.'

Dr. Whyte went on to say that twelve of the letters were from young men, of whom four had already entered the [pastoral] ministry. There is, I repeat, ample room for a spice of ingenuity in the Savior's service.

F. W. Boreham, *Boulevards of Paradise* (London: The Epworth Press, 1944), 162-163.

PRACTICED PASSION

The actor, David Garrick, used to say that he would gladly give a hundred guineas to be able to pronounce the word, 'Oh!' as movingly as George Whitefield did. The secret was that all Whitefield's soul was hungry for the salvation of all people.

F. W. Boreham, *A Casket of Cameos*, (London: The Epworth Press, 1924), 51-52.

PRAYER FOR GRACE

Among the records of the Duchess of Gordon is a story of a visit which, with a woman friend, she paid to one of the tenants on her estate. The good old Scottish body who dwelt in the cottage welcomed the two to her modest abode, and was doing her best to entertain them, when a peddler knocked at the door. It was a sultry summer afternoon, and, before opening his pack and displaying his goods, he asked if the cottager could oblige him with a glass of water. She invited him to rest on a chair just inside the door and brought him the drink that he had craved.

'I hope,' she said, as she handed it to him, 'that you know something of the water of life!' His face lit up on the instant, and he surprised the women by exclaiming with fervor that, by the grace of God, he certainly did.

They chatted for awhile, he never suspecting that he was addressing people of high degree; and then, before resuming his pack and his pilgrimage, he asked if he might pray. And this was the prayer that he reverently offered—a prayer that the Duchess never forgot.

'O Lord,' he entreated, 'Give us grace to feel our need of grace!

'O Lord, give us grace to receive your grace!

'O Lord, give us grace to be thankful for the grace we receive!

'O Lord, give us grace to ask for still more grace!

'And give us grace, O Lord, to use the grace that You do give!'

F. W. Boreham, *Boulevards of Paradise* (London: The Epworth Press, 1944), 197-198.

PREACHING WHILE WALKING

There is a famous story in the *Life of Francis d' Assisi.* 'Brother,' Francis said one day to one of the young monks at the Portinuncula, 'let us go down to the town and preach!' The novice, delighted at being signaled out to be the companion of Francis, obeyed with alacrity. They passed through the principal streets; turned down many of the by-ways and alleys; made their way out to some of the suburbs; and at length returned, by a circuitous route, to the monastery gate.

As they approached it, the younger man reminded Francis of his original intention. 'You have forgotten, Father,' he said, 'that we went down to the town *to preach*!'

'My son,' Francis replied, 'we *have* preached. We were preaching while we were walking. We have been seen by many; our behavior has been closely watched; it was thus that we preached our morning sermon. It is of no use, my son, to walk anywhere to preach unless we preach everywhere as we walk!'

F. W. Boreham, *The Crystal Pointers* (London: The Epworth Press, 1925), 19-20.

PRESENCE BEYOND THE SENSES

The Rev. D. M. Ross, of Glasgow, tells a lovely story of Henry Drummond. A woman whose husband was dying came to Drummond late on a Saturday evening, and begged him to come to her house.

'My husband is deein,' sir; he's no able to speak to you, and he's no able to hear you; but oh, *do* come!'

'But if your husband can neither hear nor speak, it's of no use my coming,' the professor reasoned.

'Oh, yes, sir, do come,' the woman pleaded. 'I'd gie anything for him to hae just *a breath o' you* aboot him afore he dees!'

F. W. Boreham, *The Golden Milestone* (London: Charles H. Kelly, 1915), 105.

PRICKING PRIDE

The ancients treasured with a chuckle a story concerning the behavior of Diogenes when that eccentric cynic called upon Plato the philosopher. Plato was, of course, as much the superior of his visitor in ability as in modesty. Finding Plato pleasantly housed, Diogenes stamped upon the luxurious rugs at his feet, and exclaimed, 'Thus do I trample under foot the pride of Plato.'

Plato was too good and too great a person to take much notice at the time, but, shortly afterwards, he returned the visit. Finding Diogenes living in ostentatious poverty, he languidly observed that he could see the pride of Diogenes peeping through the holes in the carpets! It is possible for the poor to be proud of his poverty; for the devout to be proud of his piety; for the prayerful to be proud of his supplications; for the idolater to be proud of his obeisance; for the fasting to be proud of his fasts; for the donor to be proud of his gifts; for the penitent to be proud of his penitence; for the lowly to be proud of his lowliness.

F. W. Boreham, *The Heavenly Octave* (London: The Epworth Press, 1935), 17-18.

PRIVILEGE OF SERVICE

When the Archbishop of York preached at the Coronation of King Edward, he chose as his text the words, '*I am among you as one that serves.*' It is the supreme dignity of the king to be of service to his people. On the crest of the Prince of Wales are inscribed the words '*I serve.*'

When the Prime Minister calls together the members of the Imperial Cabinet, the official summons reads that 'the servants of the King are commanded to meet.' The King—a servant; the Prince—a servant; the Prime Minister—a servant!

The apostolic epistles begin '*Paul, a servant.*' Service is the luxury of life. I was reminded of this the other afternoon. On entering Port Phillip Heads [Melbourne], after a short voyage across the Straits, the steamer on which I happened to be traveling passed a tiny little tug which was heroically pulling a huge but helpless vessel immensely larger than itself. The tug looked ridiculously small, yet we all raised our hats to it. It was made great by the service that it rendered.

I thought of [Thomas] Huxley, who used to say, if he could not be a man, he should like to be a tug.

F. W. Boreham, *The Nest of Spears* (London: The Epworth Press, 1927), 247.

PROVIDENCE, FATE AND DESTINY

I was reading the other day Commander J. W. Gambier's *Links in my Life*, and was amused at the curious inconsistency which led the author first to sneer at Providence and then to bear striking witness to its fidelity. As a young fellow the Commander came to Australia and worked on a way-back station, but he had soon had enough. 'I was to try what fortune could do for a poor man; but I believed in personal endeavor and the recognition of it by Providence. *I did not know Providence.*'

'I did not know Providence!' sneers our young bushman....

But on the very same page that contains the sneer Commander Gambier tells this story. When he was leaving England the old cabman who drove him to the station said to him, 'If you see my son Tom in Australia, ask him to write home and tell us how he's getting on.' 'I explained,' the Commander tells us, 'that Australia was a big country, and asked him if he had any idea of the name of the place his son had gone to. He had not.'

As soon as Commander Gambier arrived at Newcastle, in New South Wales, he met an exceptionally ragged ostler [person that takes care of horses]. As the ostler handed him his horse, Mr. Gambier felt an irresistible though inexplicable conviction that this was the old cabman's son. He felt absolutely sure of it; so he said, 'Your name is Fowles, isn't it?' He looked amazed, and seemed to think that his questioner had some special reason for asking him, and was at first disinclined to answer. But Mr. Gambier pressed him and said, 'Your father, the Cheltenham cab-driver, asked me to look you up.'

He then admitted that he was the man, and Mr. Gambier urged him to write to his father....

And a dozen pages farther on I came upon a still more striking story. Commander Gambier was very unfortunate, very homesick, and very miserable in Australia. He could not make up his mind whether to stay here or return to England. 'At last,' he says, 'I resolved to *leave it to fate.*' The only difference that I can discover between the '*Providence*' whom Commander Gambier could not trust, and the '*fate*' to which he was prepared to submit all his fortunes, is that the former is spelt with a capital letter and the latter with a small one! But to the story.

'On the road where I stood was a small bush grog-shop, and the coaches pulled up here to refresh the ever-thirsty bush traveler. At this spot the up-country and down-country coaches met, and I resolved that I would get into whichever came in first, *leaving it to destiny* to settle.

'Looking down the long, straight track over which the up-country coach must come, I saw a cloud of dust, and well can I remember the curious sensation I had that I was about to turn my back upon England for ever! But in the other direction a belt of scrub hid the view, the road making a sharp turn. And then, almost simultaneously, I heard a loud crack of a whip, and round this corner, at full gallop, came the down coach, pulling up at the shanty not three minutes before the other! I felt like a man reprieved, for my heart was really set on going home; and I jumped up into the down coach with a great sense of relief!' And thus Mr. Gambier returned to England, became a Commander in the British Navy, and one of the most distinguished ornaments of the service. He sneers at '*Providence,*' yet trusts to '*fate,*' and leaves everything to 'destiny'!

F. W. Boreham, *Mushrooms on the Moor* (London: Charles H. Kelly, 1915), 205-208.

PURSUING THE SARATOGA

The problem was an acute one. It all happened at Parattah Junction in Tasmania. I was traveling on the south-bound express. Having enjoyed a good dinner in the refreshment rooms, I discovered that I still had five minutes before the train resumed its journey.

At that very moment, the north-bound express arrived. How better could I spend my spare five minutes than by strolling along the platform on the chance of meeting somebody I knew? And, surely enough, beside one of the central carriages, I caught sight of a young lady, a minister's daughter, at whose home I had often been a guest.

I saw at a glance that she was in dire distress.

'Why, Effie!' I exclaimed. 'What's wrong?'

'Oh, I'm in serious trouble,' she replied. 'I've lost my Saratoga!'

'That's dreadful,' I assented, sympathetically. 'But look, *you* take the front part of the train and *I'll* take the back, and we'll meet again here in a minute or two!'

I hurried along the carriages that I had assigned to myself, looking high and low for the elusive Saratoga. I sincerely hoped that Effie would find it in that portion of the train that I had allotted to her, for I had to confess to myself that I felt seriously handicapped in my own search by the lamentable circumstances that I had no shadow of an idea as to what a Saratoga was!

It sounded as if it might be a special breed of dog, and I poked with my stick among the bags and boxes hoping that, with a frightened yelp, the little beast would dash out at me. But then again, it might be an article of jewelry, and, for that reason, I scrutinized the asphalt of the platform and the floors of the carriages in the frantic hope that I might detect a sudden glitter.

But then, I reminded myself, a Saratoga might conceivably be some mysterious part of a lady's wearing apparel, and it was because of this possibility that, fearing to embarrass her, I had refrained from asking Effie for exact particulars of the missing treasure.

At any rate I searched my half of the train as closely as my limited time would allow, and, on returning to our appointed rendezvous, was delighted to find Effie with her face beaming and the precious Saratoga at her feet. How was I to know that a Saratoga was a species of suitcase? I congratulated her, waved her a hurried goodbye; and caught my own train by the skin of my teeth.

But, to my dying day, I shall never forget the sensation of searching eagerly for a thing without possessing the faintest clue as to what that thing might be.

My experience that day resembles the universal search for happiness. If asked what they were seeking, nine people out of ten—perhaps ninety-nine out of a hundred—would reply that they are seeking happiness. Do they know what they are looking for? Would they recognize it if they saw it? Or is their passionate quest like my own wild pursuit of the Saratoga?

F. W. Boreham, *Dreams at Sunset* (London: The Epworth Press, 1954), 22-24.

Questions

A booklet contains a collection of beautifully-finished reproductions of paintings by G. F. Watts, R.A. On the cover is the
picture entitled, *Whence? Whither?* It represents a baby-soul
issuing from the infinite sea and running towards an unknown
shore. What is the sea from which it emerges? What is the
shore towards which it hastens? The Vast Behind! The Vast
Before! *Whence? Whither?* The card that claims this pretty
booklet for its companion is a New Year motto. It has been
sent me by my friend and neighbor, Canon Gray, the rector of
St. Stephen's. Artistically embellished, the motto reads: *Jesus
answered and said, I know whence I came and I know whither
I go!*

Whence? Whither? asks the Picture. It is a two-fold Note
of Interrogation.

F. W. Boreham, *When the Swans Fly High* (London: The Epworth Press,
1931), 258-259.

Reading the Face

A single face, differing in general outline from all other faces,
is itself a fascinating entertainment; it is capable of such an
infinite variety of aspects. Each expression, as it momentarily
appears and disappears, is composed of a certain admixture
of emotional ingredients. In each such admixture, the compo-
nent parts are mingled in proportions suggested by the immediate circumstances; and that same admixture, in those identical proportions, is never likely to recur.

The face is a kaleidoscope; the variety of the passions that
play upon it is extremely complicated; the same mosaic never
appears a second time.

Herein lies the subtle secret of all superlative art. Take the
drama, for example. A first-class actor can not only mime a

man, he can mimic any man in any mood. Diderot says that he once saw Garrick pass his head between two screens and, in the space of a few seconds, the expression of his countenance ranged from mad joy to moderate joy, from this to tranquility, from tranquility to surprise, from surprise to astonishment, from astonishment to gloom, from gloom to utter dejection, from dejection to fear, from fear to horror, from horror to despair; and then re-ascend from the depths of misery to the wild delight with which he started....

We are endowed with faces so sensitive and pliable that, like the seismograph, they reflect and register the slightest internal tremor or disturbance. There is an appropriate outward expression for each inward agitation; and any attempt to prevent the facial mechanism from fulfilling its proper function is a stultification of natural law and a defiance of one of the primary principles of human existence.

The forces that build up the delicate structure of this masterpiece of organism have their roots firmly struck into a hoary antiquity. History has a hand in the shaping of our faces. Thus we speak of the Grecian face, the Asiatic face, the African face, and many anthropologists declare that there is a distinct difference between the type of face that prevailed before the Christian era and the type that has evolved since.

Under normal conditions, the face, of whatever type, becomes the automatic revelation of the personal character. Mendelssohn, the eminent London photographer, always insisted that no fretful, discontented and ill-natured woman can remain for long really beautiful.

Nobody knows how Art became possessed of the traditional face of Christ; no portrait was ever painted. Its beauty is, however, a recognition of the fact that, as Paul tells us, the glory of God is manifested in the face of Jesus. The conventional descriptions of heaven may not appeal to the average person; but, as Browning makes David exclaim to Saul:

It shall be

A Face like my face that receives thee;
  a Man like to me,

Thou shalt love and be loved by, forever;
  a Hand like this hand

Shall throw open the gates of new life to thee!
  See the Christ stand!

In the invisible world, as in the visible, a human Face represents revelation's final word.

F. W. Boreham, *Dreams at Sunset* (London: The Epworth Press, 1954), 76-77.

REFLECTIVE POWER OF STORIES

In the biblical story told by Nathan, David saw himself as he had never seen himself before. By means of Nathan's clever parable about the one little ewe lamb, and by means of the sudden personal thrust that immediately followed, Nathan introduced David to David; and David was, in consequence, a better man for ever afterwards.

Nathan is one of the pioneers of literature. Wherever statues are erected to the memory of our great novelists a monument should be set up in a conspicuous place to his eternal honor. He was the first to realize the moral potentialities of fiction. He blazed the trail along which our most illustrious dramatists have followed. By means of his touching story of the rich man who stole and slew the pet lamb from the peasant's cottage, Nathan held a mirror up to life and brought a monarch to his knees.

Shakespeare, taking the hint, produced something very like it. He has told us how Hamlet trained the strolling players to reproduce the king's crime before the royal but guilty party; and, when the monarch saw his own evil deeds enacted on the stage before him, the blood left his face, his heart stood still, the lights swam in blurred confusion before his failing sight, and, pleading sudden sickness, he staggered from the theater. What Hamlet did for Claudius, and Nathan did for David, our best novelists and dramatists have been doing for us all ever since.

It is good for a man, sitting with his novel beside a roaring fire on a winter's night, to see his own little hypocrisies reflected in the hypocrisies of Uriah Heep, to see his own petty selfishness reflected in the selfishness of Mr. Dombey, to see his own vacillations and inconstancies exaggerated yet reflected in the oddities of Mr. Micawber, and to see the possibilities of his own redemption reflected in the noble self-sacrifice of Sydney Carton.

I never expect to visit the Hall of Mirrors at Versailles; but whenever I dip into *David Copperfield* or *Bleak House* or *Little Dorrit,* I enjoy a very similar experience.

F. W. Boreham, *The Three Half-Moons* (London: The Epworth Press, 1929), 47-49.

REFRESHING THE MEMORIES AND NAMES

In Sir Walter Scott's *Old Mortality* there is a picture of a man in his blue bonnet and his hodden-gray suit, the good old Cameronian [who] wandered about the moors and valleys of Scotland, seeking out the resting-places of the martyred Covenanters. And, whenever he found one, he diligently scraped the moss and the mildew, the lichen and the fungus from the tombstone with his knife, and then, with his chisel, he made the obliterated name stand clearly forth once more.

F. W. Boreham, *A Witch's Brewing* (London: The Epworth Press, 1932), 35.

Refusal to Give Up

I heard yesterday a good criticism of Sir Luke Fildes' great painting, *The Doctor.* Oddly enough, the critic was a medical man. Everybody knows the picture—the physician bending anxiously over the child; the mother sitting in the background with her face buried in her arms, which rest upon the table; and the father standing gloomily awaiting the doctor's verdict.

'It is a very good picture,' said this medical critic, 'but untrue to life. In the course of a thirty years' practice, I have never seen a mother bow her head and give up while a breath was left in her child's body.' The criticism is sound. Women are gallant hopers. They never give us up, however sick or sinful we may be. And it is largely this refusal to abandon hope that lures us back to life and goodness.

F. W. Boreham, *The Three Half-Moons* (London: The Epworth Press, 1929), 92-93.

Reverence for Life

Has not Turgenieff, the Russian novelist, told us of his first and last taste of the sportsman's triumph? 'When I was only ten years old,' he says, 'my father took me out for a day's shooting. As we tramped across the brown stubble, a golden pheasant rose with a whir from the ground at my feet. Flushed with the excitement that sportsmen know so well I raised my gun and fired. The smoke cleared away, and, to my unbounded delight, the bird fell fluttering a few yards from me. Life was ebbing fast, but the instinct of the mother was stronger than death itself, for, with a feeble flutter of her wings the wounded bird struggled to the nest in which her young brood was huddled. And then, with a look of such pleading and reproach that my heart stood still at the ruin I had wrought, the little brown head toppled over, and only the dead body of the mother shielded her nestlings.

My father congratulated me on the success of my first shot. But as I gazed upon the ruffled heap of flesh and feathers that had a moment before seemed so surpassingly beautiful, I vowed that never again would I destroy a living thing. To my dying day I shall not forget the guilt and shame of that moment. The incident has colored all my writings.'

And so the instinct of the sportsman and the instinct of the naturalist lead us by different paths to the same goal. It is life that we love. Dead things are, after all, only the shadows of living things.

F. W. Boreham, *Home of the Echoes* (London: The Epworth Press, 1921), 81-82.

RISING AGAIN

The Great Fire of London left St Paul's Cathedral a heap of charred and smoldering ruins; and all that was left of it had to be demolished by gunpowder and battering rams. It is said that when Sir Christopher Wren was mapping out the site of the new cathedral, one of his first tasks was to fix the spot that was to represent the center of the dome. Having ascertained that vital point, he asked a workman carefully to mark it. The man glanced about him for some object suited to the purpose, and was attracted by a fragment of a shattered tombstone. He laid the broken splinter on the place that the architect had indicated; and, in doing so, noticed that it bore just one word of its original epitaph. That one word was *Resurgam!*—I shall rise again! Sir Christopher took it as an omen and an augury; and, with new heart, proceeded with the erection of the cathedral of his dreams. In its exquisite symmetry and overwhelming grandeur, it sprang, like a sublime inspiration, from the poetic genius of its brilliant designer; and it has been the pride of every loyal Briton for more than two hundred years.

F. W. Boreham, *The Drums of Dawn* (London: The Epworth Press, 1933), 216-217.

SACREDNESS OF RELATIONSHIPS

I was chatting the other day with a Jewish rabbi. We were exchanging experiences and somehow the conversation drifted round to the marriage service.

'I have heard,' I said, 'that at a Jewish wedding, a wine glass is broken as part of the symbolism of the ceremony. Is that a fact?'

'Of course it is,' he replied. 'We hold aloft a wine glass; let it fall and be shivered to atoms; and then, pointing to the fragments, we exhort the couple to jealously guard the sacred relationship into which they have entered, since once it is broken, it can never be restored.'

F. W. Boreham, *Shadows on the Wall* (London: The Epworth Press, 1922), 200-201.

SACRIFICE

Every Australian has reverently raised his hat at some time or other to Mr. McCubbin's great picture 'The Pioneer.' It holds a place of honor in the Melbourne Art Gallery [National Gallery of Victoria], and copies of it have found their way into every home in the Commonwealth. I speak of it as a picture; but it is really three pictures in one frame.

The first of the set represents the pioneer on pilgrimage. There stands the wagon! The horses are turned out to forage for food among the scrub. The man himself is making a fire under a giant blue gum. And, in the very foreground, sits the sad young wife, her chin resting heavily upon her hand, and her elbow supported by her knee. Her dark eyes are eloquent with unspeakable wistfulness, and her countenance is clouded with something very like regret. Her face is turned from her husband lest he should read the secret of her sorrow, and see that her heart is breaking. She is overwhelmed by the vastness and loneliness of these great Australian solitudes; and her soul, like a homing bird, has flown back to those sweet English fields and fond familiar faces that seem such an eternity away across the wilds and the waters. The pioneer's wife!

The center picture—the largest of the trio—shows us the freshly built home in the depths of the bush. The little house can just be seen through a rift in the forest. In the foreground is the pioneer. He is clearing his selection, and rests for a moment on a tree that he has felled. His axe is beside him, and the chips are all about. Before him stands his wife, with a little child in her arms. The soft baby arm lies caressingly about her shoulders.

In the third picture we can see, through the trees, a town in the distance. In the immediate foreground is the pioneer. He alone figures in all three pictures. He is kneeling this time beside a rude wooden cross. It marks the spot among the trees where he sadly laid *her* to rest.

The pioneer! It is by such sacrifices that these broad Australian lands of ours have been consecrated.

F. W. Boreham, *Mountains in the Mist* (London: Charles H. Kelly, 1914), 75-76.

SCALLOP SHELL OF QUIET

F. W. Boreham quotes Sir Walter Raleigh's lovely lines on the night before his execution:

Give me my scallop shell of quiet,

My staff of faith to walk upon,
My scrip of joy, immortal diet,
My bottle of salvation,
My gown of glory, hope's true gage,
And thus I'll take my pilgrimage.

F. W. Boreham, *The Passing of John Broadbanks* (London: The Epworth Press, 1936), 11.

Secret of Happiness

A few months ago, a Prince and Princess stood at the altar at Westminster Abbey, and the Archbishop of York addressed to the young and happy pair some words of affectionate counsel.

'We wish you happiness,' he said, 'but you will not find happiness by seeking it. You will find it by scattering it. Let each of you make the other happy; and let both of you endeavor to compass the happiness of everybody about you; and, all unsought, happiness shall be your own!'

F. W. Boreham, *The Fiery Crags* (London: The Epworth Press, 1928), 156-157.

Secret of Some Great Lives

We have had two conspicuously successful evangelists— John Wesley and Mr. Spurgeon. The secret of their success is so obvious that he who runs may read.

I turn to my edition of John Wesley's *Journal,* and at the end I find a tribute like this:

"The great purpose of his life was doing good. For this he relinquished all honor and preferment; to this he dedicated all his powers of body and mind; at all times and in all places, in season and out of season, by gentleness, by terror, by argument, by persuasion, by reason, by interest, by every motive and every inducement, he strove, with unwearied assiduity, to turn people from the error of their ways and awaken them to virtue and religion. To the bed of sickness or the couch of prosperity; to the prison or the hospital; to the house of mourning or the house of feasting, wherever there was a friend to serve or a soul to save, he readily repaired. He thought no office too humiliating, no condescension too low, no undertaking too arduous, to reclaim the meanest of God's offspring. *The souls of all people were equally precious in his sight and the value of an immortal creature beyond all estimation.*"

In relation to Mr. Spurgeon, we cannot do better than place ourselves under Mr. W. Y. Fullerton's direction. Mr. Fullerton knew Mr. Spurgeon intimately, and the standard biography of the great preacher is from his pen. Mr. Fullerton devotes a good deal of his space to an inquiry as to the sources of Mr. Spurgeon's power and authority. It is an elusive and difficult question. It is admitted that there is scarcely one respect in which Mr. Spurgeon's powers were really transcendent. He had a fine voice; but others had finer ones. He was eloquent; but others were no less so. He used to say that his success was due, not to his preaching of the gospel, but to the gospel that he preached. Obviously, however, this is beside the mark, for he himself would not have been so uncharitable as to deny that others preached the same gospel and yet met with no corresponding success. The truth probably is that, although he attained to super-excellence at no point, he was really great at many. And, behind this extraordinary combination of remarkable, though not transcendent, powers was an intense conviction, a deadly earnestness, a consuming passion, that made second-rate qualities sublime. The most revealing paragraph in the book occurs towards the end. It is a quotation from Mr. Spurgeon himself. 'Leaving home early in the morning,' he says, 'I went to the vestry and sat there all day long, seeing those who had been brought to Christ by the preaching of the Word. Their stories were so interesting to me that the hours flew by without my noticing how fast they were going then, that I did not notice how the time passed. At seven o'clock we had our prayer meeting. I went in to it. After that came the church meeting. A little before ten I felt faint, and I began to think at what hour I had eaten my dinner, and I then for the first time remembered that *I had not had any!* I never thought of it. I never even felt hungry, because God had made me so glad!'

Mr. Spurgeon lived that he might save people. He thought of nothing else. From his first sermon at Waterbeach to his last at Mentone, the conversion of sinners was the dream of all his days. That master-passion glorified the whole man, and threw a grandeur about the common details of every day. He would cheerfully have thrown away his soul to save the souls of others.

F. W. Boreham, *A Handful of Stars* (London: The Epworth Press, 1922), 96-98.

SECRET PILGRIMAGE

The secret pilgrimage of my soul has been towards Quakerism. I am growingly impressed by the effectiveness of quiet lives. I well remember, years ago, being sent on deputation with half a dozen men representative of different churches. One member of our party was a Quaker of the old school. It was necessary that we should spend the night at the same hotel. The night chanced to be a particularly noisy and restless one. What with people arriving late and others departing early, with the attendant cranking of cars and the barking of dogs, the darkness meted out its boon of sleep with a niggardly hand. I confess with shame that I lay fretting and fuming as one interruption after another disturbed my repose; and the exercise of fretting and fuming is a poor sedative. Most of us were down early, eloquent in the expression of our disgust.

The Quaker was the last to appear. I felt sorry for him. With quietness as an integral factor in his religion I could imagine the tortures that he had endured during the noisy night. When he appeared, however, his good honest face was wreathed in smiles. He had slept like a top and was fresh as a daisy! I saw the secret at a glance. He carried his scallop-shell of quiet with him.

F. W. Boreham, *The Passing of John Broadbanks* (London: The Epworth Press, 1936), 20-21.

SEEING AS THROUGH A TELESCOPE

You never see a thing by looking at it. That is one of the most subtle and profound lessons that life is constantly striving to teach us. There are two ways of seeing everything. You may see it sacerdotally or you may see it sacramentally. You may see it sacerdotally—seeing, that is to say, the thing itself, but seeing nothing through it or beyond it. Or you may see it sacramentally—scarcely seeing the thing itself, but seeing a world of wonder as you look through it. You never see a thing by looking *at* it; you only see a thing by looking *through* it. Let me be more precise.

I hold in my hand a telescope. I draw it out; I close it up; I admire its highly burnished brasses, its beautifully polished lenses. That is one way of admiring a telescope but it is not the best way. The best way is to tuck the telescope under your arm, and set out for some green hill or tall tower. Then put the telescope to your eye. You will not see the telescope; but *you* will see a thousand things that, but for the telescope, you could not have beheld. And you will form a more just estimate of the value of the telescope by looking *through* it than by looking *at* it.

F. W. Boreham, *The Tide Comes In* (London: The Epworth Press, 1958), 63.

SELF-EFFACEMENT

Not long after the missionary William Carey lay dying, and, to his great delight, Alexander Duff came to see him. The young Highlander told the veteran of his admiration and his love. In a whisper that was scarcely audible, the dying man begged his visitor to pray with him.

After he had complied, and taken a sad farewell of the frail old man, he turned to go. On reaching the door he fancied that he heard his name. He turned and saw that Mr. Carey was beckoning him.

'Mr. Duff,' said the dying man, his earnestness imparting a new vigor to his voice, 'Mr. Duff, you have been speaking about Dr. Carey, Dr. Carey, Dr. Carey! When I am gone, say nothing, about Dr. Carey—speak only of Dr. Carey's Savior.'

F. W. Boreham, *A Bunch of Everlastings* (London: The Epworth Press, 1920), 173.

SENSITIVE TO DIVINE CONSTRAINT

I myself have had many experiences of sensing in my life a divine constraint.

I recall one, almost at random. I set off one afternoon on a round of visits. I knew exactly in which direction I was going, and had made a list of the homes at which I intended to call. On my way to the tram I suddenly thought of a home in an entirely different direction. No visit to that home was due, and there was, so far as I knew, no reason why my mind should turn that way. But as I drew nearer to the tramline the impression deepened, and, absurd as it seemed, I decided to abandon my program and make my way to that home. To my astonishment, the door was answered by Dr. Player, a medical practitioner whom I knew well. 'Oh, thank God you've come!' he exclaimed; 'Mr. B-- has just died very unexpectedly on my hands; Mrs. B--, whom I came to see, is ill in bed; there's nobody else in the house, and there's no telephone!'

I recognize that abstract impressions of this kind are treacherous. They should be treated guardedly, especially when they harmonize with one's desires and inclinations.

F. W. Boreham, *In Pastures Green* (London: The Epworth Press, 1954), 27-28.

SERVING AS A SHELTER

Robert Falconer, as lovers of George MacDonald know, is one of the noblest characters in literature. To see him was to trust him. Hugh Sutherland, the young Scottish tutor, met him for the first time on the pavement at Whitechapel. He was startled at the stranger's approach, paused, and, watching him as he passed, gazed admiringly at the striking figure as it vanished in the crowd. Hugh himself stood a full six feet in height, but he felt dwarfed by this gigantic creature. Moreover, there was something about Falconer's massive form, his lithe and upright figure, his open countenance and his lustrous black eyes that inspired confidence, almost affection. Hugh's first impression was of a strong man who knew his own mind and followed his own judgment, a man who was never in a hurry and never for a moment in doubt. And as, with the years, Hugh cultivated Robert's acquaintance, that first impression steadily deepened. Robert Falconer did not domineer or lecture or preach; yet a glance from him carried extraordinary authority. The sound of his voice, the sight of his form, the very atmosphere of his presence strangely affected and influenced all who knew him.

On one occasion he had been particularly helpful. Hugh Sutherland was at his wits' ends. He scarcely knew which way to turn. And, to make confusion worse confounded, he received at that moment a message telling him that his mother was dying in Scotland. He longed to go to her, but such a course was utterly impossible. In his desperation and distress, he instinctively turned to Robert Falconer, not to ask for help or guidance, but just because, by some spiritual magnetism of his own, Falconer naturally drew to himself all such tortured minds and aching hearts.

By the magic that seemed inherent in his towering personality, Falconer quickly unraveled the troublesome tangle, and, as a result, Hugh found himself comfortably ensconced in the Scottish express speeding swiftly to his mother's bedside. And, all through that night in the train, a proclamation of one of the ancient prophets repeated itself continuously in his brain: "A person shall be as an hiding place from the wind and a covert from the tempest; as rivers of water in a dry place; as the shadow of a great rock in a weary land."

With life-like fidelity and precision the words seemed to present Hugh with a full-length portrait of Robert Falconer.

F. W. Boreham, *Boulevards of Paradise* (London: The Epworth Press, 1944), 95-96.

SERVING IN PARTICULARS

Mr. Will Crooks told … about a man, who was always talking about the [British] Empire. He attended every Empire meeting, and joined every Empire league. Every proposal for the expansion or aggrandizement of the Empire he applauded with enthusiasm and vigor. He enlarged upon the glories of Empire at breakfast, dinner, tea, and supper, and on every available opportunity in between. The only drawback about him was that, compared with his imperial visions, his home appeared to him a rather poky place, and he treated his poor little wife with some impatience.

One day he arrived before dinner was ready. The baby had been fretful; the stove had been troublesome; and everything had gone wrong. The imperial brow clouded, and there was thunder and lightning. The poor wife winced and wept beneath the storm; and then, smiling through her tears, she went towards her lord, laid the peevish baby in his arms, and said: "There, now, you mind *your little bit of Empire,* while I dish the potatoes!"

It is a fine thing to dream heroic dreams either of the future Empire or the future Church, but, in order to make those dreams come true, it is just possible that the first step towards it is to look well after the baby.

F. W. Boreham, *Mountains in the Mist* (London: Charles H. Kelly, 1914), 169-170.

SETTLE DISPUTES QUICKLY

'A shopkeeper in a fairly big way came to me just now,' a solicitor told me, 'with a bag fairly stuffed with letters, accounts and other documents. He took them out and piled them up in stacks on his side of my table, preparatory to handing them across to me in their proper order. And then he began his story.

'A dispute arose two or three years ago, it seems, between himself and one of the wholesale houses with which he deals. In the course of the argument he has written and received scores of letters and has been to see the manager of the firm quite a number of times. It took me nearly an hour to examine, even cursorily, all the papers. But that superficial investigation convinced me that, whatever the merits or demerits of his case when the dispute first arose, he is left now without a leg to stand on. Every principle involved in the original contention has been prejudiced or compromised by something that he has written in one or other of the letters, or by some admission that he has made in one or other of the interviews. If only he had come to me when matters first went awry!'

F. W. Boreham, *I Forgot To Say* (London: The Epworth Press, 1939), 112.

SHOWY HUMILITY

There is a type of hypocrisy like [Dicken's] Uriah Heep, who pretends to be meek in order that he may inherit the earth.

'I am the 'umblest person going, Master Copperfield,' explained the oily Uriah, 'the 'umblest person going, let the other be where he may. My mother is likewise a very 'umble person. My father's calling was 'umble. We live in an 'umble abode, Master Copperfield. But we have much to be thankful for, oh, so much to be thankful for!' And so on.

Uriah was everlastingly airing his humility; but in reality he was assuming this nauseous pose in order that he might worm himself into a position of authority and power.

F. W. Boreham, *The Heavenly Octave* (London: The Epworth Press, 1935), 50-51.

SILENCE OF GOD

Silence does not mean inactivity any more than noise means power.

Hume tells us that, immediately before the Battle of Hastings, the English camps were filled with shouting and revelry while an awful silence brooded over the Normans. The silence that reigned along the British battle line before Trafalgar has been the repeated subject of comment. And the most distinguished hero that European Protestantism ever claimed was known by the significant title of "William *the Silent.*"

The quietest room in a Lancashire cotton mill is the engine-room. It is called the "power room." A river steamer on the Thames is brought to her moorings amid the wildest shoutings and the vilest imprecations between the captain and the handful of men that form his crew. A ten-thousand ton liner is berthed at Liverpool docks without the slightest shouting or confusion.

Men make more noise in one hour's work in the harvest field than God's rain and sunshine and heat and cold have made in producing the crops that they harvest. A man makes more noise in clearing the snow off his front path than the sun makes in melting a million tons of it.

God is so wonderfully silent because God is so wonderfully active.

F. W. Boreham, *The Whisper of God and other sermons* (London: Arthur H. Stockwell, 1902), 17-18

SMALL AND LARGE MEETINGS

In the journal of an old Puritan divine were found these words: "Resolved that, when I address a large meeting, I shall remember that God is there, and that will make it small. Resolved that, when I address a small meeting, I shall remember God is there, and that will make it great."

F. W. Boreham, *The Whisper of God and other sermons* (London: Arthur H. Stockwell, 1902), 50.

SOLITUDE OR COMPANY

There was an historic contention between Laurence Sterne and William Hazlitt. I have referred to it as the *historic* contention, although I have no evidence to show that the two men ever argued the point. As a matter of fact, Sterne had the misfortune to die ten years before Hazlitt was born—a circumstance that may have militated against free discussion. But the two were at issue all the same.

Hazlitt felt that you avoid many of the pitfalls of life if you keep yourself to yourself. Why complicate matters by involving yourself in companionships? 'One of the pleasantest things in the world,' he says, 'is going a journey; but *I like to go by myself!'* And, in the course of an elaborate argument, he makes out a very strong case for the solitary pilgrimage. He is not exactly unsociable; but he feels that, very often, the best of companions is something of a nuisance; he gets in your way; and, at any rate, you have to pay him a certain amount of attention and thus limit your perfect freedom by the necessity of harmonizing your behavior with his. 'When I am in the country,' Hazlitt says, 'I wish to vegetate like the country. I am not for criticizing hedgerows and black cattle. Give me the clear blue sky over my head, and the green turf beneath my feet, a winding road before me, a three-hours' march to dinner—and then to thinking!' Here, unfettered by companionship, lies the summit of human felicity!

Laurence Sterne takes the opposite view. 'Let me,' exclaims that entertaining Irishman, 'let me have a companion by my side, were it but to remark how the shadows lengthen as the sun declines!'

I seem to hear Hazlitt's disdainful snort at so vapid a sentiment. The shadows certainly do lengthen along the grass, he would say, and the sight is a very beautiful one; but there is nothing to be said about it. It is one of those entrancing spectacles best enjoyed in silence. Hazlitt feels that, if he has a companion, he is doomed to talk—and to listen. If, in their conversation, he and his companion are of one mind, they might just as well have refrained from utterance: neither has contributed to the knowledge of the other. If, on the contrary, they disagree, an argument is inevitable, and an argument in the course of a ramble, is, in Hazlitt's view, a desolation of abomination. He wants to enjoy the sweetness of the wild rose without commenting upon it. He wants the daisy, set in its coat of gold, to leap to his heart without his being under any obligation to explain the enchantment that it holds for him. He wants to rest, at evening, in the wayside inn, feeling that nobody on the premises knows his name.

It is true that Hazlitt and Sterne are simply wrangling about the conditions under which a country stroll should be enjoyed. But the principle that governs an afternoon's saunter governs also life's larger pilgrimage. The presence of a companion does certainly lessen one's liberty. With a companion by my side, I am under an obligation to be at some pains to jog along comfortably with him. And yet most of us would agree with Sterne that the game is worth the candle. It is better to have a congenial friend by my side as I trudge my way down the dusty lane, even though his presence necessitates my taking some trouble to make my company agreeable to him.

F. W. Boreham, *The Passing of John Broadbanks* (London: The Epworth Press, 1936), 47-50.

SOMETHING TO LIVE UP TO

We have something to live up to.

'If you lose what I've won,' cried the old Prussian, Frederick Wilhelm, to his son, 'I'll laugh at you out of my grave!' And, in the great after days, the old man's eyes seemed to be ever upon the Emperor as he passed from victory to victory.

I like to think of those Scandinavian veterans who, when a young recruit was buckling on his armor for the first time, took him to the halls of his ancestors. As he gazed at one rugged old face after another, some scarred laureate would recite the exploits of those heroic forefathers. And as the youth heard story after story of splendid sacrifice and doughty deed, he would feel his soul glow with intense desire to prove himself worthy of so valiant a descent.

In his *Venetia,* Lord Beaconsfield, too, tells of the old tutor who, having completed the education of a young heir of a noble house, took him, before parting from him, to the picture gallery of the castle. And then, having told his pupil of

the virtues that had distinguished all his line, he implored him
to acquit himself as a worthy son of such worthy sires.

F. W. Boreham, *The Other Side of the Hill* (London: Charles H. Kelly,
1917), 194.

SOUNDS OF TRANQUILITY

On the very last pages of his *Confessions of an Uncommon
Attorney,* Reginald Hine paints an exquisite picture of the idyllic scenes amid which he is laying aside his pen. It is a beautiful estate at Minsden in Hertfordshire, the haunt of every
kind of wild flower and of every species of feathered songster.
Among countless other attractions, it boasts the ruins of an
old fourteenth-century church, the Church of St. Nicholas. So
soothing is the perfume of the flowers and the song of the
birds that Mr. Hine feels that, if all those would visit the place
whose minds and whose hearts are, like the crumbling sanctuary, in ruins, they would find healing and succor in the very
atmosphere that would there unfold them. It would, he says,
be a lovely place to die in.

Peaceful as the place is, Mr. Hine makes it clear that its
tranquility does not consist in its silence. 'The very air,' he
says, 'is tremulous with that faint murmur—call it the under-
song of the earth, the music of the spheres, the sigh of departed
time, or what you will—which only the more find attuned
spirits overhear—

> *Stillness accompanied with sound so soft*
> *Charms more than silence. Meditation here*
> *May think down hours to moments.*

'For those who have ears to hear,' Mr. Hine adds, 'how
peaceful and assuaging it is to listen to the murmur of the
breeze's call, the night wind's lovely vesper hymn!' There are

sounds so soft and satisfying that they sweeten and sanctify the silence.

F. W. Boreham, *Dreams at Sunset* (London: The Epworth Press, 1954), 102-103.

SPEAKING TO THE SIMPLEST

Lord Beaconsfield used to say that, in making after-dinner speeches, he kept his eye on the waiters. If they were unmoved, he knew that he was in the realms of mediocrity. But when they grew excited and waved their napkins, he knew that he was getting home.

F. W. Boreham, *Mushrooms on the Moor* (London: Charles H. Kelly, 1915), 154.

Lord Cockburn, who was for some time Lord Chief Justice of Great Britain, when asked for the secret of his extraordinary success at the bar, replied sagely, 'When I was addressing a jury, I invariably picked out the stupidest-looking fellow of the lot, and addressed myself specially to him—for this good reason: I knew that if I convinced *him* I should be sure to carry all the rest!'

F. W. Boreham, *Mushrooms on the Moor* (London: Charles H. Kelly, 1915), 154-155.

I was reading the other day that Dr. Boyd Carpenter, formerly Bishop of Ripon and now Canon of Westminster, on being asked if he felt nervous when preaching before Queen Victoria, replied, 'I never address the Queen at all. I know there will be present the Queen, the Princes, the household, and the servants down to the scullery-maid, and *I preach to the scullery-maid.*'

F. W. Boreham, *Mushrooms on the Moor* (London: Charles H. Kelly, 1915), 155.

Robert Louis Stevenson knew what he was doing when he discussed every sentence of *Treasure Island* with his schoolboy step-son before giving it its final form. It was by that wise artifice that one of the greatest stories in our language came to be written.

The fact, of course, is that in the soul's sublimest moments it hungers for simplicity.

F. W. Boreham, *Mushrooms on the Moor* (London: Charles H. Kelly, 1915), 156.

SPIRITUALITY MAGNIFICENTLY INCLUSIVE

True spirituality is magnificently inclusive. What is it that Edward Markham sings?

> *He drew a circle that shut me out—*
> *Heretic, rebel, a thing to flout;*
> *But Love and I had the wit to win;*
> *We drew a circle that took Him in.*

Jeff Kilbourne was a young citizen of the United States who happened to be studying art in Paris when the War broke out. He felt the thrill of the stirring movements by which he was encircled, and longed to have some part in them. Yet how could he? He could not return to America to enlist, and, anyhow, the United States had not, at that stage, entered the field of hostilities. So he joined a French battalion and soon became the most popular member of it. Everybody loved Jeff. His comrades would have laid down their lives for him; the people of the village in which the regiment was quartered became wonderfully fond of him; the old priest felt strangely drawn to Jeff, and was always the happier after catching his smile.

But one day the company was sent into action and most of its members fell—including Jeff. Next day the old priest was called upon to bury the dead in the graveyard beside the church and then a serious complication arose. For what about

Jeff? Jeff was a Protestant; how could he be buried with his comrades in Catholic ground? The good old priest was full of grief; but he saw no way out of the difficulty. He did the best he could by arranging that the men should be buried in rows across the graveyard—rows that stretched from wall to wall—and that Jeff should be buried in one of those rows but just outside the wall. He would thus be in the company of his comrades; the wall alone intervening.

The burial took place, and the old priest, weary with his labors, returned to his well-earned rest. But that night the villagers arose in the moonlight and, joined by Jeff's surviving comrades, they pulled down part of the wall and rebuilt it in such a way that it took Jeff in!

It is a great thing when we pull down our narrow walls and make them more inclusive. The religion that takes in Jerusalem, and leaves out Nineveh, the religion that takes in Great Britain and leaves out India or China, is no religion at all. I need a faith that takes in not only Europe and America and Australia, but Asia and Africa and all the countless islands of the Seven Seas.

F. W. Boreham, 'A Prophet's Pilgrimage,' *A Witch's Brewing* (London: The Epworth Press, 1932), 160-162.

SPOILED BY TOO MUCH

A few days ago, I was shown over some very extensive and very beautiful gardens, the gardens of Carnarvon Lodge. The head gardener took me through his shrubberies, his nurseries, his conservatories, and exhibited with pardonable pride his choicest blooms and most wonderful productions.

But, after a while, I came upon a plant that reminded me of one that I remembered seeing in a cottage garden in England many years ago. But, as compared with *that, this* seemed a poor, attenuated, fragile thing. I told the gardener that, if I remembered rightly, I had seen a far finer specimen growing in England under conditions that secured for it much less attention than he was lavishing upon this.

'Ah yes,' he replied, 'I dare say! It likes the English winter—the English cold, the English snow, and especially the English frosts. It is being spoiled here by too much sunshine!' ...

In the year 1886, England was subjected to the rigors of an exceptionally severe winter. During that winter, flocks of seagulls, driven by hunger, made their way up the Thames as far as London Bridge. The crowds passing to and from the city, charmed by the novelty of the spectacle, threw food to the birds. From that time to this, great numbers of seagulls visit London Bridge every winter, finding it more agreeable to throw themselves on the compassion of the public than to earn a precarious living by their own exertions. But they are not like the birds you meet at sea. They have been pauperized, humiliated, spoiled!...

As you motor through the Rocky Mountains, you may be startled by the apparition of a huge bear shambling out of the woods and standing right in the way of your car. But there is no cause for alarm. The bears are protected and they know it. He will simply arrest your progress, and, when you stop, will plant his feet on the running-board of your car and beg for biscuits. It is, of course, very entertaining; yet there is an undercurrent of sadness. For you feel that the shaggy creature before you resembles rather the performing bear that you have seen at a circus than the bears that you associate with your childhood's dreams of adventure. He stands related to the bears of your fancy as the Indians that you now meet in the native settlements of Ontario stand related to the fierce and feathered braves of the Pathfinder stories. Charity Commissioners all the world over would bear witness to this fact that this phase of corruption is by no means confined to seagulls and grizzly bears.

Among my feathered friends, at any rate, it would be easy to produce cases in which the tendency towards deterioration under such conditions is even more marked. The kea, a parrot which inhabits the South Island of New Zealand, was at one time the strictest of vegetarians. A succession of hard winters cut off, for long periods, his usual sources of supply. Driven to desperation, he settled upon the backs of the sheep and entered upon a new career as a bird of prey. Tearing aside the soft wool, he blooded his beak in the wretched animal's kidneys, and, mercilessly tearing them out, passed on to another sheep to repeat the horrible performance. Unfortunately, the expedient, adopted under stress of famine, developed within him a new and ferocious appetite, with the result that, from being a perfectly innocuous bird, he has come to be regarded as the farmer's bitterest foe.

Many such perversions, attributable in the first instance to the austerities of winter, are on record. In *Our Bird Friends,* Mr. C. Kearton observes that long terms of privation spoil the morals of some birds. 'The hard winter of 1895,' he says, 'drove rooks to the sad extremity of killing and devouring starlings; and I am sorry to say that I have since watched them trying to repeat such murderous tactics when the excuse of starvation could no longer be urged in their defense.' They were spoiled, these gentle creatures. From being shy and timid they became ravenous and fierce. They were spoiled by adversity.

F. W. Boreham, *When the Swans Fly High* (London: The Epworth Press, 1931), 56-59 (selected).

SPREADING THE FRAGRANCE

The church's mission is not to buy or to sell, to sow or to reap, to make or to mend. The church exists to create an atmosphere, to precipitate a conquest and to deliver a message.

I was told the other day of a commercial traveler who, visiting a little town in England, spent the morning in calling upon his clients, displaying his samples and soliciting orders. At noon he heard a siren sound. Shortly afterwards, he detected a most delicious perfume. He glanced around, expecting to see some little plot in which wall-flowers and musk, violets and mignonette were luxuriating. Nowhere, however, could he see anything but dusty old warehouses and offices. After a few moments, the fragrance persisting and his mystification increasing, he met a gentleman with whom he had been doing business earlier in the day. To him he unfolded his perplexity.

'I notice,' he said, 'a most delicious perfume; yet nowhere can I see a garden plot.' His friend laughed.

'Did you not hear the siren?' he asked. He confessed that he had; but what had that to do with it?

'Oh,' explained his friend, 'the siren was the signal for the workers at the perfume-factory to leave for lunch, and, in scurrying up and down the street, they distribute the fragrance everywhere!'

To say that the church's supreme mission is to sweeten the world by creating a lovely atmosphere may seem like attributing to her an extremely nebulous and ethereal task. On the contrary, nothing practical was ever achieved except in that perfumed air.

F. W. Boreham, *Ships of Pearl* (London: The Epworth Press, 1935), 77-78.

SPUR OF A GREAT EXPECTATION

'It was the great Lord Shaftesbury that made a new man of me,' exclaimed Edward Maynard at a testimony-meeting in the East End of London. 'And it wasn't by a sermon or a lecture or anything like that,' he went on. 'It was when I came out of prison for the nineteenth time. I sort of took it for granted that I'd have to go to the bad and that I should soon be back for my twentieth term; but Lord Shaftesbury walked up to me and shook hands and said, "Ah, Maynard, we'll make a man of you yet!" I felt that he really expected me to turn out well, and I pulled myself together that very day. That was forty-three years ago ... and I've never seen the inside of a cell since!"

F. W. Boreham, *Shadows on the Wall* (London: The Epworth Press, 1922), 21.

STAND BACK FOR PERSPECTIVE

I remember, many years ago, strolling among the tulip beds in Rosherville Gardens, Gravesend. I thought the flowers wonderful and admired first this blossom and then that one. The whole struck me as a dazzling riot of gorgeous color.

Passing on, I climbed to the top of a cliff, from which, although I could no longer make out the individual flowers, I could survey the general design of the lawn. And, to my astonishment, I discovered that the tulips, in their various hues, made up an elaborate pattern, amid which the words GOD SAVE THE KING flamed in letters of vivid scarlet across the entire bed.

When I was down among the flowers, I failed to notice this patriotic slogan. Like the Jews in their interpretation of the Scriptures, I was tyrannized by detail. I had to withdraw to a distance in order to decipher the general scheme woven into the pattern. The Jews were so close to the ritual of the Temple, so close to the passionate outpourings of the prophets, so close to the human personality of that pale Carpenter of Nazareth, that, seeing each fragment clearly, they missed the meaning of the whole. It is an oft-recurring disaster.

I sometimes think that the dwellers in manses and parsonages and rectories are so near to sacred things that they are in danger of seeing only the things themselves and of forfeiting the vision of the spiritual realities behind those things. They admire the blossoms but miss the motto that blazes across the bed. It is so easy to be tyrannized by detail.

F. W. Boreham, *A Late Lark Singing* (London: The Epworth Press, 1945), 153.

STARRY ELOQUENCE

When Sir Harry Lauder was in Melbourne, he had just sustained the loss of his only son. His boy had fallen at the front. And, with this in mind, Sir Harry told a beautiful and touching story. 'A man came to my dressing-room in a New York theater,' he said, 'and told of an experience that had recently befallen him. In American towns, any household that had given a son to the war was entitled to place a star on the window pane.

'Well, a few nights before he came to see me, this man was walking down a certain avenue in New York accompanied by his wee boy. The lad became very interested in the lighted windows of the houses, and clapped his hands; when he saw the star.

'As they passed house after house, he would say, "Oh, look, Daddy, there's another house that has given a son to the war! And there's another! There's one with two stars! And look! There's a house with no star at all!"

'At last they came to a break in the houses. Through the gap could be seen the evening star shining brightly in the sky. The little fellow caught his breath. "Oh, look, Daddy," he cried, "God must have given *His* Son, for He has got a star in *His* window." '

'He has, indeed!' said Sir Harry Lauder, in repeating the story. But it took the clear eyes of a little child to discover that the ... heavens themselves are telling of the love that gave a Savior to die for the sins of the world.

F. W. Boreham, *A Handful of Stars* (London: The Epworth Press, 1922), 254-255.

STEADFASTNESS AMID DISAPPOINTMENT

The story of the publication of *Jane Eyre* is, as Miss Flora Masson puts it, one of the priceless nuggets of literary history. Poor Charlotte had completed one novel—*The Professor*—and had sent it to London. But not a publisher would look at it. Sent to one firm after another, it was rejected with the most unfailing regularity.

On the very morning on which Charlotte was setting out for Manchester, taking her father to be operated upon, in the hope of removing or mitigating his blindness, the much traveled manuscript came back to her once more. 'My book finds acceptance nowhere,' she says, 'nor do I hear any acknowledgment of merit: the chill of despair begins to invade my heart.'

Yet, all this time, while authoress and publishers were playing this tiresome game of battledore and shuttlecock with the despised manuscript, Charlotte Bronte was working at *Jane Eyre!* Is it any wonder that Mrs. Gaskell likens her to Robert Bruce? 'Failure upon failure,' she says, 'daunted Charlotte no more than it daunted Bruce.

'Think of her home and of the black shadow of remorse lying over one within it, till his very brain was mazed and his gifts and his life were lost; think of her father's sight hanging on a thread; think of her sister's delicate health and dependence on her care; and then admire, as it deserved to be admired, the steady courage which could work away at *Jane Eyre* all the time that the earlier manuscript was plodding its weary round in London!' Such exhibitions of valor do not win Victoria Crosses: yet nothing ever witnessed in a military engagement is more affecting or inspiring.

F. W. Boreham, *When the Swans Fly High* (London: The Epworth Press, 1931), 153-154.

STILL HOPE

In the *Life of George Whitefield* it is recorded that on one occasion he was preaching to a congregation that included Lord Chesterfield.

Whitefield was arguing that a man who has no guide but his own reason is like a blind man being led by a dog. He described the man making his dangerous way along the brink of a precipice, clutching the string that bound him to his dog.

Suddenly, by a telling gesture and a look of horror on his face, Whitefield cleverly suggested that the blind man's foot had slipped. Lord Chesterfield sprang to his feet in alarm. 'Good heavens,' he cried, 'he's gone!'

Whitefield paused and, addressing Lord Chesterfield, exclaimed, 'No, my lord, he is not quite gone; and, since he is not yet lost, he may still be saved!'

F. W. Boreham, *A Late Lark Singing* (London: The Epworth Press, 1945), 172-173.

STORIES OF MAGNANIMITY

As a young fellow, [the historian Thomas] Macaulay was invited to dine with Samuel Rogers, the poet. 'What a delightful house it is!' he says, in his descriptive letter to his sister. And, in telling her of the innumerable beauties of the place, he selects for special mention a fine mahogany table on which stood an antique vase.

And to that table hangs a tale. For he goes on to say that, some little time previously, Sir Francis Legatt Chantrey, R.A., the eminent sculptor, had been the guest of Rogers. Sir Francis had a good look at the mahogany table on which the vase was standing, and then asked by whom the table was made. 'It was made by a common carpenter,' said Rogers. 'Do you remember the making of it?' asked Sir Francis. 'Certainly,' replied Rogers, in some surprise, 'I was in the room while it was finished with the chisel, and gave the workman directions about placing it.' 'Yes,' said Sir Francis, '*I was the carpenter!* I remember the room well, and all the circumstances.'

Macaulay remarks to his sister that the story is honorable, both to the talent which raised Chantrey from obscurity to eminence, and to the magnanimity which kept him from being ashamed of what he had been....

It is almost as good as the story that Andrew Fuller tells of William Carey. Carey was attending a reception given at Calcutta to the Governor-General of India. His lordship was struck by the missionary's appearance. 'Who is that gentleman?' he inquired. 'Oh,' drawled one of the attendants, 'that is Dr. Carey. He is Professor of Sanskrit, Bengali, and Maratha, in the College of Fort William. He was once a shoemaker.' 'Excuse me, my lord,' interposed Carey, who had overheard the conversation, '*I was only a cobbler!*'

F. W. Boreham, *The Other Side of the Hill* (London: Charles H. Kelly, 1917), 98-99.

STORING THE MIND WITH RICHES

I have just been reading the biography of Miss Annie J. Clough, the famous Principal of Newnham College, and one of the pioneers of our modern educational system. It is a beautiful and noble life. But I was impressed by the insistence with which Miss Clough urged upon the young ladies under her charge the importance of storing the mind in youth with beautiful memories. The average person can, she insisted, furnish himself with experiences that, costing neither time nor money, will nevertheless yield infinite satisfaction when seen in the retrospect of the years.

Miss Clough reminds me of Henry Ryecroft. Lovers of George Gissing will remember that when Ryecroft realized, in the days of age and infirmity, the exquisite pleasure afforded him by the recollection of youthful strolls in the fir copse, in the primrosed woods, in the poppy-sprinkled cornfields, and in the meadows full of buttercups, he was filled with remorse at the reflection that he had spent so much of his time amid conditions that provided him with no such pleasing retrospect.

I remember once chatting with a man who had lost his sight in a colliery explosion. He was telling me that, every day of his life, there rushes back to mind some little thing that caught his eye in the old days. The squirrel that he saw in the beech-trees; the daisy-chain that his sister made as they sat together in the summer fields; the column of spray that dashed skywards when the waves broke against the cliffs; the swallow that he watched as it skimmed the surface of the millpond and returned with a captured fly to the nest under the caves; the bare branches in the forest bowed down with their heavy freight of snow; the glow of sunset; the gray of dawn; the glimmer of twilight; the merry twinkle of a boy's eye; the soft crimson of a girl's blush—he could never express his gratitude that his mind was stored with thousands of such images.

F. W. Boreham, *The Uttermost Star* (London: The Epworth Press, 1919), 95-96.

STRENGTHENED BY SUFFERING

In my college days I used to go down to a quaint little English village for the weekend in order to conduct services in the village chapel on Sunday. I was always entertained by a little old lady whose face haunts me still. It was so very human, and so very wise, and withal so very beautiful; and the white ringlets on either side completed a perfect picture. She dwelt in a modest little cottage on top of the hill. It was a queer, tumble-down old place with crooked rafters and crazy lattice windows. Roses and honeysuckle clambered all over the porch, straggled along the walls, and even crept under the eaves into the cottage itself.

The thing that impressed me when I first went was the extraordinary number of old Bessie's visitors. On Saturday nights they came one after another, young men and sedate matrons, old men and tripping maidens, and each desired to see her alone.

She was very old; she had known hunger and poverty; the deeply furrowed brow told of long and bitter trouble. She was a great sufferer, too, and daily wrestled with her pitiless disease. But, like the sturdier of the poplars by my gate, she had gathered into herself the force of all the cruel winds that had beaten so savagely upon her. And the result was that her own character had become so strong and so upright and so beautiful that she was recognized as the high-priestess of that English countryside, and every man and maiden who needed counsel or succor made a beaten path to her open door.

F. W. Boreham, *Mushrooms on the Moor* (London: Charles H. Kelly, 1915), 136-137.

Success Despite Shyness

Joseph Addison achieved so much in [British] political life in defiance of the heaviest possible handicap. He was afflicted by the most excruciating bashfulness. Like Shelley, he could never enter a drawing-room without falling over a chair nor cross a lawn in company without tripping over his own feet. His agonizing timidity was the bane of his life. He loved good company and lively discussion; nothing pleased him better than to stretch out his legs and talk; he was a very prince among coffee-house men. In his day the coffee-houses were in the hey-day of their illustrious career. A galaxy of the most eminent statesman and scholars of his time would sit with him until the dawn came stealing through the windows; he would hold them entranced hour after hour; and when at last the company broke up, it broke up with a sigh. Yet if, at any moment, the door opened and a strange face appeared, the sparkling conversationalist shrank into instant silence; shyness paralyzed his tongue; and his obvious discomfort threw a pitiable awkwardness over his entire behavior.

He became a Member of Parliament, and even a Cabinet Minister; yet he was too nervous to address the House. If he could have talked at Westminster as he talked at Button's Coffee-house, he would have bequeathed to posterity a reputation that would have eclipsed the shining records of Pitt, Fox, Sheridan, and Burke. But it was impossible. Just once he rose in his place; stammered out one or two broken and incoherent sentences; blushed, coughed, apologized, sat down; and never ventured on a second attempt. Yet he held several important portfolios. In that respect his case is quite unique.

Macaulay attributes his political ascendancy to two causes. In days in which parliamentary speeches were not reported, and in which the orator could hope to influence none but those who actually heard his voice, a Prime Minister was glad to have in his Cabinet a man who, by the skillful use of his pen, could lay the case for the Government before the country in pamphlets as cogent and convincing as those written by Addison. And any Prime Minister in any age would be glad to have in his Cabinet a man in whose unimpeachable integrity and untarnished honor the English people had such implicit confidence as they had in Addison. For, in spite of his defects as a speaker, Addison was the most trusted statesman of his time.

F. W. Boreham, *A Temple of Topaz* (London: The Epworth Press, 1928), 202-203.

TELLING THE STORY OF YOUR LIFE

For, in actual fact, each of us is sitting by the wayside reading aloud. Every day of his life since the day of his birth he has sat there reading a short installment of a great and thrilling story. Every wayfarer who has passed along the dusty road has been compelled to listen to a little bit of it; everybody who, by any chance, has come within earshot, has caught a sentence or two. And those who, like the members of our holiday party, attend us day after day in our pilgrimage through life, know the story intimately. I am thinking, of course, of that spacious romance—the romance of our own lives. *We send our years as a tale that is told.* It is a marvelous and masterly narrative. Nobody can listen to it all without being moved, sometimes to bursts of laughter and sometimes to floods of tears. It contains all the ingredients that make up a literary classic—humor, pathos, weakness, strength, sin, goodness, travel, adventure, coincidence, suffering, joy, struggle, mortification, triumph, love, hate—*everything!* It is the romance of reality; and fiction only approximates to sublimity when, catching that atmosphere, it becomes strangely and convincingly life-like.

So here I sit by the side of the road telling my story— *spending my years as a tale that is told!* Passers-by catch a stray sentence or two; those who sit beside me see the plot gradually unfold. Sometimes it pleases: sometimes it vexes: sometimes the listeners smile: sometimes they turn away their faces or brush from their eyes a tear. And, all the while, they are wondering how the story will end. And that is exactly what I wonder. For I notice, in reading aloud, that nobody is quite as engrossed as the reader. The listeners have distractions— one drops a stitch; another has to thread a needle—but, in the nature of things, the reader is compelled to mark every word and to see every point.

And so, as I sit reading aloud by the side of life's road— *spending my years as a tale that is told*—I catch myself trembling with subdued excitement. How will it all end? As the pages under my left thumb increase in bulk, and as the pages under my right thumb grow fewer and fewer, the question becomes increasingly acute. How will it end? *How will it end?* … Some stories, to be true to themselves, *must* end sadly. And I wonder if that will be true of the tale that I am telling—the romance that I am writing in breaths and heart-throbs and drops of red, red blood. I do not know. It is too soon to say. I only know that, notwithstanding all that the novelists may say, that living volume will be a failure, and worse than a failure, unless it culminates in a joyous and triumphant close.

F. W. Boreham, *A Tuft of Comet's Hair* (London: The Epworth Press, 1926), 271-272.

TETELESTAI!

It was a *farmer's* word. When, into his herd, there was born an animal so beautiful and shapely that it seemed absolutely destitute of faults and defects, the farmer gazed upon the creature with proud, delighted eyes. 'Tetelestai!' he said, 'tetelestai!'

It was an *artist's* word. When the painter or the sculptor had put the last finishing touches to the vivid landscape or the marble bust, he would stand back a few feet to admire his masterpiece, and, seeing in it nothing that called for correction or improvement, would murmur fondly, 'Tetelestai!' 'Tetelestai!'

It was a *priestly* word. When some devout worshipper, overflowing with gratitude for mercies shown him, brought to the temple a lamb without spot or blemish, the pride of the whole flock, the priest, more accustomed to seeing the blind and defective animals led to the altar, would look admiringly upon the pretty creature. 'Tetelestai!' he would say, 'Tetelestai!'

And when, in the fullness of time, the Lamb of God offered Himself on the altar of the ages, He rejoiced with a joy so triumphant that it bore down all His anguish before it. The sacrifice was stainless, perfect, finished! 'He cried with a loud voice Tetelestai! and gave up the ghost.'

This divine self-satisfaction appears only twice, once in each Testament. When He completed the work of Creation, He looked upon it and said that it was very good, when He completed the Work of Redemption He cried with a loud voice *Tetelestai!* It means exactly the same thing.

F. W. Boreham, *A Handful of Stars* (London: The Epworth Press, 1922), 102-103.

THE ADVENTURE OF FOLLOWING JESUS

The one factor that the lives of all the Church's heroes possess in common—whether they were martyrs, missionaries, reformers or what not—is the element of daring. At some stage in his career, each person hazarded everything; in many cases these people lived lives of continual risk.

We have all been stirred by the story of Dr. Albert Schweitzer, the brilliant young student who, before he was thirty, had made himself Professor at Strasburg, organist to the Paris Bach Society and the author of some famous books. Then, all at once, he decides to give a number of organ recitals, to use the proceeds in taking a medical course, and to become a missionary. He relinquishes his chair at the university, turns his back on Europe, and takes up work as a medical missionary among the natives of Equatorial Africa. And, in the closing sentences of his book, he tells us how it all came about.

He heard, he says, the call of Christ, challenging him to a superb adventure. The call was as vivid and as real as when, beside Gennesaret, the fishers heard the Savior's 'Follow Me!' The brilliant young musician, now a brilliant young physician, followed the beckoning Finger, and, as a consequence, life became lustrous.

Christ calls every person to a superb adventure; and, when people realize it, that quality in them that responds to the hazard of crime will vibrate in response to a still more thrilling challenge, and they will flock to the Cross like doves to their windows.

F. W. Boreham, *The Ivory Spires* (London: The Epworth Press, 1934), 252-253.

THE ART OF STILLNESS

In instructing us as to the best way of catching bream, [Izaak Walton] says that, at about four o'clock in the afternoon, we must repair to the bank of the stream, and, as soon as we come to the waterside, must cast in one-half of our ground-bait and stand off. 'Then, while the fish are gathering together, for they will most certainly come for their supper, *you may take a pipe of tobacco;* and then, in with your three rods!'

Now why that *pipe of tobacco?* There is a certain interval to be filled in; a period in which it would be disastrous to say anything or do anything.... Now half the art of life lies in being able on occasions to do nothing—and to do it easily.

Newman found this grace so difficult of acquirement that he gave it up as a bad job. 'He filled up,' says Mozley, 'his whole time, taxed his whole strength, and occupied his whole future. He reduced retrospection to a very narrow compass, to a few faces, to flowers on a bank or a wall, to a fragrance or a sound. He never took solitary walks if he could help it. He would not be alone and left to his own thoughts when he was neither studying nor writing nor praying.'

Darwin was as bad. His one defect was an utter incapacity for idleness. 'I wish,' writes his wife, 'I wish he could *smoke a pipe* or ruminate like a cow.' There is such a thing as a genius for repose. It is a great thing for a man to be the captain of his soul; to have every faculty under command; and to be able to drop anchor and be perfectly at ease when nothing is to be gained by continued activity. Here, then, is the problem—how to be still?

I shall never be satisfied until I can possess my soul in perfect poise and restfulness; until I can do nothing, and do it well, and do it easily ...

F. W. Boreham, *The Other Side of the Hill* (London: Charles H. Kelly, 1917), 248-251.

THE BLESSING OF HUMILITY

When, some years ago, the Government irrigators were at work in Southern India, they were troubled by one man, a native farmer, who resisted their efforts on the ground that his land was quite hopeless.

'It is hard, dry, incapable of verdure,' he said, 'is it possible that it can be watered?'

'Yes,' replied the officials, 'it can be made rich and fruitful *if it lies low enough!'*

There stands the crucial test! The one who walks open-eyed through a wheat field, notices that it is the drooping ears that are heavy with grain; the stems that hold their heads erect are the empty and worthless ones.

It is always so. Our choicest blessings invariably come to us by descending; our richest benefits come by going downward. We stoop to conquer. The farmer bows his face toward the earth both to sow the seed and to reap the harvest; the miner goes below for the precious things of the earth; the loveliest streams flow along the lowliest valleys; the sweetest flowers flourish in the shadiest dells.

> The saint that wears Heaven's brightest crown
> In deepest adoration bends;
> The weight of glory bows him down,
> The most when most his soul ascends;
> Nearest the throne itself must be
> The footstool of humility.

Marcus Quintilanus remarks of his contemporaries that they would doubtless have become most excellent scholars had they not been so fully persuaded of their own scholarship. 'He is the wisest man,' says Plato, 'who knows himself to be very ill qualified for the attainment of wisdom.'

When Dr. Andrew Bonar was visiting Mr. Moody at Northfield, the two were walking together one morning when they met a band of students. 'We've been holding an all-night prayer meeting,' exclaimed one of their number; 'see how our faces shine!'

Turning to him with a quiet smile and a wise shake of the head, Dr. Bonar quoted a text. 'Moses knew *not* that the skin of his face did shine,' he said; and the students understood.

F. W. Boreham, *The Heavenly Octave* (London: The Epworth Press, 1935), 20-21.

THE CHALLENGE OF CLOSED DOORS

I was minister at Mosgiel [New Zealand] but I had aspirations to serve in a city church. In aspiring to a city church,

I was thinking, of course, of the four New Zealand cities—
Auckland, Wellington, Christchurch and Dunedin. In these I
was well known, while, so far as I was aware, my name had
never been heard in any city outside the Dominion. During
the later stages of my Mosgiel ministry, the pulpits of Wellington, Christchurch and Dunedin each in turn fell vacant.
In each case my name was introduced, discussed, submit-
ted—and rejected. I felt no resentment. How could I? After
all, I was merely the minister of a small country church, and
it had become the established practice of the city churches to
send to England for their ministers. I recognized at the time
that a call to myself would have been a daring and hazardous
experiment. Viewing the experience in the mellow perspective of the years, I am convinced that these churches were
rightly guided in the decisions that they then reached. And I
am no less certain that the discipline of disappointment did
me a world of good. At the same time, the ordeal was a little
embarrassing and disturbing, for my people at Mosgiel soon
heard of the movements in the larger churches and, by ques-
tioning me, made my position extremely uncomfortable.

During the Wellington vacancy, I actually received a telegram from the Church Secretary informing me that a unani-
mous call was certain, telling me of the date of the meeting
and asking me to be prepared with a prompt reply. I was at
the post office when it opened on the morning following that
meeting in Wellington. The fateful telegram arrived a few
minutes later. It was to tell me that another issue had been
unexpectedly introduced, and that, whatever happened, it was
now extremely unlikely that I should be invited.

The city church in which we ourselves were most interested
was, of course, the church in the city nearest us—the church
at Hanover Street, Dunedin. During a prolonged interregnum,
my name was three times introduced; and the speeches made
in the city overnight were discussed on the street corners of

Mosgiel next day. At last a vote was taken—by ballot and by post—as to whether the church should call me or send to England. We were, at the hour at which the votes were counted, spending our annual holiday at the Nuggets, a romantic little place on the wild Otago coast. The hour drew near that was to decide our destiny, for we both felt that, if Dunedin rejected me, we must either spend all our days in Mosgiel or else leave the land that we had learned to love.

On the morning following the closing of the ballot, I walked four miles along the beach to the nearest post office. The telegram was there! With a trembling hand I tore it open. On a poll of some hundreds, the voting was almost equal—so nearly equal as to compel the officers to drop both alternatives for the time being. We behaved, I blush to confess, like a pair of silly children. I began to feel like a much-handled and badly-soiled remnant on a bargain-counter. We spent the remainder of that holiday strolling amid scenes of the most bewitching loveliness with tears in our eyes and fierce rebellion in our hearts.

Yet, looking back upon it all, nothing on the horizon of the past stands out more clearly than the fact that, had our dream been realized, and our desire granted, we should have missed the best all along the line. We can see now, as plainly as if it were written across the skies, that the opening of any of the doors that were then slammed in our faces would have spoiled everything. It would have represented, for us, an irretrievable disaster. Later on, each of the three churches that unconsciously humiliated me in those days did me the honor of approaching me concerning its pulpit. They were delightful people and I could have been perfectly happy with either of the three; but, by that time, I had found my life work; and a return to New Zealand was out of the question.

F. W. Boreham, *My Pilgrimage* (London: The Epworth Press, 1940), 174-176.

THE DELICIOUS HUNGER

My book, which happened to be a *Life of Abraham Lincoln,* was still upon my knee. I picked it up and read again the story of the profound spiritual experience that marked the last days of the great President's life. As blind people long for light, Lincoln groped after a fuller, sweeter, more satisfying faith. He tried many of the gates by which other pilgrims had entered the city; but, wistfully as he had approached them, he was compelled to turn away with a heavy heart and a sad shake of the head. Then, on the page lying open on my knee, I come upon this: 'I have been reading the Beatitudes,' Lincoln says to a friend, 'and can at least claim *one* of the blessings therein unfolded. It is the blessing pronounced upon those who *hunger and thirst after righteousness.'*

F. W. Boreham, *The Heavenly Octave* (London: The Epworth Press, 1935), 78-79.

THE DIVINE COMPANION

Sir Ernest Shackleton was speaking at a banquet given in London in his honor, and was describing the thrilling adventures of the Rescue Expedition, as, after the sinking of the *Endurance,* they made their way in an open boat—a twenty-foot whaler—over eight hundred miles of storm swept sea, and then crawled and clambered over the dizzy peaks and slippery glaciers of South Georgia—the gate of the Antarctic—in order that they might obtain succor for their twenty comrades marooned on Elephant Island. As Sir Ernest told his story, the listeners held their breath. That lonely voyage on a polar sea, and that intrepid climb over uncharted ranges, was the wildest adventure of the speaker's life.

Mr. Edward Marston, the well-known artist, accompanied Shackleton to the South, and was one of the men who owed their lives to that astounding journey. Mr. Marston declares that his leader's voyage in the open boat is one of the most magnificent feats of courage ever performed, while his climb across the frozen heights of South Georgia, never before accomplished by man, was one of splendid, almost incredible endurance. 'His repeated attempts to reach and rescue us,' Mr. Marston adds, 'and his ultimate success in the face of apparently insuperable difficulties, proved the indomitable perseverance of his mind.'

At that London banquet Shackleton said nothing of these historic heroisms of his; but he said something no less notable. 'You could have heard a pin drop,' says one who was present, 'when Sir Ernest spoke of his consciousness of a Divine Companion in his journeyings.'

Happily, the explorer afterwards wrote a book, and, in the stirring pages of *South,* he has left the story on imperishable record. 'When,' he says, 'I look back upon those days, with all their anxiety and peril, I cannot doubt that our party was divinely guided, both over the snowfields and across the storm swept sea. I know that, during that long and racking march of thirty-six hours over the unnamed mountains and glaciers of South Georgia, it seemed to me, very often, that we were, not *three,* but *four!*

'I said nothing to my companions on the point, but afterwards Worsley said to me: "Boss, I had a curious feeling on the march that there was *Another Person* with us." Crean confessed to the same idea.'

One feels the dearth of human words, the roughness of mortal speech in trying to tell of things intangible …

F. W. Boreham then goes on to compare this with the experience of Shadrach, Meshach, Abednego and the recognition that there was Another with them in the fiery furnace.

F. W. Boreham, *A Casket of Cameos,* (London: The Epworth Press, 1924), 32-34.

THE DIVINE LINK

I remember a farmhouse in New Zealand at which I was often a guest. By way of grace before meat, the farmer at one end of the table bowed his head and repeated Dr. Maltbie D. Babcock's familiar lines:

> Back of the loaf is the snowy flour,
> And back of the flour is the mill,
> And back of the mill is the wheat and the shower,
> And the sun, and the Father's will.

Whereupon his wife, from the other end of the table, would respond:

> For mill and flour,
> And sun and shower,
> We give Thee thanks, O Lord. *Amen.*

The farmer is the last person on the face of the earth who can afford to leave God out of his calculations.

F. W. Boreham, *I Forgot To Say* (London: The Epworth Press, 1939), 175-176.
(This was the grace that F. W. Boreham prayed regularly before meals.)

THE DOWNSIDE OF CONTROVERSY

F. W. Boreham writes about finding himself in controversy with these personal words:

You know how, when one dominating idea holds all your mind, everything that you see and hear seems to stand related to it. So was it with me.

I was reading at the time an old classic by Isaac Barrow, Newton's famous preceptor. I had scarcely opened the book that morning before the old professor began on this very theme. "Avoid controversy at any cost," he says. "The truth contended for is not worth the passion expended upon it. The benefits of the victory do not atone for the prejudices aroused in the combat. Goodness and virtue may often consist with ignorance and error, seldom with strife and discord."

With a heavy heart, I laid the volume aside; and took down Richard Baxter, who first taught me how to be a minister. But—would you believe it?—I had not got through half a dozen pages before my old master burst out upon me. "Another fatal hindrance," he said, "to a heavenly walk and conversation is our too frequent disputes. A disputatious spirit is a sure sign of an unsanctified spirit. They are usually men least acquainted with the heavenly life who are the most violent disputers about the circumstantiality of religion. Yea, though you were sure that your opinions were true, yet when the chiefest of your zeal is turned to these things, the life of grace soon decays within. The least controverted truths are usually the most weighty and of most necessary and frequent use to our souls." I felt that my old master had but rubbed brine into my smarting wounds, and I returned him sadly to the shelf.

That very afternoon I had occasion to dip into John Wesley's *Journal,* and under date October 9, 1741, I stumbled upon this: "I found Mr. Humphreys with Mr. Simpson. They immediately fell upon their favorite subject; on which, when we had disputed two hours, and were just where we were at first, I begged we might exchange controversy for prayer. We did so, and then parted in much love, about two in the morning."

In sheer despair I returned Wesley to his place, and forsook the theologians altogether. I picked up a volume of Darwin which, newly purchased, lay uncut on the desk. But, to my amazement, he was harping on the same old theme. "I rejoice," he said, "that I have avoided controversies, and this I owe to Lyell, who many years ago, in reference to my geological works, strongly advised me never to get entangled in a controversy, as it rarely did any good, and caused a miserable loss of time and temper." I put the volume back on the desk; and, fancying that relief would surely come with fiction, I slipped a novel into my pocket and, after tea, went out into the fields. It happened to be Mark Rutherford's *Revolution in Tanner's Lane*. Imagine my consternation on finding one of the characters, Zachariah Coleman, talking on this very subject! No controversy can be of any use, he says. "It leads to everlasting debate, and it is not genuine debate, for nobody really ranges himself alongside his enemy's strongest points! It encourages all sorts of sophistry, becomes mere maneuvering, and saps people's faith in the truth."

I went back to the house. How I spent the rest of the evening does not matter much to you or anybody else; but from that day to this I have never entangled myself in controversy again.

F. W. Boreham, *The Uttermost Star* (London: The Epworth Press, 1919), 156-158.

THE GOODNESS IN GOOD INTENTIONS

We often sneer at good intentions, forgetting that God is content to judge the intention while people judge only the resultant deed. The intention is by far the best criterion of the character.

Thomas à Kempis found infinite comfort in the thought that 'Humans consider the deeds while God weighs the intentions.' Edith Cavell marked that sentence in her copy of the *Imitation* on that bleak October morning when she walked out to be shot.

As some of our noblest rivers run sparklingly clean from their sources, only to be sullied and defiled further down, so a purpose may rise pure and sweet from the heart, and yet be marred by a forgetful mind or a clumsy hand. We may find consolation as well as condemnation in the declaration that the Lord sees not as humans see, for humans looks at the outward appearance, but the Lord looks on *the heart.*

F. W. Boreham, *The Heavenly Octave* (London: The Epworth Press, 1935), 113-114.

THE NIGHT COMES

According to custom, the novelist, Sir Walter Scott had a motto engraved upon his sundial, a motto of his own selection. It consists of three Greek words: 'The Night Comes.'

Scott was not morbid; he was a great human. But in the sunshine of life's morning he solemnly reminded himself that high noon is not a fixture. The brightest day wears away to evening at last. He horrified his bride-elect by arranging, before his marriage, for a place of burial. 'What an idea of yours,' she says in a letter written a few days before the wedding, 'what an idea of yours was that to mention where you wish to have your bones laid! If you were married I should think you were tired of me. A very pretty compliment before marriage! I hope sincerely that I shall not live to see that day. If you always have those cheerful thoughts, how very pleasant you must be!' Poor, distressed bride!

But she soon found that her apprehensions were unfounded. Her lover was not as gloomy as she feared. He was reminding himself that the sunshine does not last for ever, it is true; but, just because the sunshine does not last for ever, he was vowing that he would make the most of it. 'The Night Comes' he wrote upon the sundial on the lawn. 'The Night Comes' therefore revel in the daylight while it lasts! 'I must work the works of Him that sent me while it is day; the night comes when no one can work.'

The inscription on Sir Walter Scott's sundial must have been suggested by the inscription on Dr. Johnson's watch. Scott was a great admirer of Johnson. In some respects there is a strong resemblance between them…. Scott had read Boswell's account of the glimpse that he once caught of the old doctor's watch. As Dr. Johnson drew it from his pocket one day, Boswell noticed that on its face it bore a Greek inscription. The inscription consisted of the three Greek words, 'The Night Comes.'

It reminded the doctor, whenever he consulted his watch, that the daylight does not last forever. 'Work while it is day,' the watch seems to say, 'for the night comes when no one can work.'

F. W. Boreham, *A Bunch of Everlastings* (London: The Epworth Press, 1920), 76-78.

THE ODDITY OF MEMORY

In ninety-nine cases out of a hundred it is the big things that elude our minds, while a conglomeration of trifles remain.

In one of his soliloquies *The Poet at the Breakfast Table* [Oliver Wendell Holmes] tells how, an old man now, he distinctly remembers being cheated out of sixpence by an old strawberry-woman at an English fair fifty years ago. Yet a hundred matters of really first class importance have failed, during that half-century, to make any lasting impression on his memory! 'What an odd thing memory is,' he exclaims, in telling the tale, 'to have kept such a triviality and to have lost so much that was invaluable!' …

A man remembers the first fish that he ever caught long after many more vital events in his career have faded from his mind. With perfect clearness he will recall to his dying day the shining, scaly trout, flapping in its death-flurry on the green banks under the willows. The winning hit that a man once made for the school eleven lingers in his thought long after the twists and turns of his later history have passed into the obscurity of forgetfulness. The thrill of that glorious moment will rush back upon him in his last illness. These are the happenings that haunt the memory.

F. W. Boreham, *The Uttermost Star* (London: The Epworth Press, 1919), 185-186.

THE OTHER SIDE OF THE FOOTLIGHTS

I shared a train journey with a man who was a well-known actor, whose grotesque appearances in light comedy kept his crowded audiences in ceaseless convulsions of laughter. Now, if there was a world of which I knew absolutely nothing at all—a *terra incognita*—a realm that I had never invaded—it was the stage. Here, to my delight, I found an opportunity of exploring it. I smiled at my short-sighted stupidity in supposing when I bought my ticket, that I was merely on my way to Adelaide.

'The thing that one has to remember,' he said, in one of the confidential outbursts with which he favored me during that long and delightful evening, 'the thing that one has to remember, and the thing that an actor is most tempted to forget, is that reality lies on the other side of the footlights.' He went on to explain that the actor, in playing his part, is hedged in by four sharply-defined boundaries. *Behind* him is the scenery at the back of the stage, *on either side* are the wings, and *in front* of him is the glare of the footlights.

'I dare say,' he continued, 'that some actors and actresses can see the public to whom they are playing; but, unfortunately, my eyes are not as I could wish'—he wiped his pince-nez as he spoke—'and to me the theater beyond the footlights, is a, huge black vault. The footlights dazzle me. I sometimes fancy that I am apt to ignore the thousands of eyes that are fixed so intently on me; I am prone to forget the hearts that, out there in the void, are beating in sympathy with the part that I am endeavoring to portray. And, mark my words, as surely as an actor forgets the invisible multitude on the other side of the footlights, he will lose touch with reality.... But as long as he remains conscious—or even subconscious—of the real men and real women on the other side of the footlights, it will help to correct such tendency. He will feel that he is among realities and not among shadows; he will talk as real men talk and will act as real men act. And only thus can success be achieved in our profession or in any other.'

If it be true that the actor tends to become artificial, it is no less true that the minister tends to become cloistral, the poet fanciful, the philosopher hypothetical, the scientist chimerical [imaginary], the schoolmaster theoretical, and the artist technical. Breaking on the shore of every life there is an undertow that threatens to sweep a man off his feet and carry him away from the practical, the actual, the real. He who can hold his own against that insidious tendency is not likely to fall far short of high success....

It is so easy to lose our way among the stars. The pulpit is very much like the stage after all. We are apt to think of it as a thing of three dimensions. We forget the realities. We lose touch with real men and real women and real life. It was said of a certain eminent divine that he was invisible all the week and incomprehensible on Sundays. The one is the inevitable result of the other. The minister who gets out of touch with people will soon forget how to speak their language. He will speak a language of his own, and nobody else will understand it. Too often we ministers call our people indifferent, and all the time they think, with perfect justice, that the boot is on the other foot. It is *we* who are indifferent. We pursue the even tenor of our dreamy way—dogmatic, idealistic, evangelistic—and we appear to them to be like summer sailors gliding over shimmering seas, while they are fighting their fearful way through black tempests and cruel storms. There is no place in all the wide, wide world like the pulpit. But the pulpit is no place for any of us unless we are prepared to fathom, and appreciate, and grapple with, the pathos and the tragedy of those real problems and difficulties and riddles that are harassing the minds of so many of our hearers. When people are in the throes and agonies of the terrible temptations which start out of their domestic, social, and commercial relationships, it is not enough to answer their plea for help with the cheap platitudes of theological technique.

Our Master took upon Himself real flesh and real blood that He might appeal convincingly to real men and women…. Let him—a creature of flesh and blood—cultivate the friendship of flesh and blood! Let him get to know men; let him take pains to understand women: let him laugh with the young people and romp with the children! Let him beware of taking his theology too strong! He must dilute it liberally with plenty of histories, plenty of biographies, plenty of novels—anything that will keep him in touch with the throbbing, pulsing mass of life on the other side of the footlights….

Beyond the footlights everything seems dark, and we forget the teeming life that the darkness conceals. We are all tempted to imagine that the things on which all the lights are streaming are the substances, and that the invisible things are merely shadows. The actor knows better…. He is conscious of the unseen throng.

F. W. Boreham, *The Crystal Pointers* (London: The Epworth Press, 1925), 12-21.

THE PROBLEM WITH APPLAUSE

Applause is a doubtful compliment. It is very pleasant, when the chairman calls your name, and you rise to address your audience, to be received with a prolonged thunder of handclapping. It makes you feel that you are welcome and—which is more to the point—that you and your audience are on the best of terms with each other at the start. That is extremely important. And, as a mark of appreciation of an honest effort, it is very nice to sit down amid a tumult of cheers. But that is about all. In my time I have done my full share of public speaking, and have received my full share of public approbation, but, when I find an audience punctuating a speech with constant outbursts of applause, it leads to anxiety and heart-searching.

As a rule, people only applaud when you express the convictions that they brought with them to the meeting, or when you assail the doctrines against which they were already prejudiced.... I have heard such speeches; I blush to say that I have delivered such speeches. I make this shameful and humiliating confession only in order that I may arm myself with the authority that a writer always wields who can convince his readers that he knows what he is talking about. In this particular case, I do. And I know that, when such speeches are delivered, an extraordinary thing happens. The audience and the speaker go home and turn a somersault. I do not mean that, in their excitement, they perform such antics in a physical sense. I mean that they become the subjects of a violent emotional reaction. On the way home the people comment on the magnificence of the speech to which they have just listened. The speaker, they say, was an out-and-outer; he believes in hitting straight from the shoulder; he calls a spade a spade; it's a pity we haven't more public speakers with equal courage; and so on.

I have made speeches that have cost me a great deal of thought in their preparation; and that, in their delivery, involved me in a vast expenditure of nervous energy. Not to put too fine a point upon it, they were fairly good speeches. But, except for a cheer at the beginning and a cheer at the end, they were very little applauded. When people are hanging on every sentence, they do not interrupt you by clapping their hands. When they are thinking hard, when they are revising their superficial and hasty conclusions, when they are being coaxed and persuaded into a better state of mind, they are as quiet as mice. When a man has had twenty or thirty years of public speaking, he knows that the silent audiences are the finest tribute to his influence and power.

F. W. Boreham, *A Tuft of Comet's Hair* (London: The Epworth Press, 1926), 86-87, 92-93.

THE PROBLEM WITH LONELINESS

To the poet C. J. Dennis, Australia is always a land of bright days and starlit nights, a land in which one feels that it is good to be alive. His poem, the *Sentimental Bloke* ... represents, and represents accurately, the more cheerful and attractive phase of Australian life.

But those who have studied our Australian literature at all carefully know perfectly well that there is another and less pleasing phase. Marcus Clarke knew Australia at least as well as Mr. Dennis knows it. But he was not impressed by that aspect of Australian life upon which Mr. Dennis has laid such stress. He saw the same things, but he saw them from another angle. 'What,' he asks, 'is the dominant note of Australian scenery? That which is the dominant note of Edgar Allan Poe's poetry—weird melancholy. The Australian mountain forests are funereal, secret, stern. Their solitude is desolation. They seem to stifle in their black gorges a story of sullen despair.' Even the fauna and flora of Australia intensify, Marcus Clarke feels, the somber character of the general outlook. 'From the melancholy gums,' he complains, 'strips of white bark hang and rustle. The very animal life of these frowning hills is either grotesque or ghostly. Flights of white cockatoos stream out, shrieking like evil souls. The sun suddenly sinks, and the morepokes [owls] burst out into horrible peals of semi-human laughter. All is fear-inspiring and gloomy. No bright fancies are linked with the memories of the mountains. Hopeless explorers have named them, out of their sufferings, Mount Misery, Mount Dreadful, Mount Despair. Placed before the frightful grandeur of these barren hills, the soul drinks in their sentiment of defiant ferocity and is steeped in bitterness.' If this experience were singular, and the testimony were without corroboration, one might be pardoned for suspecting that such sentiments were but the outpourings of a misanthropic spirit incapable of seeing brightness anywhere. But others have felt in the same way. Marcus Clarke penned his impressions in 1884. At just about that time, Commander Gambier was in Australia; and, in his *Links in my Life,* he tells us what he thought of it. It is, he declares, the ugliest and most uninteresting country in the world! I was nearly driven mad, he says, by a desperate ruse of social loneliness.

A desperate sense of social loneliness! It is in those words that Commander Gambier unconsciously offers us the key to the solution of the problem.

F. W. Boreham, *The Three Half-Moons* (London: The Epworth Press, 1929), 64-67 (selected).

THE SPONTANEOUS JOY OF LIFE

From one of Madeline Cope's beautiful letters in M. E. Waller's *Woodcarver of 'Lympus* [is this excerpt]:

"Before I knew it, Hugh," she says, "I was dragging anchor, losing the dear, sweet, childlike faith I had kept as my best heritage from my father and mother, and, with it, losing; much of *the spontaneous joy of life.*"

That is it exactly. 'Dragging anchor.' 'Losing the spontaneous joy of life.'

F. W. Boreham, *Mountains in the Mist* (London: Charles H. Kelly, 1914), 87-88.

THE STRAIGHT STICK

On a beautiful Sunday evening in midsummer, I walked through St James's Park, past Buckingham Palace, to hear Dr. John A. Hutton at Westminster Chapel. It was the only occasion on which I ever enjoyed that privilege. His text was: 'I judge no one … but if I judge.'

His point was that the gentle and gracious souls who would never dream of criticizing us are the very people whose silent and unconscious condemnation is the most devastating. A straight stick, lying beside a crooked one, does not judge its twisted neighbor, yet its very straightness is the crooked stick's most terrible exposure.

Dr. Hutton employed a homely but singularly effective illustration. A man sits grimly in a crowded tram while a girl stands near him, clutching at the strap. He mutters to himself that he has paid his fare just as she has, that he is probably quite as tired as she is, and that he is in every way entitled to his seat. She, of course, neither utters a word nor casts a glance in his direction. Yet her very presence makes him thoroughly miserable and covers him with shame. 'I judge no one … but if I judge.'…

It seems to vindicate the contention of Francis of Assisi, who held that he who lives a beautiful Christian life has no need to resort to *words* in order to rebuke the iniquities that disfigure the Church and the world around him.

F. W. Boreham, *The Tide Comes In* (London: The Epworth Press, 1958), 21-22.

THE THING ABOUT ABSENCE

An admirer of Charles Dickens once sent him, as a token of appreciation and gratitude, an elaborate and beautifully-worked table-center. The design was made up of artistic representations of the seasons. Summer occupied the center, with spring on the left hand and autumn on the right. But no winter.

The donor explained that he shrank from including any reminder of that gloomy season in a gift to one whose pen had proved a ceaseless ministry of brightness. But winter declined to be left out in the cold.

'Do you know,' said Dickens, as he pointed to the gift long afterwards, 'I never look at that table-center without thinking more about winter than about any of the other seasons. Its very absence from the design only serves to accentuate the thought of it in my mind.' And so winter had its revenge: and it was a just revenge.

F. W. Boreham, *A Witch's Brewing* (London: The Epworth Press, 1932), 245.

THIS IS THE DAY

At first I thought it was just scribbled on the window with a fluid of some kind, but I soon discovered that it was cut in the glass with a stone. It was in my college days. I had been asked to conduct the anniversary services at a village chapel in Sussex. I arrived by train on the Saturday afternoon, and was met by a young farmer—the secretary of the Sunday school—and driven to the cottage at which I was to stay. It was a quaint old place, smothered by a tangle of creepers, and its sole occupant was Old Bessie, the widow of a former minister. She was a most lovable hostess. When I retired at night I saw at once that I had been given the room that she usually occupied. Everything was spotlessly clean and as cosy as could be. I slept like a top; and it was when I rose in the morning that I made the discovery of which I have already told. It was a perfect June morning. I sprang from the bed to pull up the blind and throw open the window. I had done the former, and was about to do the latter when I noticed the mark on the glass. It was just this: THIS IS THE DAY.

At first, as I say, I thought it was just scrawled with a fluid of some kind; but I soon found on examination that it was cut right into the glass. I determined to ask Old Bessie about it at breakfast.

'Everybody asks about that!' she said with a laugh, as soon as I broached the subject. 'I never thought when I wrote it there it would lead to so many questions. But, you see, I have had a lot of trouble in my time, and I am a great one to worry. I was always afraid of what was going to happen tomorrow. And each morning when I woke up I felt as though I had the weight of the world upon me. Then, one day, when I was very upset about things, I sat down, and read my Bible. It was *his* Bible once,' she said reflectively, glancing at a photograph of her late husband. 'It happened that I was reading the one hundred and eighteenth Psalm. When I came to the twenty-fourth verse, I stopped. *"This is the day that the Lord has made: we will rejoice and be glad in it."* I looked again to see what particular day was referred to. But I could not find it. And then it occurred to me that it means any day, every day—this day! *"This is the day* that the Lord has made." And why should I be afraid of the days if He makes them? It flashed upon me like a burst of sunshine on a gloomy day. I happened to notice that Tom, who is apprenticed to a glazier, had left his tools in the kitchen. I snatched up his diamond, ran upstairs and scrawled the words as well as I could on the windowpane.'

'There!' I thought, 'now I shall see that little bit of Bible there every morning when I draw up the blind, and I will say to myself, "*This* is the day! *This* is the day! *This is the day that the Lord has made!*"

'And many a time since, when things were looking black, I have been glad that I did it. Somehow, you don't feel afraid of the day if you feel that *He made it!*'

F. W. Boreham, *Shadows on the Wall* (London: The Epworth Press, 1922), 75-76.

TILTING AT WINDMILLS

Cervantes in *Don Quixote* saw to his sorrow that chivalry was running wild. The stories told by the men who were returning from the wars were inflaming the imagination of the youth of Castile to a positively dangerous degree. Hot-headed young enthusiasts were swept off their feet by an insatiable desire to cover themselves with glory. They would fight something or somebody, whether that something or somebody needed to be fought or not. Cervantes wrote his book to show that it is better to stay at home breaking stones by the roadside than to rush forth and hazard one's life in tilting at windmills.

F. W. Boreham, *A Witch's Brewing* (London: The Epworth Press, 1932), 94-95.

TOO OLD TOO YOUNG

I was out visiting a few days ago and met a man of eighty.

I said: "My friend, will you not trust the Savior?" "No, no," he answered. "I'm too old, too old."

It so happened that the very next day I met a youth of sixteen. "My friend," I said again, "Will you not trust the Savior?" "No, no," he answered. "I'm too young, too young!"

And between that "TOO OLD" and that "TOO YOUNG" we all go dancing to our everlasting doom. What a strain on the mercy of God!

F. W. Boreham, *The Whisper of God and other sermons* (London: Arthur H. Stockwell, 1902), 98.

TORMENTING DREAMS

Here is Sir Douglas Mawson, our own Australian explorer! He is in the depths of the Antarctic; has lost both his companions; and, in his lonely struggle, has little hope of fighting his

way to safety. Again and again he stumbles at some particularly perilous place; several times he falls into crevasses; but
each time he contrives to extricate himself from the danger
zone and battle on. 'I never really slept,' he says, 'but now
and then I dozed; and, as surely as I did so, I was tormented
by dreams of the most luxurious food and visions of the most
impossible banquets.'

F. W. Boreham, *The Three Half-Moons* (London: The Epworth Press,
1929), 95.

TRAINING AN UNDERSTUDY

Amid scenes of extraordinary enthusiasm, a very popular
musical comedy reached its final performance at one of our
great Melbourne theaters.... The phenomenal run of this play
has established a record for Australia; but it is not this fact
that attracts me as I approach my desk this morning.

I am impressed, rather, by the circumstance that, in con-
gratulating the actors and actresses on their triumph, the newspapers emphasize one particularly interesting circumstance.
The principal actress, it seems, had an understudy whose duty
it was to hold herself in readiness to take the name-part in the
play at a moment's notice. For more than a year, however, the
leading lady took her place at every performance—afternoons
and evenings. A few minutes before the time arrived for each
presentation of the play, the understudy visited the theater.
'Is Miss Bennet quite all right?' she inquired with monotonous regularity, and, with equally monotonous regularity, was
assured that her assistance would not be required. This, in
itself, was remarkable; but this was not all.

For, after *Rose Marie* had run its hectic course for more
than twelve months, the leading lady suddenly failed. On the
arrival of the understudy at the stage door, she was told to
dress at once for the principal part; and, to the surprise and

delight of the entire cast, she romped through the performance with such ease and verve and skill that very few people in the crowded building suspected that the principal role was being taken, not by the leading lady herself, but by Marie Bremner, the understudy!

This struck me as being very notable—creditable alike to the principal actress and to her understudy—and when, early last evening, my genial friend, Mr. Gordon Crisp, dropped in for a chat, I casually mentioned the matter to him. Mr. Crisp is an outstanding figure in the commercial life of the city; and, as soon as I introduced the theme, he gave it a turn for which I was quite unprepared.

'Splendid!' he exclaimed, slapping his knee in an ecstasy of enthusiasm. 'Splendid! That's the doctrine I've been preaching for years, but I can get nobody to pay much heed to it!'

Too blind at the moment to discern anything in this theatrical record that could reasonably be denominated 'a doctrine,' I begged my ardent companion to be a little more explicit.

'Well,' he explained, removing the ashes from his cigar, 'it's one of the fundamental principles of the business world that a person should provide against all kinds of contingencies that must—or may—arise. Recognizing the devastation that may be wrought by fire, the loss that may be sustained through the depredations of a dishonest servant or the intrusion of a thief, people take out fire policies, fidelity policies, burglary policies, and what not? Why, even if we make a business trip in the car, we foresee the possibility of vexatious delay caused by a puncture on the road, and arm ourselves with a good spare wheel. And yet, although every person knows that he cannot possibly go on for ever, very few of us take the trouble to train younger people in the tasks and duties that we are at present performing!'

'Is it not possible,' I ventured to suggest, 'that self-interest has something to do with it? Men in high office—managers, secretaries and the like—may not unnaturally feel it a some-what risky experiment to equip younger people to occupy their own positions. The directors of the company might argue that, if the younger person now knows all that his senior can teach him, in addition to all that his own observation has revealed to him, he is likely to make a more alert and vigorous and suc-cessful chief than the veteran who at present fills the post.'

'Well, there's that about it, of course,' my friend hesi-tatingly admitted, 'but in this world you never get anything without hazarding something.'

F. W. Boreham, *A Witch's Brewing* (London: The Epworth Press, 1932), 217-219.

TRANSFORMED SPEECH

Prebendary Carlile, the head of the Church Army, tells a delightful story of a Welsh miner who, in the great days of the Revival, avowed himself a disciple of Jesus Christ. He had previously exhibited an amazing facility in the use of expletives of the baser kind. With his changed life, however, it became customary for him to meet the most exasperating treatment with a manly smile and a homespun benediction. His mates, disapproving the revolution in his behavior, one day stole his dinner. But all they heard their transformed com-rade say was "Praise the Lord! I've still got my appetite!"

F. W. Boreham, *The Luggage of Life* (London: Charles H. Kelly, 1912), 18-19.

TRANSFORMING POWER OF LOVE

The never-to-be-forgotten funeral [of Fyodor Dostoyevsky] took place on February 12, 1881. On February 9, Dostoyevsky lay dying. 'When he awoke that morning,' his daughter tells us, 'my mother realized that his hours were numbered.'

Brave little mother! So this is the end of her fifteen years of romance! In the novels of Dostoyevsky there is no prettier story than the story of the meeting of these two. Dostoyevsky was forty-five at the time. Through voluntarily taking over the debts of his dead brother, his finances had become involved. Moreover, he had fallen into the clutches of an unscrupulous publisher, for whom he had contracted to write a novel on the understanding that, if it was not finished by a certain date, all the author's copyrights would fall into the publisher's hands. As the date approached, the impossibility of the task became evident, and ruin stared him in the face. Somebody advised him to get a stenographer; but no stenographer could be found. There was, it is true, a girl of nineteen who knew shorthand; but lady stenographers were then unknown; and the girl doubted if her people would consent to her taking the appointment. However, Dostoyevsky's fame removed the parents' scruples, and she set to work. On her way to the novelist's house, she used to tell her daughter afterwards, she tried to imagine what their first session would be like. 'We shall work for an hour,' she thought, 'and then we shall talk of literature.' Dostoyevsky had had an epileptic attack the night before; he was absent-minded, nervous, and peremptory. He seemed quite unconscious of the charms of his young stenographer, and treated her as a kind of Remington typewriter. He dictated the first chapter of his novel in a harsh voice, complained that she did not write fast enough, made her read aloud what he had dictated, scolded her, and declared that she had not understood him. She was crushed, and left the house determined never to return. But she thought better of it during the night, and, next morning, resumed her post. Little by little, Dostoyevsky became conscious that his Remington machine was a charming young girl and an ardent admirer of his genius. He confided his troubles to her and she pitied him. In her girlish dream, she had pictured him petted and pampered; instead, she saw a sick man, weary, badly fed, badly lodged, badly served, hunted down like a wild beast by merciless editors, and ruthlessly exploited by selfish relatives. She perceived the idea of protecting Dostoyevsky, of sharing the heavy burden he had taken upon his shoulders, and of comforting him in his sorrows. She was not in love with this man, who was more than twenty-five years her senior, but she understood his beautiful soul and reverenced his genius. She determined to save Dostoyevsky from his publishers, and succeeded. She begged him to prolong the hours of dictation, spent the night copying out what she had taken down in the day, and worked with such good-will that, to the chagrin of the avaricious publisher, the novel was ready on the appointed day. And, shortly afterwards, he married her.

And now, fifteen years afterwards—the funeral was on the anniversary of the wedding—Dostoyevsky is dying!

'He made us come into the room,' his daughter says, 'and, taking our little hands in his, he begged my mother to read the *Parable of the Prodigal Son*. He listened with his eyes closed, absorbed in his thoughts. "My children," he said in his feeble voice, "never forget what you have just heard. Have absolute faith in God and never despair of His pardon. I love you dearly, but my love is nothing compared with the love of God for all those He has created. Even if you should be so unhappy as to commit a crime in the course of your life, never despair of God. You are His children; humble yourselves before Him, as before your father, implore His pardon, and He will rejoice over your repentance, as the father rejoiced over that of the *Prodigal Son*." '

A few minutes later Dostoyevsky passed triumphantly away. 'I have been present,' says Aimee Dostoyevsky, 'at many deathbeds, but none was so radiant as that of my father. He saw without fear the end approaching. His was a truly Christian death. He was ready to appear before his Eternal

Father hoping that, to recompense him for all that he had suffered in this life, God would give him another great work to
do, another great task to accomplish.'

F. W. Boreham, *A Faggot of Torches* (London. The Epworth Press, 1926),
96-98.

TREASURE IN MUD

For what is mud? The dictionary says that it is 'mire, slime,
sediment, soft earth as in a puddle, etc.' That is all the dictionary knows!

But let us go back to Ruskin. He knew something of the
maxims of the mud as well as of the ethics of the dust. The
great philosopher was one day walking along the streets of an
English manufacturing town. The weather had been very wet,
and the mud was most abundant and tenacious. The thought
occurred to him that he would have the mud analysed to find
out its organic elements. This was accordingly done, and the
black and grimy mud was found to consist of sand, clay, soot,
and water. Musing upon them, the thought occurred to him
that these are the very substances from which our precious
gems are formed. From the *sand* or silica are formed the onyx,
chrysolite, agate, beryl, cornelian, chalcedony, jasper, sardius,
amethyst; from the *clay* are formed the sapphire, ruby, emer-
ald, and topaz; from the *soot* is formed the diamond; and the
water is the same as that which, in the form of a dewdrop,
sparkles in the heart of a rose.

So that, in wading through the ugly mud, he had really
been splashing among sapphires. Here, therefore, is the true
meaning of mud. It tells us that the toothless epigrams of
our common chatter are true in letter but false in spirit. It
tells us that 'all is not gold that glitters,' simply because that
which glitters may be much more precious than gold. It tells
us that 'things are not what they seem' because they may

be a thousand fold better than they seem. It tells us that, instead of being so swift to suspect the angel of being a devil disguised, we should rather suspect the ragged stranger of being in truth an angelic visitant. The mud of life may be jingling with jewels.

F. W. Boreham, *The Other Side of the Hill* (London: Charles H. Kelly, 1917), 153-154.

TREASURING WITHOUT POSSESSING

I am very fond of that fine passage in the *Compleat Angler* in which the gentle author [Izaak Walton] tells of the delight that he found in thousands of things that did not strictly belong to him. The actual owner of the estate on which he fished was worried to death by vexatious disputes and threatened litigation; but, as for Izaak, he was in the seventh heaven. He strolled down through the leafy woods and shady groves; he crossed the fragrant meadows in which he saw a tousle-haired school-boy gathering lilies and a rosy-cheeked lassie with an armful of cowslips; he cast his line into the sparkling stream and saw the great silvery trout flash through the laughing waters; and he was in bliss without alloy. 'As I sat thus,' he says, 'joying in my own happy condition, and pitying this poor rich man that owned this and many other pleasant groves and meadows about me, I did thankfully remember that my Savior said that the meek possess the earth. Anglers and meek, quiet-spirited people are free from those high and restless thoughts which corrode the sweets of life, and they therefore enjoy what others possess and enjoy not.'

F. W. Boreham, *The Other Side of the Hill* (London: Charles H. Kelly, 1917), 268-269.

TRUTH

Truth, in any setting, has a Grace of its own. Nothing can be too true to be good. The world that a person sees with his own eyes is the only world that he is qualified to commit to glowing canvas, to rapturous stanzas or to sturdy prose. It is distinctively his world, and, in it, he is monarch of all he surveys. It is the bounden duty of every person charged with the onerous responsibility of expressing his soul for the public good, whether in art, literature, politics or religion, to convey a faithful articulation of his own vision.

Each sees as nobody else sees. Within the framework of his craftsmanship he must therefore express himself as nobody else can possibly do. First and last, he must be himself; must see things as he alone can, and then describe what he witnesses in the palpitating terminology of his own personality. As Rudyard Kipling would say, he must paint the thing as he sees it for the God of things as they are. And, expressing his naked and diaphanous [nearly transparent] soul by means of his palette, his pulpit, his platform or his pen, he will find, sooner or later, real truth, like wisdom, is justified of all her children.

F. W. Boreham, *The Last Milestone* (London: The Epworth Press, 1961), 30.

TRUTH IN A NUTSHELL

In describing his experiences as a junior reporter on a great London journal, Harold Fortescue tells how, on the very first day of his engagement, he handed in an elaborate and carefully-compiled record of a social event that he had been designated to cover. Secretly proud of some of his more colorful and picturesque touches, he awaited the judgment of his chief. With a wry face the old man counted the sheets.

'Sorry,' he grunted, 'but you must cut it down to one sheet!'

Fortescue pleaded that it would be extremely difficult to tell the story effectively in so small a space.

'Young man,' retorted the sub-editor grimly, 'you have evidently failed to notice that the story of the Creation of the Universe is told in ten words: 'In the beginning God created the heaven and the earth.'

F. W. Boreham, *Boulevards of Paradise* (London: The Epworth Press, 1944), 68.

TRUTH IN PACK OF CARDS

F. W. Boreham writes about a man who had never even mastered the alphabet; books and papers were meaningless to him.

Hence I saw nothing of the kind in his cabin on the sands. Just a pack of cards on the table! I questioned him one day about that pack of cards. Would he explain to me the game that, in his bare and lonely room, he was always playing?

The pack of cards, it appeared, was his quaint means of memorizing and recalling the things that he stored away in his heart on the occasions on which he so furtively visited the sanctuary. To him the pack of cards was a magic mirror in which he saw reflections of all things under the sun and over it. *Spades* spoke to him of Labor; *Hearts* of Love; *Clubs* of War and *Diamonds* of Wealth. He would go through the pack again and again, each card reminding him of some precept or parable that he had imbibed from the lips of Mr. Creed, Dr. Burns or some later preacher. Thus, he would look intently at the ace and would say to himself, 'O*ne!* There is *one* God and *one* Mediator between God and men, the Man Christ Jesus!' And then he would pause for a moment, reflecting on all that was involved in those tremendous words. *One!* Only *One* God! Only *One* Mediator! But, thank God, there is *one!* What would life be like if there were *no* God? What if there were *no* Mediator, *no* Redeemer, *no* Savior?

The *two* would remind him of all that he had heard of our first parents; of the entry of the animals into the ark; of the two tables of the law; of the sending forth of the disciples in pairs; of the two men who went up to the temple to pray; of the poor widow and her two mites; of the two thieves on their crosses; of the two angels at the sepulcher; of the walk to Emmaus; of the two shining ones at the Ascension; and of the two immutable things by which the heavenly covenant is sealed!

The *three* would set him coveting the three essential graces—Faith, Hope and Love—and pondering the awful mystery of the Trinity: the *four* would recall the four evangelists and suggest the glories of the City Four-square: the *five* would lead his thoughts to the parables of the Virgins and the Talents: the *six* would remind him that, in six days, God created the heaven and the earth; and would induce a reverential mood by a thought of the six wings of the seraphim: the *seven* would suggest the Day of Rest; the seven cardinal sins; the candlesticks, the stars and the churches of the Apocalypse; and—especially in view of all that he had suffered at the hands of the unfeeling world outside—of the necessity of forgiving until seventy times seven. The *eight* would remind him of the eight souls saved from the Flood: the *nine* would recall the story of the lepers who forgot to give thanks: while the *ten* would suggest the Ten Commandments and the full-orbed praise that can be rendered with an instrument of ten strings.

Even the court cards—king, queen and joker possessed mystical meanings for him; the two colors—black and red—seemed, in his eyes, to speak of Sin and Redemption; while the totals were freighted with striking significance. There were thirteen cards in each suit—a card for each moon of the year. There were fifty-two cards altogether—a card for each week of the year. And, on the cards of his pack, there were, in all, three hundred and sixty-five dots—a dot for each day of the year. Each dot seemed to Curly to be an assurance that, as his day, so also his strength should be.

In one way and another, the cards brought him infinite comfort. All this is, of course, extremely fanciful and almost absurdly fantastic; yet it meant all the world to Curly. It was the only Bible that he possessed—the only Bible fitted to his circumstances and training. As he expounded it to me, I wondered how many of the people who regarded him as a card-playing and self-centered old hermit had the slightest inkling of the celestial treasure of which his cards were the key.

F. W. Boreham, *The Drums of Dawn* (London: The Epworth Press, 1933), 115-118.

VALUE IN THE EXTREME

In the stirring chapter in which Sir Ernest Shackleton tells of the loss of his ship among the ice-floes, he describes an incident that must have set all his readers thinking. In the grip of the ice, the *Endurance* had been smashed to splinters; and the entire party was out on a frozen sea at the mercy of the pitiless elements. Shackleton came to the conclusion that their best chance of eventually sighting land lay in marching to the opposite extremity of the floe; at any rate, it would give them something to do, and there is always solace in activity. He thereupon ordered his men to reduce their personal baggage to two pounds weight each. For the next few hours every man was busy in sorting out his belongings—the treasures that he had saved from the ship. It was a heart-breaking business. Men stole gloomily and silently away and dug little graves in the snow, to which they committed books, letters, and various knickknacks of sentimental value. And, when the final decisions had to be made, they threw away their little hoards of golden sovereigns and kept the photographs of their sweet-hearts and wives!

F. W. Boreham, *Rubble and Roseleaves* (London: The Epworth Press, 1922), 226-227.

VALUE OF FAILURE

I dabble in photography. The other evening I was showing my album to a friend who proposes to learn the black art. After he had admired my pet prints, he reduced me to abject humiliation.

'You have taken other photographs besides these?' he asked.

I confessed that he had correctly stated the case.

'Then would you mind,' he went on, 'would you mind showing me your failures—your spoiled negatives and your poorer prints? I fancy,' he explained, 'I fancy I could learn more from *them* than from *these.*'

It was rather a come-down, but I have forgiven him now; for I have discovered that while he has abased my pride he has enriched my philosophy. I have come to see, as a result of that uncomfortable experience by the fireside, that failures are really very fine things. Is it not by means of our breakdowns that we discover our hidden weaknesses and is it not by removing the lurking frailties thus revealed that we ultimately reach our goal? The amateur photographer learns very little from his successful prints. But whenever, instead of a clear image, he is confronted by a hazy blur, he patiently investigates the matter, discovers the reason for the defect, and thus attains one further degree of proficiency in photographic art.

When motorcars were first introduced, every main road was dotted with cars that had vexatiously come to grief. But each such humiliation constituted itself a revelation, either to the owner, or to the maker, or to both. One by one, the causes of misfortune were removed, with the result that today such discomforts are comparatively rare.

When the first airships fell, we did not abandon the conquest of the air as a hopeless chimera. We carefully investigated the cause of the collapse, and were grateful for the instruction that led us one step nearer to our ultimate goal. James Watt declared that the thing most wanted in mechanical engineering was a history of failures. 'We want,' he said, '*a book of blots!*'

John Hunter, the eminent Scottish surgeon, used to say that medical science would never make much headway until professional people had the courage to publish their failures as well as their successes. Did not Wenzel spoil 'a hatful of eyes' in learning how to operate for cataract? Then, at last, he mastered the secret, and taught surgical science how to do it. Like me, he produced his perfect negative. But if only he had brought out his spoiled negatives as well! If only he had recorded the melancholy histories represented by that 'hatful of eyes!' If only he had told of his failures and shown the world how *not* to do it! What a multitude of fruitless experiments, and what 'hatfuls of eyes' he might have saved! But no, we keep our spoiled negatives in the dark. It is a sad mistake.

I am coming to think, in view of all this, that a failure is a pretty difficult thing to define. Without those crude attempts of mine, I could never have produced a photograph that was really worth while. Was I then failing while I was learning? Moreover, the fact that my ruined negatives helped my friend by the fireside to turn out some capital portraits leads me to take a cheerier view of them. They were not, after all, such dismal disasters as I had supposed. That is worth thinking about. There are entries in James Watt's *Book of Blots* that are themselves crepuscular intimations of a coming glory. There are splendid failures that immeasurably outshine many of our paltry successes. The pathfinder does not really fail, even though his bones lie on the track. Has he not blazed a trail along which others may press to the hidden goal? Did Moses fail because he never entered the Promised Land? Did David fail because he never built God's house? Did Columbus fail because he never found India through the gates of the golden west? Did Livingstone fail because, dying in the trackless jungle, he never saw the fountains of Herodotus? To ask these questions is to answer them. Moses made it possible for Joshua to enter Canaan! David made it possible for Solomon to build the temple! The failure of Columbus to find India gave us a new hemisphere! Livingstone opened a continent to the commerce and traffic of the world! These men may have fancied that they had failed.

But—like me with my negatives—they did not recognize their own success even when it stared them in the face. There is surely success in the failure that makes success possible to another. Life holds fewer failures than we often think.

I read the other day of an artist who, on taking a final look at his favorite picture before sending it to the Academy, discovered to his dismay several blots on the blue sky. To erase them was impossible. So, quickly, he seized his brush, and turned each blot into a bird. I fancy that we shall find at last that many of our blots have been transformed by the Great Artist after a similar fashion.

'The Bible is a strange book,' says Dr. Matheson. 'It puts a blot upon all its portraits; and it does so, not by mistake, but by design. Its blots are as much a bit of the art as are its beauties.' Let us have *a book of blots,* then, by all means! In some modest corner there may be a reference to my spoiled negatives. And, in blazing splendor, you will find the story of the Crucifixion there.

F. W. Boreham, *The Nest of Spears* (London: The Epworth Press, 1927), 176-179.

VALUE OF KEEPING A JOURNAL

Thousands of men and women have kept diaries; and have intended what they wrote for no eyes but their own. It is part of our deep, deep instinct for the confessional. The soul must utter itself somewhere.

Claudius Clear declares that the most remarkable diary in the English language is that of Sir Walter Scott. He began it on November 20, 1825. He was then fifty-four, and he had but seven years to live. The clouds were gathering about him; ruin stared him in the face. 'Why,' asked our essayist, 'did Scott write that journal? It was, I think, because he had to express himself, and there was no friend to whom he could tell the whole bitter truth. He could not tell it to his son-in-law, Lockhart, for he had kept Lockhart very much in the dark. The same was true of his Edinburgh friends. His wife—never much of a companion—broke down absolutely under her trial, and soon passed from the troubled scene. He was too chivalrous to burden the minds of his children with any trouble he could spare them. What is most distressing in the whole tragical yet glorious business was that Scott, the friend of all, had no friend in the day of his dire distress with whom he could be perfectly frank.' And so, a broken man, he took a paper book, made it his father-confessor, and poured out his anguished soul to it.

But the singular thing is that the diaries that were written in the first instance for only one pair of eyes, have, in the end, proved the enrichment of the world. People like Bunyan and Wesley and Baxter were great believers in putting things down. And, as a consequence, Bunyan's *Grace Abounding,* and Wesley's *Journal,* and Baxter's *Autobiography* form part of the Church's priceless heritage. Here we have religion expressed in the terms of actual experience; there is a ring of reality about it; and we would rather lose all our philosophies and theologies than allow one of these artless but invaluable documents to perish.

Especially do I admire, in this connection, the amazing sagacity and insight of John Wesley. Wesley believed that, like bees in amber, the soul's experiences should be embalmed for the inspection of subsequent generations. Acting upon this conviction, he not only gave us his own journal—a work that runs into thousands of printed pages—but he moved all his comrades and associates to follow his example. He encouraged Charles, his brother, to keep a record of everything. Is it not possible that to his influence we owe the journals of George Whitefield and John Fletcher?

However that may be, it is certain that Wesley required all his preachers—Nelson, Haime, Olivers, Hopper, Jaco, Mitchell, and the rest—to reduce to writing the story of their spiritual travail. Wesley was astute enough to know two things. He knew that it would do *those men* a world of good to set their experiences down, and he knew that it would do *me* a world of good to read what they had written.

'It was not my intention,' says John Haime, 'to write any account of these things. I put it off from time to time, being conscious that I had no talent for writing, until my peace was well-nigh lost. At last I was prevailed upon to begin. I had not written many lines before I found my soul in perfect peace!' Precisely! John Haime's soul began to glow as soon as he began to write; and my soul caught fire as soon as I began to read. The pen was a means of grace to him; the paper was a means of grace to me. John Wesley was so astute, and so shrewd, and so far-seeing that he deliberately engineered this twofold benediction—the writer's and the reader's. The world has never seen such a believer in diaries as John Wesley.

F. W. Boreham, *Wisps of Wildfire* (London: The Epworth Press, 1924), 107-109.

VALUE OF TRAVEL

Lord Chesterfield was asked by an anxious father as to the proper education for a son who had just left school. 'He needs three things!' replied his lordship. 'And those?' inquired the man. 'In the first place he needs travel,' said his lordship. 'And the second?' 'Travel!' repeated Lord Chesterfield. 'And the third?' 'Travel again!' replied the peer....

Charles Darwin says that there are priceless *moral* gains [from travel]. The illustrious naturalist's voyage in the *Beagle* is one of the most notable and most fruitful journeys ever undertaken, and we have all made that wonderful trip with him again and again. To see the world through his magic spectacles is in itself a liberal education. But it always seems to me that the paragraphs with which the book closes are the most significant in the entire journal. 'Nothing,' he says, 'can be more improving than a journey. In a moral point of view, the effect ought to be to teach the traveler good-humored patience, freedom from selfishness, the habit of acting for himself, and of making the best of every occurrence.' Produced in such rapid succession, the eye is dazzled by these sparkling gems. What are curious animals, odd plants or gaily colored birds compared with these? I pick them up one by one and handle them tenderly, lovingly, reverently, as a man would finger the Koh-I-Nor.

'Good humored patience'—why, I would tour Europe from Gibraltar to Lapland if I were sure of finding such a jewel! 'Freedom from selfishness'—I would range the American continent from Alaska to Cape Horn if I were certain of finding it! 'The habit of acting for myself'—when I think of the tortures of indecision, the agonies of uncertainty and the wearisome counsel-hunting I have known, I feel that I would turn every stone in Asia, from Jerusalem to Japan, if I stood a ghost of a chance of discovering it! And 'the habit of making the best of everything'—why, the man who hit upon such a treasure would be happier than if he had come upon the philosopher's stone! I would search Africa from Capetown to Algiers if I were sure of unearthing so splendid a nugget! And these, our scientific traveler says, are the gains of a journey.

'In a moral point of view, the effect ought to be to teach him good-humored patience, freedom from selfishness, the habit of acting for himself, and of making the best of every occurrence.' Not among the golden sands of Mexico, nor among the glittering diamond fields of Golconda, did hungry-eyed prospector ever light upon a treasure-trove like this! Shame on me, if, with such gems studding my path, I reach the end of my journey with *nothing but the hair upon my head!*

F. W. Boreham, *The Passing of John Broadbanks* (London: The Epworth Press, 1936), 195-197.

VICTORY OF FAITH

There is no painting in our Melbourne Art Gallery of which I am more fond than of Mr. St. George Hare's *Victory of Faith.* It presents two young girls—one of white skin and one of black—awaiting martyrdom in an ante-room of the arena. Tomorrow they are to be thrown to the lions. And how are they spending their last night on earth? With their arms lightly thrown about each other's shoulders, they are fast asleep.

And Mr. St. George Hare calls it 'The Victory of Faith.' Victory over what? Victory over all the might of the Caesars: what do they care for the tyranny of their persecutors? They are sweetly sleeping! Victory over all their feminine frailties: the lions have lost their terror; they are in the land of lovely dreams! Victory over all racial prejudice: black and white are in each other's arms! Victory over death, for, to them, death has no more terror than the slumber in which they are now indulging.

I have sometimes thought that Mr. St. George Hare must have had this passage of Paul's open before him as he painted his noble picture. 'Who shall separate us from the love of Christ? Tribulation? Distress? Persecution? Famine? Nakedness? Peril? Sword?'

Here is a terrifying array of antagonisms! And *every one of them* is to be seen in the painting. And to this formidable list, Paul bravely answers, 'No, in all these things—the things in the list; the things in the picture—we are more than conquerors through him that loved us.'

As I glance once more at the picture of these two girls, whose nakedness is but the emblem of the fact that they have been stripped of everything, I see three possibilities open to them. They might have spent that last night bemoaning their lot and conjuring up horrifying visions of the coming day. That would have been the defeat of faith. They might have huddled together, clasping each other's hands, grimly resolving to be loyal to their Lord, come what might. That would have been the triumph of faith. But they did neither of these things. They just lay down and slept! And, sleeping, they revealed themselves as 'more than conquerors' through Him whose love and care they never for a moment doubted.

F. W. Boreham, *A Late Lark Singing* (London: The Epworth Press, 1945), 178-179.

VIRTUE OF UNTIDINESS

Let every minister be thankful that his study needs tidying: let every barrister be thankful for the bustle and confusion of his office: let every carpenter be thankful for the heap of shavings on the floor: let every mother be thankful for the tumult in the nursery: let every farmer be thankful for the crib that needs cleaning out! It shows that there is something doing.

In exactly the same way, let every man be thankful when his conscience cries out against him: the evil day is the day on which conscience resolves to speak no more. And, above all, let every man be thankful at having discovered the defilement and contamination of his own soul. As with the defilement in the farmer's stall, it is a sign of life.

F. W. Boreham, *The Crystal Pointers* (London: The Epworth Press, 1925), 185.

WAIT AND SEE

'Wait and see!' we say. To wait is to see.

When John Linnell, the famous artist, was painting the picture that he regarded as his masterpiece, some of his friends displayed a tiresome anxiety to view it before it was ready. Linnell was particularly sensitive on the point, and, fearing that, in his absence, some curious visitor might invade the sanctity of his studio, he kept the easel veiled. And across the veil he threw a streamer bearing the inscription 'Wait and you shall see!'

That inscription across the veiled picture is the inscription that is written across all veiled things. Our mysteries yield to patience, and to patience only. Waiting is the secret of seeing. The vision that will banish my perplexities may tarry, says the prophet; but, *though it tarry, I will wait for it.*

F. W. Boreham, *A Faggot of Torches* (London: The Epworth Press, 1926), 236.

WAITING BEFORE MYSTERY

I once spent the closing days of the old year at the homestead of Andrew Wallace, at Twilight Glen, near Mosgiel. Andrew was a sturdy young Scotsman who had only been ten or twelve years out from Ayrshire. He had married a New Zealand girl and they had two children, Ian and Pearl. I found the youngsters great fun. One evening they were showing me the presents that Santa Claus had brought them. The assortment included a picture-puzzle. We all set to work fitting together the fantastically-shaped fragments; but as the task approached completion it became evident that some of the pieces were missing.

'Oh,' exclaimed Pearl, in impatient disgust, 'we must throw them all away; they're no good now!'

'Oh, yes they are,' replied her wiser brother, 'the other pieces may turn up some day; we'll keep these in the cupboard till they do!'

That is the biblical argument exactly. When the soul is confronted by a perplexity that is too baffling for her, she is tempted to throw everything to the winds. But let her pause and think! Shall she fling away the answers to ninety-nine questions simply because there is one problem that she cannot satisfactorily solve? Shall I hurl into the void my hoard of golden yesterdays simply because I cannot understand God's inscrutable tomorrows? ... When, at some one point, faith is assailed, the time has come to guard her priceless hoard.

F. W. Boreham, *A Faggot of Torches* (London: The Epworth Press, 1926), 232-233.

WANTED

I took up the newspaper and was bewildered by the ocean of advertisements. The paper contained, I found, exactly two hundred and fifty-two columns; and, of these, two hundred and two were devoted to advertisements. I ran my eye down these two hundred and two columns. I seemed to be surveying a wilderness of want.

'Wanted, a house!' 'Wanted, a tenant!'

'Wanted, a master!' 'Wanted, a man!' 'Wanted, a maid!'

'Wanted, borrowers!' 'Wanted, lenders!'

'Wanted, buyers!' 'Wanted, sellers!' 'Wanted, a husband!' 'Wanted, a wife!'

It was 'Wanted!' 'Wanted!' 'Wanted!' all the time! The whole world seemed to be in want. I scanned these eager and clamorous columns until everything about me seemed to be echoing their petulant, insistent cry. I discovered at last what it is that the wild waves are always saying. As they broke at my feet they were all saying 'Wanted!' 'Wanted!' 'Wanted!' The sea birds were screaming excitedly to each other 'Wanted!' 'Wanted!' 'Wanted!'

The winds that were playing with the gum leaves overhead were sighing sadly 'Wanted!' 'Wanted!' 'Wanted!' The huge breakers that were thundering over the distant reef boomed out 'Wanted!' 'Wanted!' 'Wanted!'

I turned back to the paper on my knee, but its cry was still the same. Everybody seemed to be wanting something—or wanting somebody who wanted something!

In these two hundred and two columns I fancied that I heard one half of the world crying pitifully for the other half; and I saw what Paul meant when he said that we are members one of another....

These people want things; but they make no secret of it that they deserve the things they want.

F. W. Boreham, *A Reel of Rainbow* (London: The Epworth Press, 1920), 149-150.

WEEPING OR WHISTLING

The biographer of Sir William Osler, Regius Professor of Medicine at Oxford, tells how, one day, Sir William was passing along the ward of a children's hospital. Around him were some really desperate cases, children in the grip of horrible and painful diseases for whom nothing could be done.

Suddenly the great doctor turned away from this distressing group and strode, whistling, from the ward.

A companion ventured a remonstrance. 'How,' he asked, 'can you whistle, seeing what you have seen?' 'My dear sir,' replied Sir William, 'I just had to whistle or weep; so I whistled.'

More often than we think, the apparent frivolity of people is a subterfuge to conceal their real emotions. If we had ears to hear, we should catch the deeper notes....

F. W. Boreham, *Dreams at Sunset* (London: The Epworth Press, 1954), 103.

What Are We Doing With Life?

Mr. H. G. Wells, in *Marriage,* paints a very pitiful picture … [in which] his hero, Trafford, a clever scientist, discovers the secret of synthetic rubber. He sells it, making a large fortune. He soon finds himself the husband of a charming wife, the father of beautiful children, and the possessor of a lovely home. Nothing that heart could wish is denied him. But, somehow, all these things merely accentuate life's deepest failure; and, looking round upon his wealth, he cries out bitterly, "What are we doing with it? What are we doing with it?"

F. W. Boreham, *Mountains in the Mist* (London: Charles H. Kelly, 1914), 64.

What is the Soul?

When Laura Bridgman, deprived alike of hearing and of sight, was a small inmate of Dr. Howe's School for the Blind at Boston, her teacher one day made some reference to *the soul.*

A look of bewilderment overspread the girl's face and she slowly spelled out on her fingers the question, 'What is *the soul?*'

'The soul,' replied Dr. Howe, in the complicated language used in dealing with blind mutes, 'the soul is that which thinks and feels and hopes!'

A look of rare discernment mantled the blind girl's face. 'And is it,' she immediately inquired with eager fingers, 'is it that *which aches so?*'

F. W. Boreham, *The Heavenly Octave* (London: The Epworth Press, 1935), 66.

WHAT MOTIVE ADVENTURE?

In the early pages of *Hereward the Wake,* Kingsley describes his hero as he first becomes conscious of his insatiable craving for adventure. Longing for a hectic and perilous career, he looks this way and that way in search of some opportunity of performing desperate and doughty deeds. He wearies of the humdrum of home. Out in the wide, wide world, beyond the borders of the too-familiar Bruneswald, he fancies that every hill and valley is swarming with dragons, giants, dwarfs, ogres, satyrs and similar weird and fantastic creatures. Where shall he go? To Brittany where, in the depths of the forest, beautiful fairies may be seen bathing in the fountains, and possibly be won and wedded by a sufficiently bold and dexterous knight? To Ireland, and marry some beautiful princess with gray eyes and raven locks and saffron smock and enormous bracelets made from the gold of her own native hills? No, he will go to the Orkneys and join Bruce and Ranald and the Vikings of the northern seas! Or he will go up the Baltic and fight the Letts upon the water and slay the bisons on the land! Or he will go South; see the magicians of Cordova and Seville; beard the Mussulman outside his mosque and perhaps bring home an Emir's daughter! Or he will go to the East, join the Varanger Guard, and, after being thrown to the lion for carrying off a fair Greek lady, will tear out the monster's tongue with his own hands and show the Orient what an Englishman is made of!

At this stage, it will be observed, Hereward is seeking adventure for its own sake. The purpose of the exploit may be admirable or execrable: it does not matter. It may leave him a hero or a cut-throat: he does not care.

Happily, Hereward discovered, comparatively early in his career, that a deed can only derive its luster from its motive and its aim. No deed, however audacious, is worthwhile unless it relieves the oppressed, raises the fallen, and makes the world a better place for everybody. This discovery represents the spiritual development of Kingsley's massive hero; and it is to trace this subtle evolution in Hereward's character that Kingsley wrote the book.

F. W. Boreham, *A Witch's Brewing* (London: The Epworth Press, 1932), 93-94.

WHAT'S IN A NAME?

In the stirring annals of the Melanesian Mission, [there is a story] of a native boy whom Bishop John Selwyn had in training at Norfolk Island. He had been brought from one of the most barbarous of the South Sea peoples, and did not promise particularly well.

One day Bishop Selwyn had occasion to rebuke him for his stubborn and refractory behavior. The boy instantly flew into a passion and struck the Bishop a cruel blow in the face. It was an unheard-of incident, and all who saw it stood aghast. The Bishop said nothing, but turned and walked quietly away.

The conduct of the lad continued to be most recalcitrant, and he was at last returned to his own island as incorrigible. There he soon relapsed into all the debasements of a savage and cannibal people. Many years afterwards a missionary on that island was summoned post-haste to visit a sick man. It proved to be Dr. Selwyn's old student. He was dying, and desired Christian baptism. The missionary asked him by what name he would like to be known 'Call me John Selwyn,' the dying man replied, 'because *he taught me what Christ was like* that day when I struck him.'

F. W. Boreham, *Mushrooms on the Moor* (London: Charles H. Kelly, 1915), 253-254.

WHEN ADDITION IS SUBTRACTION

There are times when any addition is a subtraction. Some years ago, [the] White House at Washington—the residence of the American Presidents—was in the hands of the painters and decorators. Two large entrance doors had been painted to represent black walnut. The contractor ordered his workers to scrape and clean them in readiness for repainting, and they set to work. But when their knives penetrated to the solid timber, they discovered to their astonishment that it was heavy mahogany of a most exquisite natural grain! The work of that earlier decorator, so far from adding to the beauty of the timber, had only served to conceal its essential and inherent glory. It is easy enough to add to the wonders of Creation or of Redemption; but you can never add without subtracting. '*It is finished!*'

F. W. Boreham, *A Handful of Stars* (London: The Epworth Press, 1922), 108.

WHEN ENCOURAGEMENT IS ABSENT

Who that has once read the *Autobiography* can ever forget the story of Mark Rutherford's induction to his first church? He had been there for four weeks on probation; and the narrowness of the people's intellect and spiritual outlook had appalled him. But he interpreted it as a call to him to broaden their sympathies and enlarge their vision. He therefore accepted their invitation.

'The first Sunday on which I preached after my settlement was a dull day in November, but there was no dullness in me. The congregation had increased a good deal during the past four weeks, and I was stimulated by the prospect of the new life before me.'

He goes on to tell of the ardor with which he preached. The great truths that he uttered meant everything to him; and he poured out his soul with a pent-up intensity of passion. And then? Everybody went home. Except that the chapel-keeper observed laconically that it was raining, nobody said a word to him. He went home in agony, every highly strung nerve quivering to the breaking point. His health collapsed, and he abandoned the ministry. If only some good, earnest soul had shaken hands with him that first Sunday night, and expressed agreement with, or interest in, the words that he had uttered! But there was only the chapel-keeper; and he only said that *it was raining!*

F. W. Boreham, *The Fiery Crags* (London: The Epworth Press, 1928), 72.

WHEN THE STRINGS BREAK

When Paganini appeared for the first time at the Royal Opera House in Paris, the aristocracy of France was gathered to hear him. In his peculiar ghostly manner he glided on to the stage amid the breathless silence of the expectant throng. Commencing to tune his violin, a string snapped. The audience tittered. Commencing again, a second string broke; and, a moment later, a third gave way. The people stared in consternation. Paganini paused for just a second, and then, giving one of his grim smiles, he lifted his instrument, and, from the single string, drew music that seemed almost divine.

F. W. Boreham, *The Nest of Spears* (London: The Epworth Press, 1927), 151.

WHEN YOU PASS THROUGH THE WATERS

A heap of books and bones—and that was all! One after another, no fewer than forty intrepid navigators had invaded the awful solitudes of the Arctic seas in quest of some trace of Sir John Franklin and his gallant men; and *this* was the tardy and the meager reward of those long, long years of search! On the snow-bound coast of a large but inhospitable island, Sir Francis McClintock discovered an overturned and dilapidated boat. Underneath it, together with a few guns and watches˙ they found a collection of bones and of books. The men had been more than ten years dead.

Sir John Franklin, it was known, from documents found elsewhere, had died upon his ship. His last moments were cheered by the knowledge, which came to him just in time, that the expedition had been successful, and that the long-dreamed-of North-West Passage had been proved to be a fact. The other members of the expedition, more than a hundred and twenty men, had made an attempt to save their lives by an overland dash.

The locals had seen that shadowy and wavering line of wanderers. They were very thin, the Eskimos said, and could with difficulty stagger along. With every mile, some fell out and lay down in the snow to die. Others, according to an old native woman who met them, seemed to die upon their feet, and they only fell because death had already overtaken them.

But, of all the members of the Franklin expedition, these were the first whose bones were actually found. And, with the bones, some books! It was the *bones* that principally inter-ested their discoverers; it is the *books* that must principally interest us. For some of these saturated and frozen volumes were once the personal property of Sir John Franklin. Do they not still bear his name? One of them is a battered copy of Dr. John Todd's *Student's Manual*. Sir John has turned down a leaf in order to mark a passage that appears on almost the last page of the book.

"Are you not afraid to die?"

"No!"

"No! Why does the uncertainty of another state give you no concern?"

"Because God has said to me: '*Fear not; when you pass through the waters, I will be with you; and through the rivers, they shall not overflow you!*'"

There, as though his frozen finger pointed to it, stands Sir John Franklin's text.

F. W. Boreham, *A Bunch of Everlastings* (London: The Epworth Press, 1920), 31-32.

WILLING AND ABLE TO SAVE

A dramatic episode marked the historic ministry of Philip Doddridge at Northampton. An Irishman named Connell was convicted of a capital offence and sentenced to be publicly hanged. Mr. Doddridge, at great trouble and expense, instituted a most rigid scrutiny, and proved, beyond the possibility of a doubt, that Connell was a hundred and twenty miles away when the crime was committed. The course of judgment could not, however, be deflected. Connell was asked if he had any request to make before setting out for the gallows. He answered that he desired the procession to pause in front of the house of Mr. Philip Doddridge, that he might kneel on the minister's doorstep and pray for the man who had tried to save him.

'Mr. Doddridge,' he cried, when the procession halted, 'every hair of my head thanks you; every throb of my heart thanks you; every drop of my blood thanks you; for you did your best to save me!'

F. W. Boreham concludes the story by saying:

Mr. Doddridge was willing to save.

Mr. Doddridge did his best to save.

Mr. Doddridge was not able to save.

But the Bible declares: "He is able to save to the uttermost them that come to God by Him!" That is the glory of the Gospel.

F. W. Boreham, *A Bunch of Everlastings* (London: The Epworth Press, 1920), 109-110.

WINDOW DRESSING

Few of us do our window-dressing well. We do not arrange our windows in such a way that people will be eager to do business with us. We do not sufficiently study the look of the thing. I am not now referring to the subject of dress. Dress is important, just as it is important that the front of the shop should be kept painted and varnished and cleaned. But, strictly speaking, dressing is not window-dressing. There must be an essential connection between the things in the window and the things in stock. The paint and varnish on the front of the draper's shop are all very well: there can be no effective window-dressing without them yet the paint and varnish are not intended to convey the impression that the shopkeeper is an oil and color merchant. Similarly, it is imperative that a man should pay some attention to the matter of clothes: unless he dresses becomingly he cannot hope to make his behavior and speech agreeable: yet, for all that, the wearing of good clothes is not, in the strict sense, window-dressing, since, by wearing a well-made suit of clothes, a man does not mean to suggest that he is a tailor.

The vital principle in window-dressing is that the articles displayed in the window shall adequately and enticingly represent the goods that are kept in stock. A tradesman cannot stand on the pavement and show passers-by all the goods stocked away on his shelves; but by means of the window he endeavors to convey a hint of their beauty and variety.

It is so with all of us. We each carry a prodigious stock. Stacked away on mysterious and invisible shelves at the beck and call of anybody who will take an interest in them, there are thoughts in thousands, memories in millions, sentiments, opinions, convictions, ideas, and emotions galore. We occasionally indulge in a little stocktaking and are bewildered by the immensity of the collection that we have amassed. This vast hoard is not for ourselves. It is like the piles of silks and satins in the draper's shop. If he bolts his shop door, and tries to keep it all to himself, he will be ruined in no time. His wealth depends upon its distribution. He sells it, and, with the money, obtains more. He exchanges it, that is to say. He likes to sell all that he has upon the shelves, not that the shelves may be depleted and exhausted, but that they may be loaded with fresh purchases and importations.

The commerce of the soul follows identically similar lines. My stock of thoughts, memories, opinions, and ideas must be kept fluid. They must constantly be flowing in and out. I must traffic in them with as many people as possible. If I close the doors of my mind and attempt to keep my present stock to myself, I shall quickly be involved in intellectual and spiritual bankruptcy. My prosperity depends on constant traffic. People must elbow each other as they surge in and out of my shop. The more I give out from my stock, and the more I receive from those who take my goods, the richer I shall in consequence become. But, in order to attract those tides of traffic, it is a man's duty to convey to the world such an impression of himself as shall excite a desire for the stock that he carries. Therein lies the art of window-dressing.

There are, I know, some extremely lovable people whose exterior appearance is forbidding and repulsive, just as there are shops that do a brisk business in excellent commodities in spite of their unattractive windows. But this is not the normal order of things. Ordinarily, pleasant people look pleasant, kind people look kind, good people look good; and it is their duty to convey by means of their looks an accurate impression of their characters. That is what looks are for: they are the shop-windows of life. There is something wrong somewhere when people of a sunny faith wear gloomy countenances, and when people of a sweet and genial disposition look sour. At some point or other they are mismanaging the business of life. There is no reason why the best shops should have the worst windows.

Commonplace people with commonplace souls, commonplace tasks, and commonplace faces, will feel disposed to toss all this aside as a mere counsel of perfection. How can they, doing business in such ordinary stock, and handicapped by such ordinary windows, make an effective and alluring display? And yet, when you come to think of it, it is wonderful how picturesque the most mundane things may, in skillful hands, be made. A butcher might reasonably say that it was all very well for a florist or a draper to talk about window-dressing. A florist deals in sprays and nosegays and bouquets; a draper can deck his window with beautiful silks and delicate embroideries; but what is a man to do who earns his living by killing things, cutting up the carcasses, and selling the flesh for human consumption? And yet, think of a butcher's shop on Christmas Eve! The good man has deliberately set himself to make his shop window attractive, and, as a result, the crowd hurries past the florist's and the draper's to look at his imposing and appetizing display.

We all know lots of people with very commonplace souls and very commonplace brains and very commonplace tasks and very commonplace faces who, unless they took some pains with their windows, would attract and influence nobody. But because, recognizing their handicaps, they do....

If ever I become wealthy enough to found a Theological Seminary, I shall certainly endow a Chair of window-dressing. It will be the duty of the Professor of window-dressing to instruct divinity students in the art of announcing their subjects. I was talking the other day to the Rev. Theophilus Truman. He was telling me of the discouragement that was shadowing his work. Although he preaches fervidly evangelistic sermons every Sunday, none but the elect, he says, ever go to hear him. Out of sheer curiosity, I turned to his church advertisement on Saturday, and found that he was announced to discourse on *The Mermantic Theory of the Atonement.* Within a few hours of my interview with Mr. Truman, I chanced to meet Harry Twelvetrees. I made some inquiry about the church, and he startled me by saying that he hadn't been for weeks.

'Well, you see,' he explained, 'the week after Sir Ernest Shackleton died, Mr. Newcombe advertised a special address on *A Gallant Sailor on a Lonely Sea.* The church was packed. But Mr. Newcombe said not a word about Shackleton he preached on Noah! I regarded it as a pious hoax; and don't intend to go again.' A Professor of window-dressing would have saved Mr. Truman and Mr. Newcombe from such unhappy experiences.

An attractive window should indicate an excellent assortment of attractive goods; and a rich assortment of attractive goods should be heralded and announced by a dainty and attractive window. That is why religion—in all its forms, manifestations, and expressions—should be made to appear so beautiful.

It is designed as a means of enticing people to Him from whom none ever turned away dissatisfied and disappointed.

F. W. Boreham, *A Tuft of Comet's Hair* (London: The Epworth Press, 1926), 146-148, 152-153.

WORK IN PROGRESS

When Charles Simeon, of Cambridge, lay dying, he turned to those beside his bed and asked, with a beautiful smile, 'Do you know what comforts me just now?' They begged him to tell them. 'I find infinite consolation,' he replied, 'in the fact that, *in the beginning, God created the heaven and the earth!*' How, they asked, could that thought bring him solace in the Valley of the Shadow?

'Why,' he answered with another characteristic smile, 'if God can bring all the wonder of the worlds out of nothing, God may yet make something out of me!'

In dying, Mr. Simeon was thinking of the glorious transformations of the life to come—changed from glory unto glory.

F. W. Boreham, *Boulevards of Paradise* (London: The Epworth Press, 1944), 74.

YOU ARE WANTED

It is wonderful to be wanted, as Horace Vachell makes Cicely Chandos, the heroine of *Whitewash,* reflect:

"I want you," cries her lover. "I want you more than all the world. I have always wanted you, from the first day that I saw you."

"It is wonderful to be wanted," thought Cicely....

Happy are all those who have felt the thrill of the divine appreciation!

F. W. Boreham, *The Prodigal* (London: The Epworth Press, 1941), 15.

COVER STORY

"All this, to me, was enfolded in a golden haze." These words from the first story, "All the Blessings of Life," served as the inspiration for the front and back cover.

A photo of Boreham also captured the attention of cover designer, Laura Zugzda. She tells the story. "I came across a Boreham photo that really touched me. I kept coming back to it. It's a picture of him sitting with an open book in his lap, looking at the camera. His face says so much. It was like Boreham inviting me to come and sit down, so that he could share his treasures. The scripture that comes to mind is,

> 'Therefore every teacher of the law who has been instructed about the kingdom of heaven is like the owner of a house who brings out of his storeroom new treasures as well as old' (Matthew 13:52 NIV)."

Beneath the picture of Boreham, superimposed on the waters of the lake, are the letters of his name, "fwb." This logo appears on the *Dreams at Sunset* dust jacket. It adds mystery and reminds me of Celtic artwork. We may include it on future covers.

The dark sunset was so striking that it won out over the back cover photo, which we considered for the front. The colors, with their fiery hues, in both picture and design, blend well with the black and white photo.

Sunset also marks the time when stories are often read. Today they are acted out on movie screens. In the past they were told at night around a fire. Boreham cherished the

Sunday evening gatherings with his mother. "It always ended with a story. And, of all the stories that I have since heard and read, none ever moved me like those stories that, in the flickering firelight, Mother told."

The setting sun also suggests what Sir Walter Scott said so eloquently:

> Those evening clouds, that setting ray, and beauteous tints, sure to display their great Creator's praise;

> Then let the short-lived thing called man, who life's comprised within a span, to Him his homage raise.

Boreham would be pleased if his stories served to inspire praise to God, who is behind every beautiful sunset and every wonderful story.

Michael Dalton

Publisher's Note

We are grateful to Dr. Frank Rees at Whitley College for the permission to publish this book and for the practical support given by the College. Permission to reproduce significant portions of this book can be obtained from Whitley College, 271 Royal Parade, Parkville, Australia, 3052.

A portion of the sale of each book will go toward the training of pastors and missionaries at Whitley College, a ministry that F. W. Boreham supported during his lifetime.

The stories in this volume are drawn from books written by F. W. Boreham and were previously published by Epworth Press.

Sincere thanks to Laura Zugzda for the cover design, Stephanie Martindale for layout and Jeff Cranston for proofing.

Further information about the life and work of F. W. Boreham is available on the Internet at *The Official F. W. Boreham Blog Site*: http://fwboreham.blogspot.com.

Your comments and questions are welcome and they can be addressed to:

Michael Dalton
John Broadbanks Publishing
2163 Fern Street, Eureka, CA 95503, USA
dalton.michael@sbcglobal.net

Geoff Pound
c/o HCT, PO Box 4114, FUJAIRAH, United Arab Emirates
geoffpound@gmail.com

TOPICAL INDEX

Name Index